H D M

C B M D

The Bowen Family Theory and Its Uses

C. Margaret Hall

JASON ARONSON INC.
Northvale, New Jersey
London

to Dr. Murray Bowen,
with thanks

New Printing 1991

ISBN: 0-87668-373-1

Library of Congress Catalog Number: 79-51905

Manufactured in the United States of America. Jason Aronson Inc. offers books and cassettes. For information and catalog write to Jason Aronson Inc., 230 Livingston Street, Northvale, New Jersey 07647.

CONTENTS

FOREWORD

Michael E. Kerr, M.D.

When I was asked to write a foreword for this third printing of Dr. Margaret Hall's book, *The Bowen Family Theory and Its Uses,* which was first published in 1981, I was delighted to do it. The publishers asked that, in addition to making some comments about Dr. Hall and her book, I discuss some of the developments in Bowen theory during the past decade.

I first met Margaret Hall around 1970 at Georgetown University, where she was a sociology professor and I was, at that time, a psychiatric resident. Dr. Murray Bowen had been in Georgetown's Department of Psychiatry about ten years at that point, so his family program was well established. Both Dr. Hall and I were regular participants in Bowen's various teaching conferences. Murray Bowen lived by the principle, "You only have what you give away," so, from the time of his arrival at Georgetown in September 1959 until his death in October 1990, he was extremely available to medical students, residents, hospital staff, faculty, and others in the community.

Dr. Hall made numerous presentations about theory and about her own family at these teaching conferences and at other meetings. She also had many private discussions with Bowen about his theory and therapeutic approach. These discussions enabled her to write about aspects of Bowen's ideas that he did not have time to write about himself. This material gives her book a unique value. People who had done a reasonable job of learning the theory and of integrating it into their lives were frequently prodded by Bowen to write. He could not do it all himself, and Margaret Hall was one of the first to accept his challenge. Others had written papers, but she was the first to do a book. Bowen never said he necessarily agreed with all of her interpretations of his theory, but he helped her as much as he could to understand his ideas. Dr. Bowen took a similar stance with me when I wrote my part of *Family Evaluation: An Approach Based on Bowen Theory* (W.W. Norton & Co., 1988), a stance he described in the epilogue of the book. He supported and respected my effort, but he left it to the reader to distinguish any differences between Kerr and Bowen.

Learning Bowen theory requires an emotional change in the learner, because in the absence of such a change, the tendency is to modify the theory to fit one's pre-existing mindset rather than to critically examine that mindset. It is easier to view Bowen theory through the lens of conventional theory—to see it as a simple extension of Freudian theory—than it is to allow Bowen theory to be a stimulus to reevaluate the lens. A long-term, disciplined effort to "live" Bowen theory, both personally and profession- ally, inevitably confronts a person with his tacit assumptions (acquired from family, culture, and professional training) about the nature of people and their problems. Dr. Hall was among the first at an annual Georgetown Family Symposium to do a presentation about her effort to act based on theory in her own family. Her presentation was both interesting and informative. It reflected a willingness to "own" her part in the family's problems and an ability not to run from tough situations. It "spoke" to everyone, because everyone who wants to progress in his emotional func- tioning faces the same basic tasks.

The decade of the 1980s has produced some amplifications and extensions of the theory and also some changes in the therapy. In regard to the therapy, Bowen continued to refer to his approach as family "psychotherapy" as opposed to family "therapy." His retention of the term *psychotherapy* is particularly significant because many family therapists make a distinction between individual problems and family problems. These therapists hold that individual problems can have such deep roots that individual psychotherapy is required to uncover those roots. Family problems, in contrast, are more superficial and more connected to relationships, so they can be modified with a less in-depth approach such as family therapy.

Bowen held that compartmentalization into individual or intrapsychic problems (to borrow a term from Freud) and family or relationship problems is artificial, the two being too highly intertwined to separate. Furthermore, the same degree (if not more) of intrapsychic change can result from success at defining more of a self in one's own family as from psychoanalysis. When one family member can function as more of a self while relating actively to the family, not only do family relationships change, but profound psycho- logical and physical changes occur within individuals as well. Thus the term *psychotherapy* is retained to emphasize that intrapsychic process can be modified with a family approach.

One of the most important developments in the decade of the 1980s has been the effort by Bowen and others to emphasize that the family movement has produced much more than family therapy; it has produced a new theory of human emotional functioning and behavior, one that will likely replace Freudian theory. During the past twenty years, much of the family world has become splintered into schools of therapy, schools that generally reflect a particular admixture of Freudian concepts, relationship concepts, and novel therapy techniques. Bowen and the Georgetown Family Center have re- mained steadfast in drawing an identity from a new theory rather than a new therapy. Despite Bowen's efforts to emphasize theory, he has frequently been categorized as having developed a unique method of therapy that concentrates on the multigenerational family. He is credited with providing some theory for the family field, but, in most instances, this has amounted to tacking concepts such as cut-off, triangles, the poorly understood differentiation of self, and the genogram onto the basic assumptions of Freud.

The goal of moving toward a science of human behavior has also been emphasized in recent years. Bowen had a fairly straightforward definition of science, namely that science pertains to earth, the tides, the biomass, the solar system, the universe; it pertains to *what is* rather than to the content of what human beings think, feel, or say. For example, because the organ we call the brain is as real as the planet Mars, it is in the realm of science. However, because the content of the functions or productions of the brain are not necessarily factual, they are not in the realm of science. In other words, it is factual that subjective experience exists, but the content of subjectivity is not necessarily factual. Moving toward a science of human behavior, therefore, requires keeping subjectivity out of the theory.

Bowen addressed the problem of subjectivity early in the development of his theory. It is axiomatic that beliefs and the meaning people attach to their lives have an enormous impact on their functioning and behavior, yet the content of the beliefs and meaning often stems from imagination rather than fact. The question Bowen had to address, therefore, is how to incorporate the influence of subjectivity into the theory without including the content of that subjectivity.

He dealt with this issue in some early writings through a discussion of love and hate, which are subjectivity concepts of enormous influence. There are numerous nonfactual interpretations of what love is, none of which can be verified. However, Bowen noted that the impact of one person saying, "I love you," to another person can be highly predictable. The impact of statements about the presence or absence of love or hate can *function* to perpetuate certain patterns of interaction between people. While these patterns are not easily measured, their predictable repetition is easily observed. Given this action–reaction predictability, Bowen referred to the patterns as functional facts. Functional facts can be a basis for theory building.

During 1982, Bowen began expanding his ideas about how to deal with subjectivity in the theory. He had been involved in two national conferences that spring, one with Gregory Bateson and the other with Al Scheflen. Both Bateson and Scheflen had been diagnosed with cancer, but both seemed to be doing well at that time. Exposure to the thinking of these men about how they were managing their cancers led Bowen to a ninth concept in the theory, a concept about which he did several presentations, but none were ever written and published.

My understanding of Bowen's budding ninth concept is that it represents an extension of earlier writings. The idea is that the content of a belief may not be verifiable, but the belief's effects on the functioning of the individual and the family are potentially verifiable. By separating the *function* of a belief from its content, it can be incorporated into the theory, at least to the extent that that function is verifiable. Someone may recover from a cancer on the basis of holding a false belief, but he does recover. Bowen extended the function of belief concept to dealing with spiritual and other supernatural phenomena.

The opposite of subjectivity is objectivity, the meaning of the latter term being the subject of much debate in the mental health field. Bowen was specific about what he meant by objectivity, preferring the term *emotional objectivity*. Emotional objectivity implies that intellectual functioning can be sufficiently separate from emotional reactions, feelings, and other subjective experience to describe these phenomena factually. It is possible to study human emotional functioning in a way similar to studying plate tectonics, ant behavior, or the solar system. Obviously, it is more difficult to separate facts from feelings in reference to studying ourselves as opposed to the ants, but we have the capacity to move toward such objectivity. It is possible for a person to be reacting emotionally to others, to have his thinking deluged with subjectively based notions, and to *know* that this is happening. The therapy is based on using factual knowledge about emotional process to make decisions for self that are not governed by the emotionality of self and others.

People committed to the conventional notion that it is the ability to be aware of and to express feelings that is important in therapy sometimes equate emotional objectivity with the psychological defense mechanism of intellectualization. A frequently heard criticism is that therapy based on Bowen theory does not deal with feelings adequately. There is a difference between emotional objectivity and intellectualization, but this difference is not easily explained to someone steeped in conventional thinking.

The feeling and subjective side of human beings obscures a view of human relationship systems. Strong feeling reactions can narrow the observing lens, limiting the number of variables taken into account in the description of a family or social problem. This is not to say that feelings are bad, but they can have this narrowing effect, especially during periods of heightened anxiety. In an anxious environment, it requires significant intellectual discipline to see all sides of the problem. Automatic feeling responses compel people to take sides, to assign blame, to get judgmental, and to cut off. People have known this down through the ages, but Bowen has built a coherent theory around the idea, making differentiation of self the cornerstone of the theory.

One aspect of the concept of differentiation that has been amplified in recent years is the distinction between Bowen theory's concept of self and conceptualizations of self by various psychological and philosophical theories. Grasping this distinction depends on understanding the concept of the emotional system.

The theory posits that all forms of life have an emotional system. The emotional system pertains to what an organism does automatically to promote its well-being and survival. Cells react emotionally, and so do ants and people. Experience during the developmental years can shape emotional behavior, especially in forms of life with complex nervous systems and social organizations. Feelings are not equivalent to emotional reactivity in that feelings are only those aspects of emotional reactivity that are experienced subjectively. Most emotional reactivity is not felt. For example, one does not feel one's cells dividing; it would be too distracting. So while psychological and feeling processes are important influences on human behavior, such processes do not adequately explain behavior.

The emotional system is the basic driving force for the patterns of interaction observed in relationship systems. Differentiation of self makes sense only in the context of the emotionally governed relationship system. Differentiation refers to the capacity to be an emotionally separate person *while in contact* with the forces in the relationship system that promote the opposite, namely emotional fusion. In some respects, concepts of self in various psychological and philosophical theories describe characteristics of the individual similar to Bowen's concept of differentiation, but these other concepts of self are not the same because they do not conceptualize *both* differentiation and the emotionally governed relationship system. Bowen's concept of self also differs from other theories in that it is much more than a psychological concept; it is rooted in man's evolutionary heritage. Emotional distance is not equivalent to emotional separateness or differentiation. Emotional distance is a reaction to emotional fusion.

The concept of the emotional system underlines a fundamental assumption of Bowen's, namely that to move toward a science of human behavior, a theory must be consistent with knowledge about evolution and natural systems. Most theories of human behavior emphasize what makes man different from other forms of life. The assumption is that our enormous reasoning capacity and complex culture so surpass other forms of life that we constitute a special case. This viewpoint generally goes on to state that human beings have retained certain biological imperatives such as sexual and aggressive urges, but most mental illness is created by *psychological* aberrations. The dimension of "brain disease" has been emphasized in recent years to help explain serious mental illness, but even the biological psychiatrists fall back on psychological explanations for the majority of human problems. Bowen, in contrast, continued to hold that physical, emotional, and social dysfunctions are a product of that part of man he has in common with the subhuman forms. This theoretical point remains one of the most difficult to grasp. It broadens the conventional psychiatric notion of biological beyond the brain and brain disease to include all the forces that govern natural systems.

One other point about theory that has been emphasized during the 1980s is the distinction between natural systems theory and general systems theory. Bowen began emphasizing that his theory is a natural systems theory in response to others in the field claiming that general systems theory is the basis for understanding the family. The laws that govern natural systems are not necessarily included in general systems theory. For example, apart from the general notion of systems, none of the concepts of Bowen theory are in general systems theory. Bowen theory came from "whole cloth," not from general systems or cybernetics.

The methods and techniques of family psychotherapy based on Bowen theory have not been static during the past decade. However, some of what appears to have changed is related, in part, to correcting misconceptions about the therapy. Two important misconceptions pertain to the therapist–family relationship and to the focus on family of origin.

Bowen built a theory that includes the factual parts of Freud's ideas, knowledge about evolution, and natural systems thinking. He considered Freud's description of transference and countertransference to be factual. Given time, people predictably think about and relate to a therapist in ways similar to the ways they related to their own parents. Therapists are vulnerable to reacting to transference, which is countertransference. Bowen has often been mistakenly perceived not to deal with transference, not to even permit it to occur.

No therapist can prevent some degree of transference from developing. However, the therapist does not have to encourage it to do effective treatment. This does not make a therapist's focus on his own emotional functioning any less important than it is in psychoanalysis. In fact, most therapeutic failures probably result from the therapist's inattention to his own functioning. In family psychotherapy based on Bowen theory, the goal generally is to keep the focus on the "patient's" pre-existing transferences, such as with his parents and/or spouse. However, if significant transference and countertransference do enter into the therapy relationship, the therapist must be able to recognize it and to deal with it.

Focus on the family of origin as part of an effort to increase one's basic level of differentiation is as important now as it was when Bowen first presented the idea publically in 1967, but the ways in which this idea has been misheard are now better appreciated. Probably the biggest misconception is that people can change what they do in their families without changing the way they think. A corollary notion is that people can be told how to differentiate. Just going to see one's great aunt accomplishes little. It takes time to build a relationship (especially when one has been fairly cut off), it takes time to really know the family, and it takes time to develop sufficient conviction to have the courage to think for oneself and to stand alone. There are those who "visit" their parents and proclaim, "I am a person, recognize me as such!" Well, that is making a demand on the family, which is the opposite of differentiation of self. There are countless other examples of how the approach to family of origin has been bastardized.

Another major misconception about family of origin is that one can be become a more differentiated person solely through efforts in that arena. Differentiation is something people must pay attention to in their extended family, nuclear family, work situation, and social network. Undifferentiation is ubiquitous, always there to counterbalance differentiation, whatever the life situation. Differentiation does not mean having a better relationship with one's mother, although that usually occurs; it means trying to get more objective about self and others, and living as much as possible on the basis of that objectivity. Among other things, this means examining one's beliefs, attitudes, and values, and becoming aware of beliefs that are discrepant. Differentiation is not a set of techniques for changing relationships; it is a process in which people examine the way they think, gradually building conviction about a different way of thinking. To accomplish this, people must distinguish between the feeling/subjective side of themselves and the more thoughtful side, and be able to act on the basis of that distinction when they decide it is important to do so.

Bowen believed that family systems theory may contribute as much to all of medicine as it does to psychiatry and mental health. By keeping a focus on how to think rather than on what to think, the theory is open to modifications, amplifications, and extensions based on factual knowledge derived from multiple disciplines. I believe that the next hundred years will witness considerable fleshing out of Bowen theory, much as Darwin's theory of natural selection as a basis for evolutionary change has been fleshed out since 1859. I also believe that Bowen's basic blueprint of the family emotional system, just as Darwin's basic blueprint of evolutionary change, will survive the test of time.

PREFACE

The Bowen Family Theory and Its Uses is an exploration and series of applications of a pioneering family theory. My early professional work was in the area of general social theory development. In the early 1970s, I began to specialize in family theory construction through my work with Murray Bowen, M.D., The Family Center, Department of Psychiatry, Georgetown University Medical Center. The Bowen theory is the basis of the conceptualizations and propositions presented here.

Although I have been familiar with some of Dr. Bowen's ideas for more than ten years, the manuscript of *The Bowen Family Theory and Its Uses* has been in gestation for only seven years. As my professional work in theory construction advanced, I realized the need for a book-length description of Dr. Bowen's original contributions to family theory. In the early stages of writing, I worked with Dr. Bowen to coauthor a book of this kind.

After more than five years of discussion, for the most part with Dr. Bowen himself, and after closer reading of his works, I concluded that my interpretation of the Bowen theory was problematic. I could not, as I had hoped, follow the details of Dr. Bowen's thinking. My rote repetition of some of his ideas and illustrations still reminds me that I have been unable to digest various meanings and implications of his work.

The ideas expressed in *The Bowen Family Theory and Its Uses* could not have been formulated without my own gripping interest in, and fascination for, one of Bowen's major hypotheses: Human beings' perceptions of self and others are more strongly influenced by the quality of their emotional dependency in family relationships than by any other social or environmental factor. In developing this interest, I was unable to explore the manifold aspects of these issues without changing my own perceptions and behavior.

Thinking in terms of family emotional systems may become for the reader, as it did for me, more than an academic exercise. I pondered for many hours my understanding of the Bowen family theory, as my attention was necessarily drawn to a little-researched order of social and behavioral phenomena. The concepts used are both professional and personal. When new ideas in the theory make sense, change of self through action may follow a modified perception of self and others.

The Bowen family theory is also a practical theory of emotional systems. The range of applications described in *The Bowen Family Theory and Its Uses* does not do justice to the theory's versatility, although some of the broad-ranging discussions and illustrations included may convey the intrinsic flexibility of the concepts. The theory has many implications for further research on a wide range of general human behavior.

This is not a simple how-to-do-it book. It touches on such divergent subject areas as evolution, healing, business management, aging, and religion. In it are many practical suggestions, implicit if not explicit, for the family researcher and the family caseworker, as well as for those interested in theory construction or just in new ideas. New approaches to business management and social policy decision making are also presented.

It is my hope that *The Bowen Family Theory and Its Uses* will be more than food for thought. Optimally, the principles I present will be sufficiently meaningful to encourage the creation of additional applications to self, to families, and to various aspects of social interaction.

My indebtedness to Murray Bowen, M.D., Clinical Professor of Psychiatry and Director, The Family Center, Georgetown University Medical Center, Washington, D.C., is overwhelming. Dr. Bowen answered many questions I put to him and left many unanswered. He spent long hours discussing theoretical issues with me and left me wanting to continue each exchange. Dr. Bowen's ideas have changed my life, even though I have not been able to capture their essence and describe them clearly in many places in this book.

The faculty and staff of The Family Center played a significant part in the development of *The Bowen Family Theory and Its Uses*. Besides finding supportive colleagues— especially Dr. Lillian Winer—Ruth Riley and Elaine Trogdon worked directly with me to make my interpretation and description of Dr. Bowen's ideas more intelligible.

Brenda Broz Eddy, a faculty member of Georgetown Business School, originally coauthored the work that I subsequently revised as Chapter 8, "Formal Organizations," and Chapter 13, "Toward a General Theory of Human Behavior." Without her generous and thoughtful contributions in the early stages of drafting the applications and implications of the Bowen theory, these particular chapters might not have been completed. I am also indebted to Brenda Eddy, who has now joined The New

TransCentury Foundation in Washington, D.C., for selecting salient references from the literature in formal organization theory.

Dr. Marvin Sussman, Bowman Gray School of Medicine, also coauthored the discussion of alternatives to institutional care that now appears as the second part of Chapter 6, "Aging and Institutionalization." Our joint effort was presented at the Committee on Public Issues and the Family Session at the 1975 annual meeting of the American Sociological Association. I am indebted to Dr. Sussman for his contributions based on his past experience in making policy recommendations to government agencies.

The first part of Chapter 6, which has been revised, was originally published as "Aging and Family Processes" in *Journal of Family Counseling* 4 (1976): 28-42. This article is reprinted by permission of Transaction, Inc.

Pat McMahon and Nell Anderson read drafts of my work and made editorial suggestions. Ellen Dorosh and Samantha Hawkins assumed the primary responsibility for typing the manuscript at different stages. They gave me significant assistance in my efforts, as a book is much more than a series of discussed ideas, and it takes on a life of its own as it is drafted and redrafted.

Colleagues and students in the Sociology Department at Georgetown University and the staff and families I worked with at Frederick Community Mental Health Services from 1971 to 1976 influenced my work, as did members of my own family. I am also grateful for the sabbatical leave granted to me by Georgetown University for the 1977–78 academic year. The impact of these various contributions is impossible to assess. My intent is to communicate that this book is by no means a solo performance, and that I cannot take credit for all the value *The Bowen Family Theory and Its Uses* may have for its readers.

INTRODUCTION

The field of family research is too new to have a body of clearly defined knowledge about which there is general agreement. Any author who attempts to survey family studies as they now exist will produce a theoretically biased evaluation, as each investigator is so immersed in a selective way of thinking that it is difficult to really know, or even hear, the work of others.

A variety of principles, methods, and techniques have been used to understand behavioral processes in families. These approaches to family research are frequently based on a conglomerate of vague and contradictory theoretical notions. A lack of awareness of the assumptions which have been accepted and incorporated into the different working hypotheses has tended to result in treatment of these assumptions as facts.

At present, the family field is a theoretical maze. The Bowen theory is described here in the belief that the dilemma of incompatible orientations will be resolved more quickly and more fruitfully if investigators present their thinking as clearly as possible.

The Bowen theory consists of a series of eight working concepts and hypotheses, which together provide a description of processes in emotional systems. The basic concepts of this theory include the following: differentiation of self, triangles, nuclear family emotional system, family projection process, emotional cut-off, multigenerational transmission process, sibling position, and emotional process in society. The Bowen theory describes some of the more predictable aspects of human emotional behavior. Individuals are viewed as biological beings who behave in ways inextricably related to the behavior of other animals.

Bowen suggests that people can become more maturely dependent in different kinds of intimate and social relationships. However, independence from emotional needs is considered a theoretical and empirical impossibility. The Bowen theory can be summarized as a general theory of emotional processes in human relationship systems, with an emphasis on biological rather than cultural variables.

One important difference between the Bowen theory and other family theories which are applied clinically to emotional problems is the express attempt of Bowen family therapists to operate as much as possible outside the emotional field of a person or a family. Conventional family theory and psychotherapy train therapists to work inside this emotional field. The Bowen theory communicates what it means to be in or out of an emotional system, and one of Bowen's hypotheses is that family therapists will achieve effective clinical results to the extent that they remain outside the emotional field of the family in the clinical setting.

History of the Family Movement

Family movement refers to the emphasis on family theory and family therapy that began in the United States in the mid-1950s, although it could be argued that a family movement began in the United States during the early decades of this century. For example, some family studies and clinical work were attempted in the 1920s, in response to the problem social conditions of rapidly growing cities. However, the thesis that the family movement developed as an evolutionary process may be more accurate, as some examples of early antecedents of family work were discovered in retrospect, following the beginnings of the later and more influential *family movement*.

The family movement is a more direct development of psychoanalysis, which introduced concepts describing the actual and potential influences of one human life on another. In most respects, the family as a unit of study was outside the immediate field of interest of psychoanalysis. The focus in psychoanalysis was on a single patient and on personal retroactive memories about the patient's family life.

Sociologists and anthropologists studied families and contributed to the professional literature on family research before the family movement began in the 1950s. These sociological and anthropological contributions were largely descriptions of cultural differences observed in families, rather than accounts of predictable patterns of interaction in families. Such research generally did not provide a solid theoretical base for the conceptualization of different kinds of family emotional processes, nor did it recognize emotional processes common to families in different cultures. Although sociologists and anthropologists have made several attempts to focus on specific kinds of family behavior, such as the allocation of roles and the division of labor, they have not conceptualized the family as an emotional system.

Another influence in the evolution of the family movement was the development of general systems theory following the pioneering work of Ludwig von Bertalanffy in the 1930s. This general systems orientation questioned the logic and assumptions underlying the cause-effect paradigm utilized in most scientific disciplines at that time. The systems focus, which aims to replace the cause-effect schema, is a model of a whole unit composed of the complex interaction of many variables. Each set of variables is conceptualized as inextricably related to the other sets. A change in any part of the complex unit is accompanied by predictable changes in other parts of the system. The general systems frame of reference produced a new way of describing fairly predictable sequences of events. This model pinpoints the ineffectiveness of conceptualizations which arbitrarily label one set of phenomena as "cause" and another as "effect." The fact that B follows A no longer suggests that B is caused by A.

Before the burgeoning of the family movement in the mid-1950s, several family researchers and therapists had worked independently on similar themes. The formation of the Committee on the Family by the Group for the Advancement of Psychiatry in 1950 was another step in the evolution of the family movement. The committee, formed at the suggestion of William C. Menninger, worked for several years without much knowledge of parallel developments in the field until family movement therapists more openly articulated their views at national professional meetings.

It is impossible to explain why the family movement began in the way it did at that particular time, although a few observations about some of the trends can be made. Several concepts used in the newly developing movement had been available for many years but until this period were neither a focus of interest nor a theoretical preoccupation. Another point of interest about the family movement is that many of the originators had backgrounds in psychiatry, although very few were child psychiatrists. Characteristics of the family movement seem directly related to the development of psychoanalysis, which during the 1930s gained increasing acceptance in psychiatry. However, although psychoanalytic theory had explanations for many family emotional problems, adequate treatment techniques had not been developed especially for more severe symptoms. Those who began family research and family therapy appear to have been largely motivated by a need to initiate more effective treatment methods.

Clinical observations of whole families provided a spectrum of behavioral and emotional patterns that had not yet been accounted for. Although at first each investigator reported and interpreted observations in isolation from other researchers, many of the concepts used in the early studies are still current; some have been developed into concepts central to the family field today. As new family sessions were held at several national professional gatherings, the family movement became increasingly recognized. Information about family therapy spread rapidly, and beginning in 1958 therapists crowded into family sessions at national meetings.

The rapid increase in the number of family therapists was the beginning of a healthy ferment in the family movement. The development of family theory was largely ignored, however, and most family therapists operated with the basic assumptions of individual theory, which were usually taken as scientific fact.

In 1970, the Committee on the Family of the Group for the Advancement of Psychiatry completed a report on the family movement. Among the committee's findings was the interesting fact that the overwhelming majority of family therapists used the same theory and practice used by individual therapists. Family therapy was most often used as a supplement to individual therapy; in very few instances was it the main technique. A few "deviant" therapists, who thought in terms of systems and emotional fields of relationships, viewed almost all problems in the family context and consulted with several family members during the course of treatment.

As professional experience in family therapy has increased, more and more family therapists have changed from the individualistic style of family therapy to an emotional systems orientation. With this change in orientation has come increasing use of a terminology related more closely to theory than to specific techniques.

Development of the Bowen Theory

The main thrust of Bowen's work has been to make the study of human behavior as scientific as possible. His efforts have been based on the conviction that human behavior is relatively predictable. Bowen has been developing his theory over a period of more than twenty-five years of clinical work with families. In the 1950s he took as his original research focus the symbiotic relationship between a mother and her schizophrenic child.

His first research hypothesis, based on his accumulated direct observations of families, was that the origin and development of schizophrenia was a product of the two-person mother-patient relationship. This hypothesis was elaborated in detail, and many of the relationship problems that could develop in different clinical situations were anticipated. Psychotherapeutic principles and techniques were developed for every possible clinical situation.

Bowen's first research hypothesis also predicted the kinds and rates of changes that would occur in the course of psychotherapy. When research observations were not consistent with that hypothesis, it was changed to fit the new facts, the psychotherapy was modified to fit the changed hypothesis, and new predictions were made as to the results of the psychotherapy. When an unexpected clinical crisis arose, it was handled on an interim clinical-judgment basis and the hypothesis was considered faulty for not having anticipated the situation and for not having generated effective therapeutic principles. Except in emergencies, the therapy was not changed on an ad hoc basis to fit the situation; rather, the research goals were to change the hypothesis to account for the unexpected crisis and on this basis to change the therapy and make new predictions. Failure to change self and relationships during the course of psychotherapy was considered as much a reason to reexamine and modify the hypothesis as any unpredicted crisis or situation.

Strict adherence to such organization of concepts in relation to observations resulted in the development of an integrated theoretical-therapeutic system, with psychotherapy being largely determined by theory. The discipline necessitated by the research project improved the skill of the therapists, and the research plan was designed to fit as closely as possible with other structured research in science.

The original hypothesis about the symbiotic mother-patient relationship was accurate in predicting some of the details of behavior patterns within the twosome, but did not account for the different ways the twosome related to others. A critical omission was that the hypothesis did not conceptualize how the mother and patient interacted with other members of the same family. At this point of awareness in the course of research the theoretical basis for the project became oriented more to family systems. The basic hypothesis was modified to include fathers, and families with fathers were added to the research. At the same time, a more extended method of family psychotherapy was devised to fit that hypothesis.

Although particular relationship characteristics observed in families with schizophrenia were initially hypothesized as specific for schizophrenia, once it was possible to discern their patterns of interaction similar but less intense patterns became evident in families with less severe emotional impairment. The same kinds of patterns could also be observed in "normal" families and in the work system of researchers and therapists conducting the experiment. The latter finding brought about a major change in Bowen's subsequent family research. Efforts began to be directed away from schizophrenia and toward less impaired human behavior, including individuals and families without clinical problems.

With this shift in research focus, different hypotheses were generated. Since people with less severe problems change more rapidly in family psychotherapy, new observations and further alterations of the original hypothesis were accelerated. Bowen gradually extended and modified the hypothesis, and each change was continually checked, both in and out of the clinical setting.

Interrelated concepts emerged when the hypothesis was accurate enough to no longer require significant modification. The concepts proved useful for describing and predicting discrepancies as well as consistencies in human behavior. Only after several integrated concepts were developed could the term *theory* be used to describe this unique system of ideas. The Bowen theory thus emerged as considerably different from conventional individual theory, and distinct as well from other kinds of family thinking.

Bowen's clinical work with families emphasizes the importance of emotional nonparticipation by the therapist for a successful therapeutic outcome. One advantage of emotional nonparticipation is the therapist's increased capacity for objectivity in observing behavior and gathering information. Only when a family functions as an emotional unit can its relationship patterns be relatively definite, orderly, and predictable. If an important other person participates in the family emotional system or is removed from the system, relationship patterns become atypical and important nuances in family processes are obscured. Family interaction is modified when a therapist becomes emotionally *fused* into a family. A pragmatic dividend of a therapist's emotional nonparticipation is the increased likelihood of orderly and consistent progress in the course of family psychotherapy. When the therapist can remain relatively outside the family emotional system, long-term results are more positive, and therapeutic impasses occur less frequently.

Another dividend of a therapist's emotional nonparticipation is the therapist's greater freedom to relate to any family member throughout the course of therapy. When a therapist can remain emotionally free but still in emotional contact with family members, the family becomes calmer and more flexible, and family members themselves are emotionally more free. This posture of emotional nonparticipation allows a therapist to use knowledge of family systems to guide efforts with a family more effectively. When family relationship patterns are distorted, progress slows down or family members become passive and wait for the therapist to solve problems. These signs indicate that the therapist has become fused into the family and needs to devote more attention to the quality of his emotional functioning.

The observation of similar relationship patterns in families at all levels of emotional maturity provided an added dimension to Bowen's research. Observations of functioning in the broadest range of different families led Bowen to a more accurate perspective. The delineation of essential differences between feeling and thinking and their various behavioral manifestations led to the formulation of concepts that proved central to the Bowen theory and related psychotherapy. Observations suggested that emotionally impaired individuals do not distinguish between subjective feelings and thinking. The intellectual processes of emotionally impaired individuals are in fact so flooded with feeling that they are incapable of thinking that is at all separate or distinct from feelings. They generally consider it truthful and honest to speak in terms of feelings, and insincere and false to speak of thinking, beliefs, and opinions. They strive for togetherness and agreement in relationships with others and avoid statements establishing self as different from others. Observations also suggested that more integrated persons can distinguish between feeling and thinking processes and are more accurate in their use of the phrases "I feel" and "I think."

Much study and work with a large variety of families went into Bowen's effort to clarify feeling/thinking issues. The quality of interplay between feeling and thinking came to be considered one of the most accurate indicators for assessing different levels of emotional integration in individuals and families.

Bowen's overall research hypothesis about the nature of symptomatic behavior suggests that all observable symptoms are manifestations of disorders in emotional systems. A related hypothesis is that the human emotional system is an intimate part of a phylogenetic past shared with lower forms of life and governed by laws applicable to living things. Specifically, human thought is seen as a function of the more recently developed cerebral cortex, the most essential distinguishing characteristic between human beings and less evolved forms of life. Although human emotional and intellectual systems have different functions, they are interconnected and influence each other. The connection between the two systems appears to be the feeling system, through which certain influences from upper strata of the emotional system are perceived by the cerebral cortex as feelings.

Emotion can be conceptualized as an energy or an instinct, a drive or force that governs all life processes. Emotional illness can be viewed as a deep-seated behavioral manifestation which is more than a disorder of the mind. In developing his theory, Bowen discontinued use of the term *mental illness*, which connotes a disorder of thinking, and substituted *emotional illness* to describe this kind of dysfunction more accurately.

Although the brain is an integral part of each human being's protoplasmic totality, the mind is more easily productive when it is devoted to subjects outside human experience. People have been less effective in their achievements when they have directed intellect to themselves and to their own behavior. For example, people became knowledgeable about the solar system many years before human systems were researched. Although human beings are related to all members of the animal kingdom, they have been more successful in defining ways in which they differ from lower life forms than they have in defining instances of kinship and shared characteristics.

A major hypothesis of the Bowen theory is that human emotional systems run a course as predictable as that of any natural phenomenon. Illness is viewed as behavior which is manifested by emotional systems in different states of dysfunction and impairment. Perhaps the main problem in discovering how emotional illnesses come about rests more in the ways in which people deny, rationalize, and think about emotional illness than in the nature of emotional illness itself. It is possible to predict fairly accurately the natural course of an emotional disorder and, with this knowledge, to allow for some modification of the processes of emotional impairment.

Part I

Theory

Chapter 1

THEORETICAL PERSPECTIVES

Historical Background

Bowen has been developing his family theory for more than twenty-five years. In the United States in the early 1950s, Murray Bowen, Nathan Ackerman, Virginia Satir, Don Jackson, and other pioneer family clinicians used a family perspective to examine and understand individual behavior. Bowen's early family research at the National Institutes of Mental Health focused on mother-child relationships in families with a schizophrenic child. To work more effectively with these families and to describe other family relationships and other patterns of behavior, Bowen articulated a series of concepts that represent the family as an emotional system, and schizophrenia as a family problem. Bowen postulates that these concepts describe emotional processes in all families rather than emotional processes peculiar to families in clinical populations.

Data Sources

Large clinical populations have been used for the development and substantiation of these family concepts by both Bowen and myself, and additional data have been collected from the families of mental health professionals and of undergraduate, graduate, and medical students. Genealogical records have been used for longitudinal research on family interaction with smaller populations.

Theoretical Assumptions

1. Bowen's concepts describe emotional processes thought to have a strong influence on both human and animal behavior. Human beings are perceived as having an evolutionary heritage of primitive levels of functioning, which influence all kinds of behavior. Important examples of primitive behavior are the reflexive and reactive emotional responses between human beings, which are most visible in families and intimate relationships. The Bowen theory conceptualizes human behavior in a broad evolutionary context and assumes the existence of certain universals in human and animal behavior.

2. Bowen suggests that the intense emotional interdependency in families contributes toward making family interaction more predictable than behavior in other groups or settings. Family interaction tends to crystallize in particular patterns through time, and these patterns are frequently repeated in several subsequent generations. When sufficient intergenerational data about a family are available, the degree of persistence in certain patterns of behavior or the intensity of system reactions to a disruption of established patterns of behavior and dependency can be estimated fairly accurately.

3. Families appear to exert a strong and compelling influence

for the conformity of each member's behavior, but Bowen's theory suggests several benefits in resisting this pressure by changing functioning positions in the relationship systems.

Basic Concepts

Eight major concepts have been developed from Bowen's initial conceptualization of a family unit as an "undifferentiated family ego mass." Bowen no longer uses the concept of undifferentiated family ego mass.

1. *Differentiation of self.* Self may be thought of as both *solid self*, which is nonnegotiable with others, and *pseudo-self*, which is negotiable with others. A more differentiated person behaves from a basis of a more fully integrated solid self and less pseudo-self than does a less differentiated person. It is extremely difficult for anyone to move up or down from a given level of differentiation. A lifetime of efforts to differentiate self may culminate in only slight changes in solid self. At the higher levels of differentiation, behavior is influenced by thinking and self-selected goals. At the lower levels of differentiation, behavior is more *automatic* and is largely controlled by emotions and the anxiety of the moment.

2. *Triangles.* The smallest relationship system in families and other social settings has three members rather than two. A triangle is the basic unit of interdependence and interaction in a family emotional system. When anxiety in a two-person relationship reaches a certain level, a third person is predictably drawn into the emotional field of the twosome. Where triangles in a family are not readily apparent, they remain dormant and can be activated at any time, particularly in a period of stress.

3. *Nuclear Family Emotional System.* The most intensely interdependent part of a family is the nuclear group. Three mechanisms are used in most families to deal with the overload

of anxiety that frequently amasses in the nuclear system. The adaptive mechanisms are marital conflict, dysfunction of a spouse, and projection to a child. Most families use a combination of all three mechanisms to dilute the unlivable intensity resulting from an overload of anxiety.

4. *Family Projection Process.* Parents stabilize their relationship with each other and lower the anxiety in their undifferentiated twosome by viewing a child as their shared "problem." This overinvestment of feeling in a child frequently impairs the child's capacity to function effectively in the family and other social settings.

5. *Emotional Cut-off.* In an attempt to deal with the fusion or lack of differentiation in their intimate relationships, family members or segments of the extended system may distance themselves from each other and become emotionally divorced. Cut-offs are particularly frequent between the parent and grandparent generations of a family. One direct consequence of emotional cut-off is the burdening of the nuclear system with an equivalent overinvestment of feelings and expectations.

6. *Multigenerational Transmission Process.* The strong tendency to repeat impairing patterns of emotional behavior in successive generations culminates in lowered levels of differentiation of self for certain members of the younger generations. Unless conscious efforts to modify these impaired patterns are made, such behavior is usually repeated automatically.

7. *Sibling Position.* Seniority and sex distribution among siblings in the same and related generations has a strong influence on behavior. A more differentiated individual is able to neutralize some of the programming for the typical expectations of that person's sibling position.

8. *Emotional Process in Society.* The strength of the emotional forces in society may make differentiation difficult or

impossible. When togetherness forces in society are strong, anxiety is high and problem behavior is pervasive. Extreme behavior sequences, such as violence and destructive political leadership, are more likely to occur when the anxiety level of the emotional process in society is high than when less anxiety exists in society.

Sociological Contributions

1. Bowen's concepts suggest universals in human behavior that extend beyond the descriptive studies of family cultural variations characteristic of the field of sociology. His work is an attempt to show that human nature and human behavior are components of evolutionary processes rather than products of historical or cultural contingency.

2. Bowen's family concepts have a broader scope than role analyses. According to Bowen, behavior emanates from a self which is only partly influenced by wider cultural forces.

3. As any group can be considered an emotional system, Bowen's family theory can be applied to behavior in other social settings. It may be thought of as a middle-range theory, as the empirical context of this family paradigm is a limited social setting, which can be documented more easily and accurately than other concepts.

4. Bowen's concepts suggest prediction as well as description. Although many of these predictions may remain substantively unverified for generations to come, some limited predictions can be made in individual families from accumulated case histories.

5. The Bowen theory indicates the possibility of viewing family dependency and patterns of family interaction as independent variables in research on human behavior. Although a division between independent and dependent variables may be

artificial and overly simplistic, Bowen's concepts postulate that family dependency and patterns of family interaction play a more significant role in influencing all kinds of human behavior than is reflected in current sociological family research.

6. Bowen's view of the family as an emotionally interdependent unit suggests that change in one part of the system will bring about changes in related parts and ultimately of the whole. This sequence of changes does not necessarily culminate in a return to the original position of homeostasis. Under optimal conditions, a new level of functioning or differentiation for the entire family is created. Bowen's concepts articulate a specific theory of family change and imply a broader theory of social change.

7. The analogies and theoretical models Bowen uses to describe emotional processes are drawn from biology. Sociologists may criticize this orientation as "reductionist," but a view of family as an ecological unit specifies the interrelatedness of all living phenomena more adequately than sociological models.

8. Bowen's family theory extends and modifies Freud's emphasis on instinctive behavior. Bowen attempts to describe systematically more socially expressed rudimentary behaviors, such as a human need for togetherness, than Freud did. Bowen also suggests the existence of collective automatic strivings for the survival of the human species rather than individual struggles.

9. Bowen defines some of the limits to changing individual behavior and patterns of family interaction. He is more concerned with possibilities and probabilities than with modes or norms of behavior; a preoccupation with the latter is typical of much of the sociological literature on family.

10. Bowen consistently maintains a view of a family as a multigenerational system. Longitudinal genealogical research on past generations enhances his view and neutralizes the apparent

sociological overemphasis on the importance of interaction in nuclear families.

Family Systems and Cross-Cultural Studies

The Bowen family systems theory is sufficiently versatile to be particularly useful for international cross-cultural research. Its emphasis on universals in human behavior, biological analogies, and an evolutionary context allows for a wider variety of cultural applications and international comparisons than family theories based on cultural differentials and normative descriptions.

International research in family behavior has proliferated in recent years, and systematic syntheses of the different findings (Aldous and Hill 1967) are much needed. A large part of the existing family research describes cultural variations of family behavior without reference to explicitly articulated theory. The family systems theory may be viewed as a middle-range sociological theory. The systems concepts could be used to interpret or reinterpret family data already collected, as well as to provide an alternative orientation for future international comparative studies.

Family systems theory is a beginning formulation of a general theory of emotional systems. A family system consists of human dependencies and emotional needs present in all societies at all times. Although it is extremely difficult to substantiate hypotheses that link specific family data to accurate indicators of evolutionary change, measurement problems do not nullify the significance and usefulness of these ideas for viewing family behavior. The emotional systems extension of the Bowen theory also suggests that it is possible to pinpoint common denominators of behavior in families and other social settings, as these characteristics are also present in all societies at all times.

History

Bowen's family systems theory was developed within the discipline of psychiatry (1960, 1966, 1971a). As Bowen's theoretical orientation has relieved symptoms in families and has precipitated changes in functioning in families and in the wider society, however, his propositions might be utilized successfully in a variety of research settings.

Some disadvantages of the family systems conceptualization may limit its general applicability to comparative international studies. The theory evolved in the post–World War II era in the United States from data largely drawn from white middle-class families. Such a sampling introduced a certain amount of bias and error into its formulations; however, the theory has since been operationalized in a large variety of clinical settings with a broad spectrum of different types of families. Many of the families in these clinical samples had international and intercultural backgrounds, as well as low socioeconomic status. Clinical findings indicate that there are distinct similarities in behavior and patterns of interdependency within and between the different national, cultural, and socioeconomic groups.

Theory

Bowen's family systems theory consists of eight basic interlocking concepts. No single concept can be fully understood except in relation to the other seven concepts, and each has evolved in complex and distinct ways. The following discussion describes selected meaning elements of concepts to pinpoint their applicability to international comparative studies. I will not discuss the difficulties involved in operationalizing the ideas, although this problem is inevitably a significant limiting influence in any overall evaluation of the usefulness of a family systems perspective.

Differentiation of Self. A variety of behavior is described to represent degrees of emotional strength of self. These characteristic patterns can be delineated in any cultural setting. Functioning can indicate lower or higher levels of differentiation of self. When a self is less differentiated, behavior is largely emotionally responsive or reactive and shows little or no indication of being thought directed. When a self is more differentiated, behavior is goal directed, with a clear awareness of distinctions between thinking and feeling activities.

Triangles. Following the tradition of Georg Simmel's "triadic" conceptualization of human behavior (Wolff 1950) and extending some of Theodore Caplow's findings (1968), Bowen has defined the smallest relationship unit in a family as a triangle, or a three-person system. This relationship unit can be found in any family in any society. A triangle is a relatively stable group with shifting emotional forces. The most uncomfortable participant in a dyad, or two-person system, predictably draws a third person into the twosome when sufficient stress occurs in the two-person relationship. This process creates a triangle in any family in any society.

Nuclear Family Emotional System. The inner core of a family, the two-generation group of parents and children, is the most intense emotionally interdependent part of a family. This degree of intensity exists in any nuclear family in any society. One family system has several nuclear families in its broader network. In nuclear systems where there is no clear differentiation of self between spouses, surplus anxiety must be absorbed. Mechanisms of adaptation that resolve these tensions include marital conflict, dysfunction of a spouse, and projection to one or more of the children. The surplus anxiety and mechanisms of adaptation are characteristic of all families in all societies. Many families use all three mechanisms to deal with an overload of tension.

Family Projection Process. The undifferentiation or fusion of parents can be projected to the most dependent child in a family. In some families there may be a projection to a dependent older person in the family. This projection generally has less impairing consequences than projection to a child, as the latter's ability to function may gradually be affected. These impairing consequences can occur in any society. A family projection can be considered a scapegoating process in which one person is singled out as a family "problem." In reality, the problem is not localized in that person as much as in the entire relationship system of the family, especially in key members such as the parents.

Emotional Cut-Off. Emotional divorces or estrangements in families reflect a high level of intensity. Emotional cut-offs also precipitate increased anxiety in surrounding relationships. These relationship tendencies exist in all families in all societies. Symptomatic behavior is most prevalent in families where there are many emotional cut-offs. Parents who have eliminated cut-offs with their parents are less likely to experience cut-offs with their children. Although much effort and courage is needed to contact a person who has cut off or has been cut off in a family, self can be strengthened by reestablishing such cut-off relationships.

Multigenerational Transmission Process. Repeated projection processes through several generations in a family create an extended powerful emotional force, which eventually raises or lowers levels of differentiation in members of succeeding generations. This repetition and powerful influence exist between different generations of families in all societies. Genealogical data and observations of families over several generations provide evidence of a variety of repeated patterns of dependent behavior.

Sibling Position. Walter Toman (1972) generalized profiles of expected behavior from observations of different sibling positions. These expectations cross cultural boundaries and apply to all societies at all times. The probability of this typical sibling behavior occurring appears to depend largely on the level of anxiety in the family. Bowen emphasizes that sibling position behavior can also be greatly influenced by family projection.

Emotional Process in Society. Emotional process in society represents a combination of the forces of togetherness (fusion) and individuation (differentiation). Any society manifests emotional process as a combination of these two forces. The level of anxiety in society influences how the emotional process is expressed. Emotional process in society has an impact on each family member's behavior. The pervasiveness of particular patterns of family dependency also intensify or deintensify the general level of emotional process in society. Emotional process in society may be progressively adaptive or regressively maladaptive within the context of evolutionary change.

International Comparative Studies

The following observations and propositions illustrate some of the implications of family systems for a synthesis of international comparative data from cross-cultural family research.

1. Families in any society can be conceptualized as emotional systems with a range of degrees of dependency. Family systems can be classified as relatively open or closed.

2. The degree of predictability of individual behavior in a family and in the wider society is greater if the family is relatively closed. Symptomatic and antisocial behavior is more characteristic of families with a closed relationship system.

3. Emotional processes perpetuated over several generations are influential determinants of present behavior in a family. Specific patterns of behavior in a family tend to be repeated in different generations regardless of the extent of that family's exposure to different cultural influences through time.

4. The timing of major events such as deaths, births, migrations, or job changes has a significant impact on family behavior. Much human behavior can be described as responses to the timing of shifts in dependency in family emotional systems.

5. Individuals tend to behave according to the specific expectations for the sex and rank ascribed to them in their families of origin. Some of the observed variations in the behavior of members of a particular sex in the wider society are associated with the range of behavior patterns generated by the different distributions of sex and seniority in families. In general, males appear as emotionally dependent on females as females are on males.

6. Triangles have more predictable characteristics than other relationship systems. When triangles in a family are delineated, more accurate predictions of behavior can be made about behavior in that family. Behavior in the wider society can also be predicted, to some extent, by examining the ways in which individuals participate in triangles in their own families, particularly in their families of origin.

7. An individual can be a self to the extent that he or she is aware of togetherness and individuating forces in the family and other social groups. Togetherness forces are more automatic and easier to delineate than differentiating forces. Differentiation of self is only possible when sustained conscious efforts are made. Efforts to differentiate self are more effective within the context of an individual's own family than in other social settings.

8. Most people have a moderate or mid-range level of differentiation. Each specific level of differentiation is a balancing point of togetherness and differentiation forces. Considerable changes in a person's level of differentiation are impossible. A significant move in a direction toward differentiation or toward togetherness is counteracted by the

pull of the force not currently activated. Because of the intensity of the interdependence of these counterbalancing forces, it is extremely difficult to change an individual level of differentiation.

The family systems perspective implies that research on families is more useful if longitudinal data is used. Where multigenerational data has already been collected, interpretative analyses could pinpoint the frequency of transmission processes or other repeated patterns of emotionally dependent behavior. Although Bowen does not emphasize the influence of the broader social network on family behavior as much as do some other family researchers (Bott 1957), family systems concepts suggest some social policy directives and alternatives that could improve family functioning.

The systems perspective provides a new view of family problems currently described in conventional culture-based diagnostic or social-problem terms. Systems thinking crosses national boundaries in its specific applications by highlighting the emotional processes that enter into different varieties of traditional labeling.

A family is a prototype of emotional and social systems. International comparative research on families is epistemologically significant because of its potential for contributing to a fuller understanding of broader macrosociological forces within and between societies. Such research also provides more reliable empirical indicators of evolutionary processes than research based on conventional concepts.

Chapter 2

FAMILY PROCESSES

To more clearly conceptualize family processes as an independent variable in the total social complex, selected aspects of the family systems orientation are restated. Bowen's contribution is unusual in its emphasis on the importance of documenting the degree of influence of family variables in all kinds of social research.

Behavioral Determinants

Recent research on families and the state of theoretical formulation in family studies suggest a few distinctive trends. There appears to have been a shift in emphasis from a conceptualization of families as basic social groupings with particular structures, functions, and roles (Parson and Bales 1955) to a conceptualization of families as emotionally charged intradependent units with a wide range of characteristic behavior or processes (Turner 1970, Broderick 1971).

In spite of efforts to relate the American experience to that of other countries, most family theories that originated in the United States are ethnocentric in that they were based primarily on American data. However, with the recent conceptual focus on family processes, the traditional socioeconomic and cultural characteristics of American families (Farber 1964, Parsons 1943, Schneider 1973) have been researched, together with newer "universalistic" concerns about the enduring impact of patterns of family interaction (Troll 1971), the significance of extended family influences (Sussman and Burchinal 1962), and the influence of intergenerational patterns of behavior.

Although little systematic research has been done on the nature of the interplay of family and nonfamily behavior patterns this topic is beginning to receive greater attention in family studies. Related working hypotheses are that the family can be viewed as a basic ecological unit or maintenance system in society and that the emotional climate generated by the complex interdependence between several generations of family members can have a lasting impact on how each family member behaves in nonfamily settings as well as in the family.

The Bowen family theory addresses itself to the need for a comprehensive conceptual schema to describe and define the complex interplay of emotional processes in family dependencies. Some of the assumptions of the family systems conceptualization constitute ways in which experimental and field observations can be organized to link indicators of family behavior with data from other social contexts. For more details about these assumptions, see some of Bowen's original work and reviews (1959, 1960, 1961, 1965a, 1966, 1971a, 1971b, 1972).

Family and Nonfamily Behavior

The Bowen theory suggests specific ways in which family and

nonfamily behavior may be linked. Some of these linkage
be described in terms of the family systems concepts.

1. A person who acts in accordance with others' expectations for a particular chronological or functioning sibling position tends to repeat the same interdependent behavior patterns in various social settings.

2. A person who is the object of a family projection is more vulnerable to projection or scapegoating processes in other social settings.

3. A person who is "triangled" into a family system tends to be easily triangled, or "caught up" in the emotional inter-dependencies of other relationships and social groups.

4. An individual's differentiation of self in a social group depends on the effectiveness of that person's differentiation of self in the family.

These assumptions can be used as a guide to explore the extent to which family processes may be considered primary determinants of behavior. The more general concept of emotional system can also be used to draw closer parallels between family and nonfamily behavior by documenting some of the shared characteristics of families and other groups and the shared behavior patterns of their respective members.

Emotional Systems

Any investigation of the extent to which family theory can explain human behavior suggests that family processes can be conceptualized as an independent variable in the complex array of influences on human behavior. However, the theoretical approaches used in most family studies rarely lay claim to such a view of family processes (Zimmerman 1962, Lee 1974, Martin 1974). In the relatively few studies in which family processes have been used to explain broad ranges of social behavior (Cooper 1970), conclusions have been harshly criticized and essentially dismissed as worthless. Perhaps a more useful way to describe the influence of family interaction on behavior is to view the family as an ecological unit. The family establishes the most significant emotional climate for the functioning of its members and programs its members to recreate similar emotional conditions and behavior patterns in nonfamily settings.

The degree of dependency in a family generates the intensity and "tightness" of the emotional climate of this relationship unit. The emotional climate establishes the significant postures and functioning orientations of each of its members for a lifetime. Patterns of family interaction and family programming influence past, present, and future behavior. Family systems theory is an emotional systems theory to the extent that social groups such as work, friendship, religious, and political systems manifest relationship characteristics similar to those of families.

Case History Data

Documentation of the influence of family processes on social behavior suggests that family membership is a more significant behavioral determinant than membership in a particular social class, ethnic group, or religious group. Some research findings on these linkages are illustrated by examples drawn from a sample of about six hundred detailed family case histories: three pairs of individuals with similar social backgrounds and different functioning levels, together with three pairs of individuals from dissimilar social backgrounds but with similar functioning levels.

Family Processes

Pairs with Similar Backgrounds and Different Functioning Le

1. *Individuals from the same ethnic group.* Both men were from the same black family. One was the oldest son, and the other, who was the next to the youngest, functioned as a youngest son in this family. The older son went to college and acted responsibly in his personal life and in a professional career after his education. The younger son dropped out of college. Although the younger son continued to be a "family favorite," he continually fell into "bad company" and was arrested on several occasions.

2. *Individuals from the same social class.* Two women from the same middle-class family functioned at different levels. The older woman, who was the oldest of four siblings, had been adopted. She described herself as having received much attention throughout her early childhood. The other children in this family were "natural" children. The older sister demanded much attention from others and developed problem behavior when she could not be the center of attention of others: she had an illegitimate child, became addicted to drugs, and attempted suicide. In contrast to her older sister, the younger woman in this family led a peaceful and productive life.

3. *Individuals with the same religion.* Two second sons in separate Jewish families functioned differently in relation to influences in their respective emotional systems. One of the second sons underfunctioned. He was a member of an intense family system that had experienced many deaths and cut-offs during his lifetime. He was unable either to make decisions or to act in his own interests. The second son from the other family had not been given much attention from his parents and siblings. His outside position in the family emotional system enabled him to lead a fairly independent and effective life and to follow his own interests and objectives.

**Pairs with Dissimilar Backgrounds but with Similar
Functioning Levels**

1. *Individuals from different ethnic groups.* Two second
daughters were compared, one from a black family and the other
from a white family. In spite of their different ethnic origins,
both women were effective in their social groups and both were
able to assist their elderly parents without becoming
destructively supportive through their care for them. In each
case, older brothers from birth had received most of the
emotional investment of their parents. One woman's brother
developed a drinking problem in adolescence. Each woman
consistently functioned from flexible and productive positions
in her family and other social settings.

2. *Individuals from different social classes.* Two middle
daughters from middle and lower social classes functioned at
home and in society in similar ways. Both women had fairly
autonomous positions in their families. They were able to
mature independently in relation to their parents and to their
more inhibited, "trapped-in" siblings.

3. *Individuals with different religions.* Two youngest sons,
one a Roman Catholic and the other a Protestant, functioned
similarly in their families and in other social groups. Neither
liked to assume responsibility for leadership or to make routine
decisions in day-to-day affairs. Both men had been the family
"problem" as children and disciplinary problems at school, and
they subsequently experienced marital difficulties.

Review of Observations

These brief descriptions can only suggest the possible strength
of family processes as behavioral determinants. Data on
different levels of functioning indicate that family processes are
significant variables in the complex "determination" of human
behavior.

When assessing the significance of interdependent processes in a family unit, the functioning positions of family members appear more critical in determining general behavior than rank or sex distribution. Also, the influence of family projection is increased by factors such as the frequency and number of deaths in a family and the number, intensity, and duration of emotional cut-offs in the relationship system.

The ecological unit of the family appears to establish a powerful emotional climate, which "colors" members' activities and perceptions of reality. Comparisons between ranges of emotional intensity in families and variations in societal emotional climate may be a graphic means of drawing meaningful parallels between family processes and their broader environment. The use of such models constitutes an alternative to conventional conceptualization of ecological processes and their influence on human behavior.

Differentiation of Self

Individual behavior can be considered the product of family processes. To the extent that patterns of social interaction and social institutions evolve as consequences and products of individual behavior, family processes can be viewed as an independent variable in the complex of social reality. The data on which these propositions are based are accumulated case history materials from families in psychotherapy and miscellaneous families. Some of the data are extensively longitudinal in that genealogical research has been used, wherever possible, to supplement three- or four-generation life histories of families.

The concept of self is the focus of many intellectual and research disciplines. Self is considered a family concept to the extent that self is viewed as a product of family interaction. The concept of self has implications that extend beyond an immediate focus on family interaction. A general theory of human behavior can be developed from a starting point of conceptualizing self as a product of family processes. *Differentiation of self*, a concept of the Bowen family theory, describes and defines activity considered necessary for an individual to become responsible and effectively integrated in a variety of social contexts. A detailed focus on Bowen's concept of differentiation of self distorts some of the systems aspects of Bowen's theoretical orientation. This selectiveness may serve to clarify some of the most significant variables influencing human behavior, rather than to define and describe the complex varied influences exerted on the development of self.

One of the most important premises of Bowen's theory is that a family is the most tightly bonded emotional system an individual participates in for an extended period of time. Not only do family relationships, for most people, largely define an individual's life situation at birth and in the years of early socialization, but they also strongly influence an individual's behavior at all stages of life. Even though family members may be widely dispersed geographically or separated through institutionalization or death, some degree of emotional "bondedness" between them persists, especially in relation to their family of origin (Boszormenyi-Nagi and Spark 1973).

The emotional intensity of a family system increases in relationship crises such as birth, abortion, adoption, loss, sickness, marriage, divorce, separation, institutionalization, or delinquency. According to Bowen's theory, it is more difficult to be a self in a family than to appear to be a self in comparatively transient social groups, which make fewer and less persistent emotional demands. A related hypothesis is that self can be differentiated most effectively in an individual's family, as other social contexts do not provide a sufficiently challenging, lasting, and reactive arena for this difficult sequence of behavior.

Effective differentiation of self generally creates crises in the emotional relationships of the differentiating person's family. Differentiation of self may also consist of planned responsible behavior in major crises, such as the death of a significant family member. Some preconditions appear necessary for successful differentiation. Only if relationship issues are dealt with in an emotionally reactive system that will not easily disband, can an individual respond fully to the feedback needed for long-term emotional maturation or differentiation. Only in a family network, can *solid self* most meaningfully encounter and deal with ingrained patterns of behavior which were and continue to be intimately related to self.

Bowen has clarified some of the nuances between the ideal types of differentiation, or individuation, and undifferentiation, or fusion. In more differentiated individuals, behavior is fairly well integrated at the levels of thought, feeling, and action. A more differentiated person can distinguish between thoughts and feelings and is more likely to act consistently in relation to self-selected long-range goals in life. Undifferentiated behavior is emotionally reactive and automatic. Undifferentiated behavior is generally the outcome of the pressures and demands of others and is an immediate response to the tensions of the moment, rather than an actualization of integrated inner principles and beliefs. A less differentiated person's behavior is so tied to others' responses that there are fewer options for self in selecting postures or courses of activity.

Bowen suggests that most people in contemporary American society fall within moderate ranges of differentiation of self and that members of the same family tend to have about the same level of differentiation of self. It is not possible for a person to change self to become much more or much less differentiated in a lifetime. Action that culminates in a slightly higher level of differentiation precipitates other changes in the ways an individual conducts life. Although there may be a slight momentum that accompanies increases or decreases of differentiation, movements in either direction do not necessarily precipitate further changes in the same direction.

Sequence of Behavior

Behavior patterns appear more predictable in a family than in other social groups. If an individual assumes a less emotionally dependent posture, a negative response from other family members predictably follows. This response frequently manifests itself as a direct pressure on the person differentiating self to assume the former functioning position. If this person is able to maintain the new level of differentiation, other family members are compelled to change their own levels of functioning and differentiation in the long run, and the entire family system eventually moves to a higher level of differentiation. On the other hand, the person making differentiating moves may succumb to the pressures of other family members and return to the former level of functioning. The latter choice is much easier to make and carry through in action. If this sequence of events occurs, the whole family will remain at the original level of differentiation.

Implications

Bowen's theoretical orientation and observations of family interaction suggest the following tentative propositions:

1. Families and their individual members tend to remain at the same or similar levels of differentiation through several generations, one generation, or a lifetime.

2. Behavior patterns characteristic of an individual's activities in a family tend to be repeated in other social groups

whether or not that person's level of differentiation of self changes.

3. Emotional maturation or differentiation of self is more effective when a person engages with family members than when he or she moves away from them, especially with members of different generations of the family of origin. Genealogical research on emotional relationships between members of past generations in a family can also be a phase of differentiating self.

Indicators of Family Trends

Patterns of family interaction may be conceptualized as indicators of family trends in broader processes of social change. This approach is distinct from a static focus on specific family forms or structures, as well as relatively superficial research that explores the composition of households. The quality of family processes appears to have the capacity for predicting changes and degrees of adaptation in families. To be viable, a family must manifest certain characteristics of flexibility and openness in its relationship system and transactions.

The combined findings of contemporary family researchers have not adequately verified the hypothesis that industrialized societies are moving away from extended family forms toward nuclear family forms. The value of substantiating this hypothesis and its consequences for the existing body of knowledge about families should be questioned. The operational problems involved in merely defining or describing family trends can, at best, give rise to limited results, especially given the initially postulated nuclear/extended polarity. No specific theoretical or pragmatic outcome for such efforts is guaranteed.

A research focus on family processes, or reactive emotional behavior in intimate relationship systems, generates richer sources of information and more powerfully predictive indicators than does research on family forms. Case history data from longitudinal studies of families suggest that the frequency of particular patterns of communication or of specific critical events such as deaths and other kinds of losses among different families can be compared meaningfully. Manifestations of these kinds of behavior appear to provide more accurate evidence of the nature of persisting trends and their underlying emotional processes than do data limited to a structural or geographical definition of *nuclear* and *extended* families.

A considerable variety and quantity of research on families in different cultures and societies, together with syntheses of these findings (Aldous and Hill 1967), indicate that there is a lack of precise data on family relationships in the past and over long periods of time. This state of affairs negates some of the potential usefulness and validity of discussions on the myth or reality of the "historical generalization" that a declining extended family form is being replaced by a predominantly nuclear family type (Goode 1963a). How can the "decline" of extended families be defined, or the degree of "isolation" of a nuclear family with a minimum level of reliability (Harris 1969)?

The changing structure of families may not be the most significant dimension or variable in an accurate and meaningful description of family trends and social change in short or long periods of time. A sufficient number of detailed "vertical," or multigenerational, studies of different families, based on genealogical data and other documentary or oral source materials, may provide more accurate and more valuable information on trends in families than the conventional "horizontal," or culture-based, survey studies of families at a particular point in time—which make up much of the current research.

Recent Trends

International comparative studies of kinship and families in industrial societies suggest that corporate primary groups based on kinship and neighborhood have declined, at least in terms of their ideological importance. Extended families are supposed to have been replaced by isolated nuclear families characterized by an intensification of emotional involvement and a greater sharing of activities. However, this apparent decline and replacement of one family type by another has not yet been sufficiently substantiated in empirical terms (Goode 1963b).

Research data, primarily from western industrial countries, indicate that there has been an increasing emphasis on the value of companionship in nuclear families (Blood and Wolfe 1960, Dennis 1962, Burgess, Locke, and Thomes 1963, Edgell 1972), on equality and "mutual consideration" (Fletcher 1962), and on the sharing of domestic and financial tasks and responsibilities (Young 1962). Although these quality-of-relationship emphases suggest an increase in nuclear family forms, other studies indicate that the extent and nature of the supposed decline in extended families has been greatly overemphasized (Sussman 1953, Litwak 1960a, 1960b, Loudon 1961, Rosser and Harris 1965, Adams 1968, Bell 1968).

From this discrepant data it can be concluded that the family may be changing its form, but there is no evidence that it is disappearing. This view of family trends has been shared by researchers in different academic disciplines and in different countries (Elliott 1970).

Patterns and Trends

Patterns of behavior and dependencies between different generations describe long-range changes in a family more accurately than substantive details about family structure. Process data on births, marriages, divorces, or deaths indicate trends more clearly than data that describe how individual family members are geographically located or economically situated (Boszormenyi-Nagy and Spark 1973). Place of residence and social class data are frequently used to indicate distinctions of form between nuclear and extended families.

Clinical findings suggest that one of the most significant influences on the pervasiveness of effective behavior is the intensity of family emotional processes. Extended or nuclear family structure, or any other kind of structure, appears to have fewer consequences for behavior in the family and in the wider society than the dependent processes and patterns of interaction between different family members. One variable used to formulate predictions about behavior is the nature and extent of communication in families (Bowen 1972).

Clinical findings also suggest certain negative consequences for behavior from the increasing emotional isolation between nuclear families and their extended networks. The probability of symptomatic or antisocial behavior appears significantly greater when the relationship system of the extended family is splintered through a lack of meaningful communication between the different nuclear families in the broader network.

One condition that precipitates symptomatic or antisocial behavior is the number and intensity of emotional divorces or cut-offs between different family members, particularly between members of different generations of the same family. Another influence on symptomatic or antisocial behavior is the sudden or lingering death of an emotionally significant family member. Temporary or threatened losses in a family also produce stress and generate the same kinds of behavioral consequences (Toman 1972). Incest, homicide, and deaths in fairly close succession may occur when the resulting level of anxiety in families is high (Bradt and Moynihan 1971, Andres and Lorio 1974).

Data of this kind question the significance of research that examines the structure rather than behavior of families. A family systems model (Bowen 1972) may provide a valuable frame of reference for cross-cultural family research (Broderick 1971) and the study of general behavior, especially as no meaningful comparisons of data from different societies can be made unless the same unit of investigation is used (Payne 1973). Although no precise hypotheses about evolutionary trends in families throughout the world can be formulated, a focus on communication and dependency in families is a more significant means of conceptualizing and describing trends and social change than a focus on family structures (Goody 1973).

Further Research

Although new data should ideally be collected to define trends and change in a world perspective, some of the data already compiled could be utilized for this purpose (Zelditch 1955, Britton 1971, Musil 1971). Political conditions and social stratification are significant influences on family structures and processes, but the emotional dependencies and intimate needs (Dennis 1962) expressed in patterns of behavior in families cannot be neglected, especially as these characteristics persist regardless of the particular historical circumstances (Anderson 1971). An exploration of the variety of family processes manifested and their pervasiveness in society can contribute further toward a theory of social change.

Variant Family Processes

Support for the view that effective social adaptation is accomplished through changing family forms has increased, particularly in the second half of the twentieth century. Much recent family research in experimental and nonexperimental settings has primarily focused on the range of observed differences in family forms or structures. The Bowen family theory points out some of the shared emotional characteristics of families with different structures. Data on family interaction suggest that the documentation of emotional processes in families is a more effective way to represent the salient survival characteristics of both *normative* and *variant* families than an examination of specific structures.

Variant family processes include a wide range of reciprocal family interaction patterns. Variant family processes consist of emotional or affective behavior, which initiates interaction or reacts and responds to interaction. These processes occur in the context of procreative or other enduring intimate relationships. They may be illustrated with reference to two ideal types of family or intimate relationship forms: an isolated nuclear family and a commune.

The quality of family emotional processes is hypothesized as more significant for the "viability" or effective survival of a family than a particular form or structure. Family processes are conceptualized as products of tensions between togetherness and individuation strivings within a family emotional unit. Relatively open, flexible relationships appear more conducive to constructive adaptation than relatively closed, rigid relationships. Both open and closed relationship systems and their characteristic emotional processes are found in nuclear and communal ideal types of families.

Forms and Processes

The increasingly widespread use of the term *variant family form* reflects a tendency to view families and intimate relationships as particular structures rather than processes. The recent proliferation of variant family forms has been hypothesized as an unintentional structural response to the changing composition of particular classes or groups in society (Bernard 1971, Paden-Eisenstark 1973). Emotional overload in nuclear families is also viewed as precipitating the increase in variant family forms (Ramey 1972, Whitehurst 1972), with a flexible role structure being considered more characteristic of communes and their larger living-in membership than of nuclear families (Nimkoff 1965, Kenkel 1966, Queen and Habenstein 1967, Weintraub and Shapiro 1968, Sheper 1969, Schlesinger 1970, Olson 1972, Talmon 1972, Muncy 1973, Paden-Eisenstark 1973). Although this research has not exclusively focused on the structural aspects of experimental and nonexperimental variant families, the conceptualization and measurement of processes within these units appears to have been largely ignored.

Other research on variant families has attempted to describe affective behavior in these relationship systems. Studies of commitment mechanisms (Kanter 1968, 1973) have been based on selected parts of these relationship systems. Studies of commitment mechanisms (Kanter 1968, 1973) have been based on selected parts of these relationship systems. However, this research has not been able to define the intricacies and complexities of interlocking interdependencies within a family at producing an adequate theoretical frame of reference to conceptualize the diverse characteristics and consequences of these processes (O'Neill and O'Neill 1972).

In spite of such criticisms, the studies on variant families have many valuable aspects. One generalization is that the current strong interest in structural characteristics of families appears to have led to the examination of variant family forms, such as communes, more for their differences from normative families than for their similarities to traditional or preponderant families (Kanter 1968, Lacey 1968, Bartell 1971).

The Bowen theory highlights shared similarities in emotional processes in different kinds of family structures (Bowen 1960,

1961, 1965a, 1966, 1971a, 1971b, 1974, Alexander 1973). This view of families as emotional systems is a deliberate attempt to avoid the perceptual inaccuracies that occur when families are defined in terms of cultural norms or variations from those norms.

Variant family processes are viewed as significant evolutionary processes. In this respect they can be considered necessary and intrinsic aspects of biological adaptation rather than transient historical or political phenomena (Kanter 1968, Barakat 1969, Cooper 1970, Schlesinger 1970, Taylor 1970, Ferm 1971, Olson 1972, Sussman and Cogswell 1972, Talmon 1972, Boszormenyi-Nagy and Spark 1973, Muncy 1973).

A variety of family processes are examined to discern whether they are effective and functional for the survival of a family or whether they contribute toward a family's extinction. The capacity of the processes to be effective or functional is considered the degree of *viability* of the family processes. If a particular pattern of family interaction appears destructive to a family and seems to lead toward its extinction, the family processes concerned are assigned a low degree of viability.

Propositions

Accumulated case history data from several hundred families in clinical and regular settings, which have been organized with reference to Bowen's systems concepts, suggest two propositions. These hypotheses are used as a focus for observations delineating similar family processes in the two different ideal-type family forms selected, a nuclear family and a commune.

1. The degree of a family's viability depends more on the quality of its emotional processes than on its specific form or structure. To the extent that family processes are flexible, family members will function effectively.

2. Family processes and behavior patterns of family members

are products of individuation and togetherness strivings within a family. The degree of viability of a family is directly correlated with the effectiveness of the family members' management of tension between the individuation and togetherness strivings.

Processes in Nuclear and Commune Ideal Types

The degree of viability of family processes is documented in terms of strength or weakness. *Strength* is used to denote the high degree of viability of emotional processes conducive to the survival and successful adaptation of a family unit. *Weakness* is used to denote the low degree of viability of emotional processes destructive to the continued existence of a family, eventually leading to the extinction of the family unit.

Research on kin networks suggests the existence of a permeable boundary between nuclear and extended families in many traditional families. In contrast, the ideal-type nuclear family is considered relatively isolated from the extended family. This ideal-type nuclear family has restricted membership in its intense emotional relationship system, with established patterns of interaction cut off from preceding generations. Although the possibility of opening up the intergenerational network of exchanges persists throughout the condition of cut-off (Slater 1963, Whitehurst 1972), this ideal-type nuclear family is essentially enclosed by an impermeable boundary.

Some communes have generational linkages outside the commune, and a few "three-generation" families may be found in certain types of communes. The ideal-type commune conceptualized here is defined as a lateral extended relationship system (Sussman and Cogswell 1972) that is relatively isolated from the families of origin or extended families of commune members. This ideal-type commune is a group of intimate peers that has endured through time and has maintained its own household throughout this period. Children may or may not be procreated in this group.

Strengths

1. To the extent that either an ideal-type nuclear family or an ideal-type commune allows for the differentiation of self of its members, the relationship system of either family form will be viable and adaptive. When both ideal-type family forms are flexible and sufficiently elastic to allow for the unhampered responsible activity of their members, both forms are correspondingly freer of the symptomatic and "problem" kinds of behavior that could eventually lead toward extinction.

2. A member of an ideal-type nuclear family or of an ideal-type commune who differentiates self within either family context predictably encounters resistance to this new functioning position from other family members. If the differentiating individual is able to maintain the new functioning position in face of the opposition while remaining in emotional contact with other family members, the level of functioning of the other family members and of the entire unit is gradually raised to a higher level of functioning. This predictable sequence of events can occur in either a nuclear family or a commune.

3. Viable family processes in either a nuclear family or a commune are characterized by an open communication system. Such relationships have fewer emotional cut-offs and are less influenced by seniority and sex distributions than are relationships in a closed relationship system of either a nuclear family or a commune.

Weaknesses

1. In either an ideal-type nuclear family or an ideal-type commune, the relationship system can become overburdened by excessive investments of emotions and feelings in togetherness. Role options are limited by the strong pull toward togetherness, and the relationship system becomes rigid and restrictive.

2. If a nuclear family ideal type or a commune ideal type does not allow for meaningful contacts in the most extended parts of their relationship systems, behavior problems develop in the nuclear family or commune.

3. When the most meaningful interpersonal relationships in either a nuclear family ideal type or a commune ideal type are emotionally intense and restrictive, the children socialized in this context strive to maintain a strong dependence on this group or to transfer the same intense dependency to another group. In an historical context, the emotional isolation of nineteenth-century utopian communities and the subsequent homogenization of their members' experiences are considered to have contributed toward their extinction (Kanter 1968, Muncy 1973).

Review of Observations

Some of the associations described suggest that the particular form or structure of a famly is not the primary influence determining its survival or extinction. Historical surveys of experimental families (Muncy 1973), contemporary trends toward companionate marriage (Sussman and Cogswell 1972), studies of miscellaneous types of variant families (Farber 1964, Humphreys 1970, Kirkendall and Whitehurst 1971, Ibsen and Klobus 1972, Lyness and Lipetz 1972, Olson 1972, Osofsky and Osofsky 1972, Sussman and Cogswell 1972), and clinical data on families suggest that emotional processes are essential components and functions of families. This shared characteristic of emotional processes in variant family forms such as the nuclear and communal families deserves a closer examination through systematic research.

Further Research

The emotional forces of differentiation and togetherness are more easily identified and predicted in a family than in "secondary" associations in the wider society because of the greater degree of emotional intensity and bonding between members of families and the persistence of membership through time. However, it is possible, to some extent, to observe and document togetherness and differentiating strivings in more comprehensive, transient and diverse social networks. Family processes are viewed as indicators of broad emotional and social processes in that they are a microcosm of affective behavior patterns characteristic of less intense relationship systems.

Another area of further research is to define more precisely the influences involved in the complex interplay of family interaction and social institutions. In spite of the recent pronounced interest in theoretical concerns (Christensen 1964, Aldous 1970, Broderick 1971), family processes have rarely been conceptualized as an integral part of a general theory that would relate family interaction to nonfamily events (Zimmerman 1972, Lee 1974, Martin 1974). Some of the foregoing observations and discussion suggest that family processes are a significant influence on nonfamily behavior, rather than that family processes are merely structural and functional responses to broader social changes (Berne 1967, Cooper 1970, Toman 1972, Olson 1972). People may be more conditioned and pro-grammed by patterns of intergenerational family interaction (Berne 1967) than by membership in a particular ethnic group, social class, occupational group, or religion or by location in a rural or urban environment. Family programming predisposes individuals to repeat similar kinds of behavior in both family and nonfamily settings. It is in this respect that family processes can be treated as an independent variable and as a significant behavioral determinant in a more general theory of human behavior.

Chapter 3

THE EIGHT PROCESSES

Differentiation of Self

Differentiation of self is a key concept in the Bowen family theory. Any given level of differentiation represents the extent to which a person is embedded in the emotional matrix that binds human beings together. An individual may have a relatively separate self, with a calm posture to others, or a "soluble" self in the emotional field, with intense and anxious bonds with others. Three important factors that influence differentiation are the degree of bonds with others, the level of anxiety in self and the relationship network, and the degree of emotional cut-off with others.

Bowen hypothesizes that any relaxation in efforts to be a self leads toward the obliteration of self. Anxiety in self and in the relationship system tends to annihilate self, as the more social and changing parts of self become increasingly soluble in the emotional matrix.

Bowen originally described the ranges of differentiation of self in terms of a scale with score from 0 to 100. However, this scale was merely a working hypothesis about various characteristics of human functioning, rather than a precise ranking or tool of measurement. To avoid oversimplifying the complexities of any given situation, scores and intermediate numbers were not assigned to specific levels of differentiation. In recent years, Bowen has discontinued use of the scale and has focused more on the qualitative aspects of differentiation of self.

The terms *hard-core self* and *pseudo-self* may clarify some of the complex meaning elements of differentiation of self. Hard-core self, or solid self, is nonnegotiable with others and is composed of an individual's firmest convictions and most integrated beliefs. Pseudo-self, by contrast, is negotiable with others. Pseudo-self consists of others' opinions absorbed as one's own without any personal conscious commitment to the beliefs and convictions underlying the opinions absorbed. The changes that occur through differentiation generally affect both hard-core self and pseudo-self. As a person becomes more differentiated, the importance of hard-core self increases and the influence of pseudo-self correspondingly decreases.

Although a few isolated indicators of differentiation can be operationalized in research settings (Winer 1971), it is not possible to make accurate day-to-day or week-to-week evlutions of all the complexities of differentiation. Wide shifts in the functioning of pseudo-self characterize those who are not well differentiated. Furthermore, the functioning of undifferentiated individuals vacillates considerably with small environmental changes. On the other hand, it is possible to make fairly accurate estimates of general levels of differentiation from detailed information on family behavior during time spans of years or generations.

Summary descriptions of contrasting levels of differentiation serve as a guide to further research in this area. Less differentiated people live in a "feeling-controlled" world, in which their emotions and subjectivity dominate objective reasoning most of the time. These individuals do not distinguish feeling from fact, and their primary life goals revolve around relationship characteristics such as love, happiness, comfort, or security. More differentiated people make up a smaller proportion of the population. Such individuals have a fairly clearly defined autonomous self, or basic self, and a greater capacity for goal-directed activity. They can distinguish between feelings and objective reality more accurately than less differentiated individuals.

Differentiation of self describes a range of thinking, feeling, and emotional behavior. The life-style of a well-differentiated individual is clearly distinct from that of someone who is less well differentiated. People with contrasting levels of differentiation have such dissimilar life-styles that they do not choose each other for personal relationships.

The concept of differentiation of self is a product of systems thinking. The range of behavior defined by differentiation eliminates any need for the conventional concept of "normal." The indicators of this process are not directly related to mental health, illness, or pathology, although there is some overlap between the conventional meaning elements of "emotional maturity" and those of differentiation of self. Although differentiation has social consequences, there is no direct correlation between differentiation and either intelligence or socioeconomic achievement. Higher levels of differentiation indicate responsible autonomous behavior rather than such attributes as occupational attainment or social class.

The level of an individual's differentiation represents that person's *basic* self. Basic self includes "I" position action statements such as the following: "These are my beliefs and convictions. This is what I am, who I am, and what I will and will not do." Basic self consists of integrated beliefs, convictions, and ideas—which can change from within and through new knowledge and experience. It is not negotiable in relationships and resists external coercion or pressure. Basic self is not changed merely to gain approval, enhance one's standing with others, or share beliefs with others.

A second level of self, which is related to hard-core basic self, is described as *pseudo-self* because of its fluid and shifting characteristics. Pseudo-self is a mass of heterogeneous and frequently contradictory observations, beliefs, and principles that have been acquired in the context of the prevailing emotions in an individual's relationship systems. The components of pseudo-self include what one thinks one is supposed to know and beliefs borrowed or accepted from others as a means of enhancing status. Unlike basic self, pseudo-self is negotiable with others in relationships.

Reflexive, or automatic, behavior in families moves toward undifferentiation or fusion with others. The condition of fusion is the "eclipse" of one self by another self or by a relationship system. When fusion occurs, an individual loses personal distinctive attributes and becomes lost or submerged in the characteristics of the other or the relationship system. Fusion takes place with either the loss of pseudo-self or the apparent loss of both basic self and pseudo-self. An undifferentiated person tends to manifest a greater degree of emotional fusion with others than a person who is more differentiated. The less self one has, the more one depends on a common self for direction and energy.

Fusion is an interaction process in both overcharged and undercharged relationships. Fusion generally reaches its greatest intensity in marriage. In the emotional closeness between spouses, two partial selfs fuse into a common self. Sometimes this degree of closeness is only tolerable if the spouses distance themselves from each other rather than operating as a combined self. The intensity of the resulting fusion largely depends on the spouses' differentiation before marriage.

Fusion takes place between any two or more individuals. Extreme fusion frequently occurs between a parent and child. The parent is emotionally dominant in the twosome with a child, functioning at the child's expense. In this process, the adaptive child gives up self and becomes submissive.

In his family theory, Bowen conceptualizes differentiation more clearly than he does fusion. He emphasizes the clinical importance and personal significance of differentiating self for each individual. A particular level of differentiation is considered a "balancing point" between the two major emotional thrusts of differentiation, or individuation, and fusion, or togetherness, in families and other social groups. As the level of differentiation increases, the discomfort and less effective functioning associated with fusion is partially resolved or relieved. However, much personal effort is necessary to increase differentiation of self.

Bowen suggests that a well-differentiated individual has more basic self and is less likely to fuse with others than a poorly differentiated individual. In contrast to differentiating processes, fusion is a spontaneous and automatic emotional response in a relationship setting. As many complex feelings are generated in a fused response, effective functioning by the individuals concerned is inhibited.

Research

Although differentiation is a general concept applicable to a large variety of groups, I refer to it only in the context of research on families. A family is considered a prototype of emotional system, as patterns of wide ranges of interpersonal behavior are more prevalent and more clearly delineated in families than in other social groups.

Bowen's concept of differentiation of self does not include reference points of "normal" or "abnormal." His distinctions between activities at thinking, feeling, and emotional levels suggest new dimensions of behavior for further research. Bowen's emphasis on the importance of observing and describing process in interaction highlights phenomena not usually accounted for in substantive descriptions. Behavior that demonstrates adequate or inadequate functioning, characteristics of contrasting levels of differentiation, can be used as a basis for comparing individuals and families. For example, functioning can be evaluated in terms of its contribution to adaptation, maladaptation, or extinction. Within this frame of reference, symptomatic functioning would eventually be disruptive to the development of a family, in that family needs for growth and change cannot be met.

One approach to estimating differentiation is an examination of individual and family functioning at times of crisis or during nodal events in a family's history. A *nodal* event is a significant change, such as a migration, that brings with it many related changes. In retrospect, a nodal event appears as a turning point in the intergenerational history of a particular family. Patterns of interaction in these periods generally reflect important characteristics of the overall functioning of a family.

Nodal events also include birth, marriage, death, divorce, illness, institutionalization, and occupational change. These complex major shifts in a family's relationship network trigger automatic behavior patterns that may or may not be adaptive for the family undergoing these changes. Flexible responses, rather than rigid reactions, indicate higher levels of differentiation of self. Other influences on differentiation processes include sibling position, quality of multigenerational contacts, degree of isolation between family members, and level of intensity in the relationship system.

Assessments of basic self and pseudo-self also indicate specific levels of differentiation. If an individual's beliefs are integrated and clearly defined, behavior will be more differentiated than if beliefs are confused, contradictory, and rigidly narrow.

Therapeutic Considerations

The concept of differentiation of self makes it possible to examine people and relationship anxiety more objectively. This improved facility is important for the development of the discipline and clinical success of psychotherapy. However, differentiation of self is a suggested goal of psychotherapy, rather than a diagnostic tool.

Although specific levels of differentiation cannot be precisely correlated with pathology, some generalizations about relationships between differentiation of self and symptomatic behavior are offered. Less differentiated individuals are more vulnerable to stress, and their recovery from symptoms is generally slow or impossible. However, less differentiated people do not necessarily manifest behavior symptoms when under stress, and they may keep their lives in emotional equilibrium fairly effectively. More differentiated individuals may also develop symptoms, especially when under severe stress. Unlike those who are less differentiated, more differentiated individuals are generally less vulnerable to stress and they tend to have comparatively rapid recoveries from any symptoms.

One goal of Bowen's family psychotherapy is to increase differentiation of self. As an individual becomes more differentiated, dysfunctional symptoms in individual behavior and in patterns of family interaction decrease. The general alleviation of stress and recovery from symptoms in a family are more effective when one family member becomes more differentiated.

Improved differentiation is an ideal goal of psychotherapy, rather than a goal that can be easily achieved. It is frequently not possible for an individual to become more differentiated during a course of psychotherapy. The pervasive inability to change self may result from emotional symptoms that have become rigid and immovable through time or from lack of motivation.

When there is no unusual stress in a family, any small move toward differentiation will predictably be accompanied by pressures to return to patterns of former functioning. Much of the difficulty involved in becoming more differentiated is the opposition of the thrusts of individuation and togetherness, the two major forces in an emotional system. Togetherness inhibits individuation, and individuation inhibits togetherness.

Most of the problems dealt with in a clinical setting are related to fusion or loss of self. The feeling of being trapped in intimate relationships is characteristic of fusion. Coaching the adaptive or submissive individuals in a fusion to behave in more differentiated ways optimally culminates in their becoming more able to function autonomously. Differentiation is a complex combination of processes through which awareness of personal unique qualities and of the potential for growth and autonomy is increased.

At all stages of psychotherapy, a well-differentiated therapist is more effective than a therapist who easily becomes fused in ongoing relationships. In Bowen's view, therapeutic success results from a differentiated clinician's ability to remain relatively outside the emotional field of the clinical setting. A well-differentiated therapist does not allow self to be drawn into a family's fusion. Any resolution of the intensity of this fusion generally occurs through the activation of latent relationships in the family, rather than through emotional involvement on the part of the therapist.

A primary goal of a family systems therapist is to maintain a differentiated "I" position despite any pressures to take sides on a particular family issue. The ability of a therapist to remain differentiated in a clinical setting depends on the quality of the therapist's own relationship between self and family of origin.

One's Own Family

Differentiation cannot occur in a vacuum. Differentiation describes a posture of direct meaningful emotional contact with one's family emotional system at the same time one is sufficiently outside the family fusion to be reasonably objective about self and others. Differentiation involves establishing personal relationships with extended family members and communicating with as many relatives in different generations as possible. To perceive self more objectively, an emotional "twin" in an earlier generation is identified through genealogical research. The discovery of someone in a similar functioning position and network of dependencies to self generally clarifies one's view of emotional processes in living generations. The broadened perspective also facilitates objectivity about self.

Optimal conditions for differentiating self in one's own family usually include a certain degree of unrest, anxiety, or disequilibrium. If these conditions do not already exist, one may create or respond to a "tempest in a teapot" (Bowen 1972). When tension exists, a more effective and durable "I" position can be taken. Family members tend to pay more attention to a differentiating self and to hear that person more willingly during conditions of stress than of *peace-agree* togetherness. If anxiety increases, family members are more likely to accept and respect differentiating acts than if there is a rigid status quo in the relationship system. If the individual differentiating self is able to maintain the higher level of differentiation and remain in meaningful contact with other family members, those closest to the person differentiating self eventually function at higher levels of differentiation of self themselves owing to their dependency on that person.

Pervasive change in a family may follow the differentiation of self of a single family member. This broader change occurs only if the person differentiating self simultaneously maintains emotional contact with other family members and remains relatively outside the fusion and togetherness of the family. Becoming more differentiated generally enhances one's attractiveness in the view of other family members, and that individual becomes more of a focus of interest. For example, a differentiated person's company becomes more sought after, and that individual appears increasingly indispensable to the emotional system.

Characteristics of higher levels of differentiation of self include effective functioning, goal-directed activity, and responsible behavior. As basic self is defined, there is less of a tendency or a need to put self in the position of others. By not being overly responsible for others, a differentiated self is less inclined to be irresponsible. A differentiated self focuses on "I" and "owned" beliefs and convictions and refrains from telling others what to do. Rather than spending time and energy criticizing the shortcomings or solving the problems of others, differentiated individuals examine the extent to which their own acts are motivated by the pressure of others or by inner beliefs.

Differentiation in one's own family proceeds more effectively if one acts as a self in the primary triangle, or three-person relationship system, with one's parents. As individuation generally cannot be achieved directly with one's parents, three-person relationships that include a parent, a member of that parent's extended family, and oneself are activated. Differentiation results from activating emotionally significant relationships in one's family and remaining outside the various three-person systems.

People tend to marry those who have the same level of differentiation as themselves. Also, children tend to maintain the same level of differentiation as their parents. Even though differentiation consists of a wide range of different processes and patterns of behavior, only slight changes in levels of differentiation of self are accomplished during two or three generations.

Triangles

The concept of triangles describes structural characteristics and emotional processes in relationship systems. The use Bowen makes of the terms *to triangle, to detriangle,* or *to be triangled* suggests some of the action dimensions of this concept. Triangles are considered *reflexive*, as they indicate relatively predictable emotional interdependencies and patterns of interaction in families.

Bowen's concept of triangles suggests a theoretical frame of reference for the observation of functioning patterns in families and emotional systems. This concept perhaps has more pragmatic and versatile applications and implications than other concepts in the Bowen family theory. For example, step-by-step descriptions of the functioning of the primary or parental triangle and related triangles in a family provide effective means for understanding the relationship system for psychotherapists, researchers, or family members. The nature of the distribution of flexible or rigid processes and relationships in triangles indicates overall patterns of functioning in families or emotional systems.

A family is considered a complex network of interlocking three-person relationship systems. Each triangle is related to all triangles in the overall family system. The degree of overlap or interrelatedness of the triangles influences the emergence of chains or waves of reactivity in families. Emotional forces within and between triangles operate as predictably and as automatically as reflex behavior. The extent of reactivity depends on the degree of interdependence between members of a single triangle and related triangles. A change in one triangle in a family is accompanied by predictable changes in other triangles in the same family when members of the first triangle stay in contact with members of other triangles. Knowledge of the predictability of "chain reactions" in the relationship system can assist family members in modifying their positions.

A triangle is the basic molecule of a family or emotional system. In contrast to a triangle, a dyad, or two-person relationship, is inherently unstable and cannot maintain its existence through time. Under stress, a twosome draws a third party into its emotional field, and the two-person relationship then becomes a triangle. The new three-person system has a lower level of anxiety than the original twosome.

The intergenerational network of a family is characterized by specific patterns of behavior. These regularities in interaction reflect the levels of functioning in each triangle of the family, and the patterns are crystallized over long periods. The behavior in each triangle reinforces the postures and levels of functioning of members.

Over short periods, emotional forces are observed to shift around triangles. These tensions appear in perpetual motion. Patterns and repetitions can be discerned only when interaction is observed over extensive periods. However, all triangles are emotional systems that are continually in motion. To the extent that some "focus points" of emotional forces in a family become consolidated, triangles also have relatively static qualities.

The meanings Bowen gives to the concept of triangles suggest the pervasive existence of predictable structures and processes in families and other emotional systems. Fairly accurate predictions can be formulated about moves that will be made within and between triangles when overall levels of tension in the triangles and in each member of the triangles are known. Similar patterns of triangling are found in all emotional systems. When differentiation is low and anxiety is high, the prediction of reactivity and symptoms in triangular interaction is easier to make and more accurate. Triangling is most visible in families, as these systems are highly charged with emotion and persist through time.

Functioning in triangles consists of fairly predictable sequences of events. When tension mounts in a twosome relationship, one person becomes more emotionally uncomfortable than the other and *triangles in* a third person. The first person may tell the second a story about a third. Storytelling relieves some of the tension between the first two parties and shifts it to the emotional field between the second and third. If tension arises in the outsider, that person's next predictable move is to form a twosome with one of the original parties, leaving the other original party an outsider.

The emotional forces within a triangle move from moment to moment and over long periods of time. This fluctuation is an essential characteristic of triangles and is manifested most clearly when triangles are active. A person who attempts to detriangle self in a family is in a more advantageous position for observing the triangular substructure in the family than if no moves are made.

When a triangle is calm, the relationships within consist of a comfortable twosome and an outsider. In these circumstances, the most preferred position is membership in the comfortable twosome. When a triangle is in a state of tension, the outside position is the most preferred.

The emotional forces operating in triangles are manifested most clearly as the members attempt to gain closeness with each other or to escape from tension. Each move by a member of a triangle predictably requires a compensatory move by another member of the same triangle. This high degree of interrelated activity suggests a strong human need for closeness with others.

Although any triangle can be activated fairly easily, the circuits of a triangle can lie dormant for considerable periods. Also, the field forces of one triangle can become more active in a different triangular position in the same emotional system. For example, conflicts in one triangle may be "fought out" in related triangles. A particularly anxious family triangles in more and more outsiders. Neighbors, schools, police, clinics, and others participate in the family problem. The family reduces its anxiety by triangling members of the community into its emotional system. Family tension is consequently fought out largely by the outsiders, often within their own respective groups.

The relatively "fixed," or more predictable, characteristics of triangles are easier to operationalize than their more changeable characteristics. As positive and negative emotional forces constantly shift back and forth, ranges in patterns of behavior can be documented in related triangles. The complexity of triangle formation in a family increases as these forces shift. Primary and secondary triangles alternate in importance as they become activated in response to different issues.

A pervasive triangle pattern in families, especially in the United States, is a close emotional twosome between the mother and child, with the father in an outside position. The triangle between mother, father, and child is the basic primary triangle in most families and in general is highly charged with emotion. When a symbiotic closeness and dependency builds up between two members of this primary triangle, the probability that one of the twosome will develop symptomatic behavior increases.

The flexibility and versatility of the concept of triangles make it particularly useful for describing and defining patterns of interaction and change processes in a family. Unlike many conventional relationship concepts, the concept of triangles does not focus on intrapsychic phenomena. The meaning elements that describe triangles emphasize modifiable characteristics of dependency behavior. Any pattern of family interaction can be conceptualized in terms of triangles. As basic triangular configurations of emotional functioning in a family are delineated, the probability of being able to modify positions in this network increases. For example, conflict between two siblings can be viewed as a triangle between a mother and her two children, the mother having a different amount of emotional investment in each child. Conflict breaks out between the children who attempt to adjust the imbalance in their mother's emotional investment. This unproductive sequence of reactivity is changed most effectively if the mother is able to see the triangle forces operating and changes her own input to the two relationships and the surrounding emotional system.

Detriangling self, or losing the emotional intensity of a fused twosome in a triangle, is synonymous with differentiating self. A well-differentiated family member is aware of multigenerational triangles and at the same time is able to remain relatively outside their strong emotional forces. A less differentiated family member is perpetually "caught up" in different triangles, especially in those that are multigenerational. One consequence of family triangles is an increasing tendency to automatically repeat previously established behavior patterns and symptoms. These continuing sequences appear in individual behavior or in shared patterns of behavior through several generations, and the patterns and symptoms are frequently intensified through time.

Family projection is a particular pattern of triangling found in a nuclear family. In this triangle, a "vulnerable" child is pulled into the anxious twosome of undifferentiated parents. Multigenerational transmission consists of repeated family projections or extensive intergenerational triangling. Sibling position can be a significant predisposing factor in these processes, as seniority and sex distribution frequently suggest which individuals are most likely to be triangled into the relationship network.

Research

The hypothesis that social interaction is essentially triangular rather than dyadic or linear, as is conventionally believed, is not new. Georg Simmel described properties and distinguishing characteristics of two- and three-person relationships as social systems in his writings as the turn of the century (Caplow 1968). However, the application of these principles of social interaction to families and emotional systems constitutes a new theoretical orientation and a new series of hypotheses.

Although Simmel first discussed triads or three-person relationship systems in 1890, social psychologists in the United States did not begin until the 1950s to experiment with different types of triadic interaction in a laboratory setting. Giving each person in a triad the letter *A, B,* or *C,* a triad is defined as a social system containing the three relationships *AB, BC,* and *AC.* A triad is the only social group with an equal number of members and relationships.

Some contemporary experimentation with triadic relationships suggests that one of their most significant properties is the tendency to divide into a coalition of two members against the third. Particular coalitions in triads are fairly predictable if the relative power of the three members is known. Generalizations from research findings of the study of three-person relationship systems provide a basis for a "social geometry" (Caplow 1968).

Recent social psychological research on structural and dynamic aspects of triads is only indirectly related to Bowen's concept of triangles. Caplow and other researchers who examine triads differ from Bowen in that they do not account for ranges of emotional intensity and dependency in three-person relationships. For example, their much used concept of "power" does not adequately describe the full spectrum of complexities and nuances of emotional responsiveness and reactivity in family relationships. From the Bowen theory perspective of emotional systems, power more accurately represents specific aspects of relationships.

Research findings cannot yet provide accurate assessments of the influences that different groups have on their members or on society at large. Patterns of family interaction are not usually conceptualized as significant determinants of behavior in the social sciences, even though families manifest more emotional intensity and have more clearly identifiable patterns of behavior than do other groups. Bowen's concept of triangles provides a means for strengthening and clarifying some of the research dealing with family and group influences on individual and social behavior.

Therapeutic Considerations

A therapist is constantly subject to becoming a significant participant in the emotional system of those coached in the clinical setting. A Bowen family therapists's primary goal is to remain detriangled from the family emotional field by not taking sides with individual family members in the ongoing therapy or during discussion of "hot" issues. By refusing to take sides, a therapist can more effectively encourage the involvement of family members in triangles in their own family. The Bowen theory suggests viewing transference as triangling. The development of a transference attachment or emotional alliance between the therapist and a family member results in their becoming locked or triangled into their relationship with each other. This relationship rigidifies in the transference, and little action for self can be taken by either party.

An emotionally "freeing" move in a triangle that includes the therapist is to encourage increased involvement between the other two members of the triangle. This action enables the therapist to maintain an outside position in the triangle. The therapist can achieve this effect in a clinical setting by asking a "leading" question or by making a comment that precipitates emotional reactivity on the part of one or both members of that triangle. Detriangling is achieved by actively encouraging the engagement of the other two members in positive or negative feelings. As the emotional field between the twosome intensifies, the therapist, to maintain a detriangled position, must remain outside the interdependencies expressed.

Psychotherapy based on the Bowen theory consists of coaching one or two family members to become increasingly aware of triangles in their families and to assume new functioning positions in relation to the triangles. A coached family member is given direct or indirect suggestions about how to detriangle self from "locked," static triangles or from parts of the relationship network where members are "paralyzed" in the family emotional field. Changes in self occur only very gradually and usually simultaneously with becoming more detriangled from the relationship system. Multigenerational detriangling consists of freeing moves made by family members in three different generations. Multigenerational detriangling is a particularly effective means of accomplishing change in self and in a family.

The Bowen therapy emphasizes the importance of an individual's ability to objectively observe the primary emotional system and the part the individual plays in it. Once this ability is sufficiently developed, conscious control of the individual's programmed reactiveness to the emotional system becomes possible. The degree of reactivity of behavior is largely a function of the intensity of the triangles concerned.

The observation and control of self are extremely difficult to accomplish. Observation and control are closely interrelated in that observation allows for increased control, and increased control allows for more accurate observation. As a long-term consequence of the different moves a peron makes, interaction in the entire family will gradually be modified. The intensity of the interdependency of the triangular substructure of a family is a strong influence on the quality and extent of the "chain-reaction" throughout the system.

When the therapists's own responsiveness to emotional reactivity in the clinical setting is controlled, anxiety in the others present decreases. If the therapist is able to remain in emotional contact with those in the clinical setting, their functioning will improve. If the therapist cannot remain in emotional contact in the clinical setting, the others present will try to triangle in another person to decrease their anxiety. The ability to remain detriangled while in emotional contact with clients depends on the extent to which the therapist is detriangled and simultaneously in emotional contact with his or her own family of origin. When a therapist controls emotional involvement with others, those coached are also able to control their emotional involvement.

One's Own Family

One's level of differentiation in work and social systems depends on the degree to which one is both detriangled and in emotional contact with one's own family, particularly in relation to the primary triangle with parents. Only when major triangles in the family are identified can a posture relatively outside the emotional processes be achieved.

A working knowledge of the triangles in one's family suggests which personal contacts would be most productive for establishing and improving the quality of person-to-person relationships in the family. It is frequently not possible to work directly on person-to-person relationships with significant family members such as parents. This difficulty may be aggravated conditions such as emotional resistance, "unavailability," institutionalization, or premature death. An alternative for changing the relationship between self and a key family member is to approach a family member who is emotionally close to the significant person concerned, such as the latter's parent or sibling. By establishing meaningful contact with someone who is emotionally important to the significant family member, a triangle is activated. This change in the emotional system modifies the relationship between self and the significant person who was contacted indirectly. The modification occurs when a triangle is activated between self, the person sought after for a personal relationship, and the one emotionally important to the person chosen for a personal relationship.

The activation of triangles and accompanying moves to detriangle self gradually opens an entire family system. Through these processes, a rigid emotional system with automatic reactive responses slowly becomes more flexible and has increasing numbers of meaningful emotional contacts between members. Although these changes may not be achieved in a single lifetime and certainly not in a short period of time, one can establish a direction for self in one's family that optimally will contribute toward the increased differentiation of other family members.

A prerequisite for successful application of the concept of triangles is a knowledge of the strength of emotional forces and their interdependency in an emotional system. A change in one part of a family is predictably followed by changes in related parts of the same family owing to the complex interrelatedness of the triangles in the relationship system. Changes in one's position are effective and persist over time if one is able to maintain emotional contact with other family members throughout all efforts to make changes.

Nuclear Family Emotional System

Bowen's concept of nuclear family emotional system most closely approximates what is conventionally known as "the family" or "the nuclear family" in the United States today. To some extent, the meaning of nuclear family emotional system was articulated before Bowen's other family concepts. (In the early stages of theoretical development, Bowen used the term "undifferentiated family ego mass," rather than nuclear family emotional system.) The concept of nuclear family emotional system describes qualities of the emotional field between "inner-core" family members rather than processes throughout the intergenerational network. Several nuclear family emotional systems can be identified within any given extended family.

The level of differentiation of self of spouses in a nuclear family largely determines the intensity of the triangles that make up that family's emotional system. When spouses are less differentiated, the intensity of relationships in the nuclear family system is greater than when spouses are more differentiated. The probability of certain kinds of behavior in nuclear family emotional systems also depends on complex stress factors and the overall level of anxiety in the families. Fairly accurate predictions about patterns of interaction can be made when there is intense emotional "stuck togetherness," or fusion, between spouses or between parent and child in a nuclear family. The intense fusion precipitates reactivity, and the tight interdependence between members of the nuclear family system restricts their behavior options.

Levels of differentiation of self in spouses' families of origin influence the degree of the spouses' emotional fusion in a nuclear family. The ways in which spouses handle undifferentiation largely determine the areas in which the fusion is absorbed by the nuclear system, and the kind of symptoms that are expressed in times of stress.

A nuclear family emotional system has three major mechanisms for dealing with an overload of anxiety between the spouses: marital conflict, dysfunction of a spouse, and projection to one or more of the children. Most families resort to a combination of the three adaptive mechanisms. Symptoms surface most visibly when only one means is selected as an outlet for the surplus undifferentiation. Even when a major proportion of the anxiety is absorbed by one mechanism, a certain amount of "spill" of undifferentiation is generally absorbed by the other two mechanisms.

A family's ability to deal with the fusion in the nuclear emotional field largely depends on the level of differentiation of self of the most dominant person in the system. Marital conflict, which derives from excess fusion, usually develops when neither spouse will "give in" to the other. For example, the conflict may occur when an adaptive spouse refuses to continue giving in to a dominant spouse. Marital conflict is useful to the extent that it absorbs large quantities of the undifferentiation of spouses, thereby minimizing the probability of dysfunction of a spouse or projection to a child.

Spouses may also distance themselves from each other emotionally as an easier way of coping with a situation in which the two pseudo-selfs have fused into a common self. Unlike conflict between spouses, distance between spouses is not generally viewed as a behavior symptom. Either conflict or distance (or both conflict and distance) can develop into the dysfunction of one spouse. As fusion increases, one spouse gives up pseudo-self and the other gains a higher level of functioning self. The higher level of functioning of one spouse in the fusion is thus bought at the expense of the functioning level of the adaptive spouse. These are the early stages of increased dysfunction of one spouse.

The degree of closeness and togetherness between spouses influences the extent of the more adaptive spouse's dysfunction in the nuclear family emotional system. The merger between spouses may suppress conflict and encourage increasing closeness. The dominant spouse, who gains self and does not become clinically symptomatic, is generally not aware of the problems of the adaptive one, who gives up self for the sake of the merger. Dysfunction of the adaptive spouse may include physical or emotional illness and social acting out such as alcoholism or promiscuity.

The habitual dysfunction of a spouse in a nuclear family emotional system is difficult to reverse. The dysfunction absorbs increasing amounts of undifferentiation in the spouses' relationship and encourages the fusion to perpetuate itself. The continued dysfunction of one spouse allows the other to gain strength and ascendency in the emotional exchanges between spouses. The dysfunction simultaneously inhibits the eruption of marital conflict and the projection of the undifferentiation to a child. If a projection of the parental fusion to a child occurs, it eventually results in dysfunction of the child.

A fundamental function of the nuclear family emotional system is the absorption of the immaturity, or undifferentiation, of the spouses. The amount and intensity of the undifferentiation absorbed is fairly fluid and shifting. The absorption increases during periods of stress, and more symptoms are manifested at these times. Borrowing and trading pseudo-self among members of the same nuclear family emotional system increase when the fusion is intense.

The intensity of an extended family's emotional system is less than that of a related nuclear family. However, the emotional system of the extended family is the next most intense and significant relationship system after the nuclear family. The interdependency of these two emotional systems is so great that a changed emotional input to the extended family significantly modifies the intensity of nuclear relationships. For example, a spouse's increased contact with extended family generally culminates in increased differentiation. When an increase in differentiation occurs, there is less undifferentiation to be absorbed by the nuclear family emotional system, and a reduction of symptoms in those relationships frequently follows.

Research
    The tasks of the scientific enterprise are most effectively accomplished when research efforts have a relatively restricted focus. A nuclear family emotional system is a more clearly defined area of research than a complex social form such as a political movement. When the conditions examined are limited to a small but representative group in society, research objectives and methods become increasingly manageable and productive. A nuclear family emotional system may be conceptualized as a fairly predictable unit of social interaction. When this relationship system is intense, participating members are anxious and their behavior is more clearly patterned and predictable.
    To expedite the accumulation of integrated and useful knowledge in the behavioral sciences, some delimitation of the infinite number of variables possible in any field of social interaction is necessary. To some extent, increased clarity has already been accomplished by adopting hypotheses as delimiting tools in research. If observations of facts are inductively related to hypotheses, the selection of social forms and processes to be examined is as crucial to the successful outcome of the research

effort as the selection of a particular hypothesis. A working knowledge of a prototypical emotional system such as a nuclear family, which is fundamentally significant in many kinds of socialization processes, may be a more effective basis for collecting additional data and generating further productive hypotheses about human behavior than knowledge of less influential groups.

Nuclear family emotional system is, to some extent, a developmental concept. The term describes patterns of reciprocal behavior that originate with courtship and plans for marriage and continue more or less consistently throughout a marriage or a lifetime. Past and current emotional relationships outside the immediate nuclear unit, such as those of the spouses of the nuclear family and their parents, are important precipitating factors in the development and persistence of patterns of behavior in the related nuclear family. Patterns of interaction in a nuclear system tend to be directly or inversely correlated with patterns of behavior previously established in the family of origin of one or both spouses.

Other indicators of the most significant processes in a nuclear family emotional system are patterns of behavior during the spouses' adjustment to each other before they have children. Patterns of behavior during crises in the relationship of spouses, such as births or deaths, further specify the range of intensity in a given nuclear family.

The nuclear family emotional system is an arena for many kinds of nodal events, or major turning points in microscopic evolutionary processes. The accumulation of data on nuclear family systems can contribute toward increasing knowledge of the perpetuation of society as well as of the procreation and care of its young. Scientific knowledge of processes within nuclear family emotional systems is useful for the description and prediction of human behavior in general. Although patterns of behavior in nuclear families are usually more visible and more extreme than are patterns of behavior in other social groups, similar tendencies can be delineated in all emotional fields.

Case history study is one of the most effective research methods for examining nuclear family emotional systems. When this approach is used, data are collected from a fairly small number of families, and attention is focused on the delineation of indicators to represent the variety of qualities of relationships observed. A research tool that facilitates collection of this kind of data is a diagram illustrating the range of intensity of the emotional forces in a given nuclear family system. A graphic presentation of the basic data of a family network provides a reasonably clear view of the "systemness" of a nuclear emotional field and provides a context for delineating primary triangles in a family.

Patterns of emotional reactivity in a nuclear family suggest the location of pressure points. Pressure points are junctions in the emotional network where undifferentiation tends to be absorbed, either as a routine occurrence or during a crisis in a period of stress. When the flow of emotional forces and pressures has been delineated, some predictions about the outcome of specific inputs to the nuclear family can be made, and an individual family member can then choose a posture in relation to the system rather than allow self to be absorbed or dominated by the system. Such a choice and posture are possible only when patterns of interaction in a family system are known fairly well.

The study of nuclear family emotional systems is directly related to research on broader change processes. Although some details of typical patterns of emotional reactiveness and behavior in nuclear family emotional systems can be defined through survey techniques, large-scale cross-sectional analyses of emotional systems do not provide the same wealth of multidimensional data as do longitudinal case studies. Many survey findings are subject to a considerable "built-in" distortion of facts. This bias is frequently attributable to subjects' inaccurate reporting in response to impersonal written questionnaires.

Case history studies are usually conducted by means of a fairly long series of personal interviews. These continuing exchanges can provide much data about emotional processes. The data from case history studies can be double-checked in separate interviews, especially when the information requested is invested with feelings and several family members are questioned. Detailed historical data on past behavior in a nuclear family, which can be accumulated in several interviews, also appear more pertinent in terms of accurately representing an emotional field than information collected through surveys. By contrast, survey techniques generally provide a rather arbitrary and superficial series of indicators of interaction and at best merely suggest the presence of emotional processes.

Some research findings on nuclear family emotional systems indicate that there is a direct correlation between the intensity of the systems and the specific structural characteristics of those nuclear families. For example, in the most intense nuclear systems, there may be a lack of procreation or a high incidence of premature death. An important question arising from the exploration of these kinds of correlations is: To what extent can nuclear family structures be changed by modifying the degree of intensity of emotional relationships in the system?

Therapeutic Considerations

Central concerns of the Bowen family therapy include a systems description of emotional malfunctioning and a meaningful selection of means to work toward a more differentiated level of self. A knowledge of the complex dependencies in a nuclear family emotional system is a reliable basis for specifying such therapeutic measures.

Although one family member may be singled out as a "patient," this person may not actually dysfunction or may not be undifferentiated. An "identified patient," as in the case of a child, is frequently not as emotionally impaired as those who identify the patient. It is more accurate to consider the whole family a "client" when dysfunctioning by a single member is reported. If the therapist views the entire family network as client or patient in a clinical context, the nuclear emotional system can be considered one of the most representative units of the whole, thereby indicating tendencies in characteristic behavior patterns of the wider network.

The Bowen theory suggests a course of therapy where the person coached begins to learn how to identify triangles and how to detriangle self. Although detriangling may be more easily accomplished in the extended system than in the nuclear family, knowledge of the nuclear system is indispensable for ensuring the effectiveness of moves in the extended network. The immediacy and intensity of emotional forces in the nuclear family must be dealt with to some extent to arrive at some degree of objectivity regarding the whole family. For example, multigenerational transmission processes cannot be delineated until the emotional forces in member nuclear systems have been defined.

Knowledge of the nuclear family emotional system facilitates the measurement of change in a course of psychotherapy. This knowledge is also needed by a therapist for dealing with the impact of changes in a family. For example, members of a nuclear family may be so reactive to a person who is trying to differentiate self that they may appear to an uninformed observer to be preventing, rather than resisting, change. A firm stand for self is only possible when the person attempting differentiation has a working knowledge of the emotional forces in the nuclear family.

One's Own Family

Discerning the characteristics of the nuclear family system may be so difficult that an individual member of the nuclear group may not know what it means to be either "in" or "out" of this emotional field. The degree of intensity of the nuclear processes distorts many of the perceptions its members have of each other.

The strength of the feelings invested in the nuclear system facilitates differentiation of members of the nuclear group most effectively when many meaningful person-to-person relationships are established and maintained with members of the extended family. Objectivity about the nuclear group results from a knowledge of the perceptions and experiences of extended family members. If an individual achieves differentiation, deep-seated tendencies to accept the perceptions of emotionally significant other members in the nuclear system as one's own are counteracted. "Buying" others' perceptions is characteristic of the nuclear processes. This fused exchange occurs automatically unless conscious efforts are made to act for self.

When relating to extended family members, emotional contact with members of the nuclear family should optimally be maintained at all times. Changes in the nuclear family occur following differentiating moves in the extended system to the extent that contact between the nuclear and extended systems is maintained.

An exploration of trends and patterns in births, marriages, deaths, and other nodal events in previous generations and in other nuclear systems in one's family adds significant dimensions to knowledge of the emotional forces in one's immediate nuclear system. The structure of past generations provides indicators of the pervasiveness and intensity of the family emotional processes, and a more objective view of repeated patterns of behavior and symptoms becomes possible. For example, sibling position can be considered the product of the emotional processes in a family as well as a particular structural characteristic of a family. Rank ordering and sex distribution of siblings do not appear to be as random as is conventionally believed.

Differentiation of self in one's family of origin is frequently facilitated by the greater degree of emotional and geographical distance that exists between members of the family of origin than between members of the nuclear system. By diluting the intensity of the emotional processes in the nuclear field, the emotional engagement made with members of one's family of origin automatically opens up the nuclear system. The investment of feelings in an increasing number of meaningful relationships in the extended emotional field draws emotional investment out of the nuclear group. Whatever moves one makes in one's extended family, differentiation of self in the nuclear system remains a high priority.

Family Projection Process

Family projection process is closely related to the concept of nuclear family emotional system. Family projection describes an important pattern of interaction that appears in many nuclear families. The "surfacing" and visibility of family projection within a nuclear family does not mean that the projection derives solely from this group. The emotional forces that precipitate projection are an integral part of the entire family system. A sequence of projections in different generations of the same family influences the extended family as well as a particular nuclear unit.

Family projection is a mechanism for dealing with surplus undifferentiation in a nuclear family emotional system. Family projection become symptomatic when the level of differentiation of spouses is low and the resulting need for absorption of undifferentiation is high. The differentiation level of each spouse is a precondition of the degree of fusion in their relationship and the amount of undifferentiation in the nuclear family that must be absorbed. The intensity of a projection process increases when anxiety in a family is high.

The ways in which spouses routinely handle fusion in their relationship stabilize patterns of behavior, especially in the specific areas where undifferentiation is absorbed and symptoms appear under stress. Projection to one or more children, marital conflict, and dysfunction of a spouse are areas in a nuclear family where symptoms may be manifested. Most families deal with undifferentiation in a combination of ways. Family projection is most frequently accompanied by some marital conflict and some dysfunction of a spouse.

Family projection is a mechanism through which parents transmit a substantial amount of their own emotional immaturity to a child. Immaturity is a component of the undifferentiation of fusion of the parents who use this adaptive mechanism. The most pervasive pattern of projection in families in the United States is close bonding between mother and child, with the father supporting the mother's overinvolvement. In the closely interdependent twosomes between mother and child, the mother generally overfunctions and her child reacts by underfunctioning. The mother is able to reduce her own high level of anxiety by focusing it on her child, seeing her child as a problem or in need of her help and protection.

Among the many complex factors which influence the selection of a particular child for projection are the sibling positions of parents and the intensity of the parents' dependency on their parents. Traumatic events during a pregnancy or soon after the birth of a child and the distribution of highly charged or emotionally invested relationships in a family also influence which child will be singled out for the projection process.

One of the most critical family events that influences the selection of a particular child for projection is the death of a key family member. If a birth occurs soon after the death of a close family member such as a parent, an older sibling, or a grandparent, the newborn child is more likely to become a focus of family projection than if no death had occurred at that time. Family projection may also be precipitated by other emotionally significant losses in a family, such as divorce, geographical separation, or institutionalization.

The child most trapped by a family projection is the one who is most emotionally attached to the parents. This involvement may be either an overt closeness or an intense repulsion. The recipient of the family projection eventually becomes less differentiated than the parents, largely because of an emotional response to being caught in the parental emotional field. The intensely dependent relationships between parents and between parents and child prevent the child from being able to take a differentiating posture in relation to either or both parents. Such dependent relationships are reinforced and perpetuated through the projection process. The focused child is inextricably triangled in the fused togetherness of the parents.

A child who grows up outside the projection can become more differentiated than either the child who is the object of projection or the parents. It is easier to become more differentiated outside a family projection, as the degree of objectivity necessary for differentiating moves generally cannot be attained by the principal recipient of projection.

Research

If the intensity of a family projection and the levels of differentiation of parents are measured fairly accurately, the differentiation of the children can tentatively be predicted, especially where a child is clearly focused by the family projection. To the extent that family projection represents the most intense emotional interdependency possible between parents and a child, it must be considered one of the most significant influences on behavior in a nuclear family. Although a family projection can be directed to an older relative or to a member of the extended family, the process is most frequently and most visibly generated from parents to a child. A child is usually more vulnerable to these emotional forces than other family members, as a child is, of necessity, extremely dependent on the parents.

The most critical determinants of the potency of a family projection are the level of undifferentiation between parents, which must be absorbed by the nuclear family, and the level of anxiety in that system. Other significant influences include the amounts of marital conflict and dysfunction of spouses in a nuclear family. To describe how a family projection eventually manifests itself, some assessment must also be made of the varying degrees of vulnerability to the projection of each child in a nuclear family. Whether or not a child becomes the object of a projection depends on factors such as the child's functioning sibling position, established patterns of behavior in the nuclear and extended systems, and crises or nodal events in the family relationships.

Clinical data substantiate the proposition that the child who receives the most emotional investment from parents becomes the "victim" or object of the family projection. Oldest, youngest, and only children are frequently recipients of family projections, although children who function in those roles are perhaps more vulnerable to projection than are children chronologically in those positions. Seniority is not as strong an influence as the nature of the active dependencies in the family relationship system. In contrast to extreme or symptomatic family projection processes, "healthy" projection meets a child's real needs and does not go beyond them.

Although many complex variables influence projection, the scope of scientific research on these processes is fairly clearly defined. The sampling universe that best illustrates projection is a family. Within the family, the differentiation and fusion of grandparents, parents, and children are assessed and patterns of emotional reactions and responses are examined. A proposition of the Bowen theory is that in families where there is little evidence of marital conflict and dysfunction of a spouse, projection to a child is fairly predictable.

To have a comprehensive and objective view of family interaction, the scientific description and prediction of projection within nuclear families should be accompanied by the description of patterns of emotional behavior in related extended families. These wider influences contribute directly to the maintenance and persistence of family projection over several generations. A broadly based study of this kind may indicate the ways in which the forces leading to and maintaining a projection are related to characteristics of a particular nuclear family, its extended network, or both systems. A detailed examination of family projection may shed light on the complex issue of the nature of the interdependency between nuclear and extended family systems.

Family projection is a sufficiently versatile concept to generate several hypotheses for different kinds of applied research. Further examination of this particular aspect of the interdependencies in a nuclear family emotional system might contribute toward a fuller understanding of some of the problems identified by families and society.

Formal research studies of family projection are more productive if they are longitudinal in design and multigenerational in scope. Descriptions of family projection at one point in time and within a fragment of a family network are inadequate, as they are not representative of the whole system. In addition to maintaining a broad perspective, the projection process in terms of a particular child should be studied.

A family where a child is clearly focused by projection is frequently so stable that it may be described as unchangeable. The pervasiveness of this pattern of family interaction has several implications for society. A child who is object of a family projection is more likely to have behavior symptoms or to be viewed as delinquent than is a child who is outside a projection. As society must ultimately be concerned with the effectiveness and meaningfulness of its interpersonal relationships and with its overall ability to meet group needs, research hypotheses that examine the consequences of projection for a family and for society might suggest practical measures or preventive strategies to deal with the impairing processes.

Closely related to how a child is selected by a family projection and how a family projection operates is the question of what contributes to a nuclear family's selection of projection to absorb undifferentiation or fusion rather than the alternative mechanisms of marital conflict or dysfunction of a spouse. In general, either marital conflict or dysfunction of a spouse presents fewer long-range problems for families and society than does projection. If patterns of behavior leading to the selection of a child for projection and family projection processes themselves are described more accurately, people's ability to avoid or neutralize projection may be increased.

Therapeutic Considerations

Family projection is a strong influence on the development of various forms of emotional disorders and symptomatic behavior. Much psychotherapy is an attempt to deal with the consequences of this powerful mechanism. Even if nuclear families stabilize their dependencies through marital conflict or dysfunction of a spouse, the latter may have resulted from family projection in the families of origin of either or both spouses.

A primary goal in psychotherapy is to relieve family members of the intensity and destructive effects of projection processes. A reduction of projection is a prerequisite of increased responsible behavior by key family members as well as of the alleviation of symptoms.

When family projection processes are active, one family member is singled out as a "patient" or a "problem" by those who are in strategic positions in the emotional system. A therapist or coach who works with families that have a child-focus, for example, may present alternative perceptions of the focused child to the other family members to encourage increased objectivity about the family system. If these members are able to direct their attention to the complexities and intricacies in the broader emotional network, the family "fix" on one person's behavior or on one problem may be loosened. Families with projection to one child are among the most difficult to change through psychotherapy.

Only when a parent of a child who is caught in a family projection becomes aware of some of the emotional processes involved can a first step be taken to defocus and free the child. An increase in the differentiation or functioning of one of the parents decreases the fusion between spouses that had previously been absorbed by the projection. Where there is less change in a spouse's behavior, there is no change in the projection or merely a shift in the symptoms of the projection. When a child is no longer an exclusive focus of a projection, increased marital conflict or increased dysfunction of one of the parents may occur. Although a shift in symptoms may or may not precede more permanent changes, shifting symptoms suggest less serious impairment than conditions where there is no movement of symptoms either during or following psychotherapy.

One's Own Family

Projection in one's own family may be so difficult to observe with any degree of objectivity that family members may consider such processes nonexistent until a focused child behaves symptomatically. One's position in relation to projection in one's nuclear family cannot be modified, however, until projection in one's family of origin and, to a certain extent, in the family of origin of one's spouse, is identified. Delineating projection in these contexts and taking a differentiated posture in relation to the processes precipitates changes in one's family of origin, one's spouse's family of origin, and eventually in one's nuclear family if emotional contact with these systems is maintained.

One's family of origin may provide clearer evidence of projection than one's nuclear family. It is generally easier to assess which of one's siblings has had the most symptoms over a time span of many years than to evaluate the behavior of one's own children. Indicators of adequate functioning include academic and occupational achievement, physical and emotional health, and marriage and procreation. The extent of projection in one's family of origin can be partially estimated by comparing projection symptoms with characteristics of the marital conflict between one's parents and the degree of dysfunction of one or both of them. An assessment of the potency of projection includes an examination of patterns of behavior when symptoms are manifested, a delineation of precipitating factors in symptom development, and the observation of conditions of the termination or regulation of symptoms.

It is easier to delineate details of projection behavior in one's

family of origin by focusing on relationships in the periphery of
that system than by examining only the central nuclear family.
Members in this outer network include grandparents and
relatives in the grandparent and earlier generations. The
lessened degree of emotional involvement with more removed
family members enables more accurate observation of behavior
in these relationship systems. Public records of births,
marriages, and deaths can provide at least minimum
information for a reconstruction of projection processes in the
past if substantial data on previous generations is not available
through personal contacts. In some respects, a reconstruction
from public records may be more representative and more
reliable than use of data that has been filtered through the
perceptions and memories of living family members in the
nuclear and extended emotional fields.

Data from public records indicate extreme manifestations of
family projection more clearly than milder varieties of
projection. Some of the more acute projections suggested by
public records include early death, no marriage, no procreation,
and conception or birth before marriage. The more detailed
information that appears on public records in the last few
decades, such as data on occupations or migrations, permits
clearer and more accurate descriptions of projection.

Emotional Cut-Off

The concept of emotional cut-off describes extreme cases of
distancing between family members. High levels of anxiety in
self and in the family relationship system are preconditions for
the development of emotional cut-offs. Increases in anxiety or
the perpetuation of the same degree of anxiety reinforce existing
cut-offs and predispose the system to develop new cut-offs.

Emotional cut-off may be used as a means of dealing with

fusion in intimate relationships. Each person who participates in an emotional cut-off plays a part in the complex estranging processes. Although each party has a strong need for the other, neither is able to handle that need effectively. Going away from each other emotionally and perhaps geographically is chosen as the easiest and most effective way to deal with the intensity and demands of the interdependency.

The existence of many cut-offs in a family's emotional system indicates a high level of anxiety. A considerable number of emotional cut-offs is associated with symptomatic behavior, illness, and premature deaths. In families where anxiety is low, there are few cut-offs in important relationships and between nuclear and extended parts of the family. Families with few cut-offs have few symptoms and only minor disabilities.

Although several reasons are usually given for an emotional cut-off in a family, such as geographical migration, these tend to be rationalizations for anxious reactions rather than accurate descriptions of existing conditions. Moreover, single incidents tend to be inappropriately cited as significant factors in precipitating emotional cut-offs. In reality, estrangements take long periods of time to develop, perhaps several generations.

Although it is difficult to measure the intensity of an emotional cut-off, the duration of a cut-off is an indicator of the investment of feelings each party has in continuing the repulsion. When anxiety is high in a family relationship, the probability that a cut-off will occur or will be perpetuated increases. These conditions may be inevitable unless one of the parties involved makes conscious efforts to reverse the interactive estranging processes. If one is able to bridge cut-offs in one's own family, there will be significant benefits for self and others throughout the entire relationship system. Bridging a cut-off is a differentiating move to the extent that emotional contact is maintained with other family members as the cut-off is bridged.

People find many ways to cut off from each other. A close examination of the triangular substructure of the family relationship system facilitates the prediction of cut-offs and contributes toward describing cut-offs that have already occurred.

The pervasiveness of loneliness and misunderstandings between members of different generations in contemporary society suggests high frequencies of emotional cut-offs in families and other relationship systems. Although loneliness and distance between generations have always existed to some extent, these phenomena have reached problem dimensions in contemporary society.

Before social and geographical mobility were possible for large numbers of people, cut-offs appear to have been largely handled by intrapsychic and somatic mechanisms, such as withdrawal, sickness, or accidents. Although it is difficult to determine precisely what part self plays in a cut-off, a cut-off is more than a defense mechanism for an individual. Emotional cut-offs have implications for others beyond a single individual's withdrawal from an anxiety-laden relationship.

Emotional cut-offs in families have intergenerational consequences. One of the more predictable and more visible outcomes is that when a parent generation cuts off from the grandparent generation, there is a strong likelihood that the children of these parents will also cut off. Hypothetically, the more an individual cuts off from the family of origin, the more that person's children are likely to cut off relationships in the future. A cut-off from the parent generation is frequently justified as making a break from a difficult past for the sake of living in a more ideal present. However, such reasoning is an emotional reaction to the anxiety in the relationships that have been cut off.

The ultimate emotional cut-off is death. Premature and

accidental death are ways in which a person or a family may deal with overload anxiety. One possible sequence of events is that intense emotional cut-offs are followed by symptomatic behavior and premature death. Although this pattern of events is crude and extreme, its outlines are manifested to some extent in a variety of families. It is possible to make some moves toward closing a cut-off between a dead person and self. These moves consist of contacting persons who were close to the cut-off deceased family member and trying to piece together the life-history of the deceased individual.

As with other Bowen family concepts, emotional cut-off can be considered scientific in terms of its predictive capacity. Some of the more predictable sequences of behavior related to emotional cut-off include the following:

1. Where anxiety is high in a family, there is a high frequency of intense cut-offs.

2. When a cut-off is bridged in a family and emotional contact with family members is maintained, the probability of effective differentiation increases.

3. When cut-offs exist between parent and grandparent generations, a cut-off between parents and children in the next generation is more likely to develop, especially when the children are old enough to leave their parental home.

4. As emotional cut-off is not a constructively adaptive means of dealing with fusion and intimate relationships, cut-offs may be followed by symptomatic behaviors, including premature death.

5. The degree of cut-off in a relationship is an indicator of the degree of fusion or undifferentiation in the same relationship.

6. All members of a family play some part in the cut-offs that exist and are perpetuated in that system.

To the extent that emotional cut-offs reflect the degree of

fusion and anxiety in a family, their distribution is largely determined by characteristics of the substructure of triangles in this system. Close togetherness in triangle frequently occurs at the expense of cutting off from the third member of the triangle. In this situation, emotional cut-off assists in coping with the overload of anxiety or fusion in a triangle and the relationship system.

Activity that culminates in cutting off emotional contact with other family members is frequently an ineffective effort to achieve independence. These moves do not differentiate self, and the process is almost the opposite of differentiation. Any gain in pseudo-self through creation of an emotional cut-off provides only temporary relief from the intense anxiety in a relationship system. The cut-off merely makes self more vulnerable to a new mode of intense togetherness with others, which also tends to annihilate self. The degree of cut-off oversensitizes self and predisposes the cut-off individual to participate in other fused relationships. The greater a cut-off from past relationships, the higher is the probability that intense fusion in future relationships will develop.

An estimate of the number of cut-offs in a family is easier to make than an estimate of the intensity of the cut-offs. The manifestation of symptoms in a family provides some indicators of the intensity of cut-offs in the emotional system. Children who are cut off from their grandparents generally have more problems in performing at school than children who are in meaningful contact with their grandparents. If a child becomes delinquent or is chronically sick, the intensity of the cut-off between generations tends to be greater than if a child's behavior is mildly symptomatic.

Duration through time is an indicator of the intensity of cut-offs. If a cut-off has persisted for a decade, this cut-off is more intense and is a product of a more anxious relationship system than if it had lasted for a short period of time. The stability and rigidity of a cut-off suggest the strength of the feelings invested in the cut-off. The stronger the feelings invested, the more rigidified the cut-off becomes. These kinds of indicators provide a basis for measuring and refining the concept of emotional cut-off for further research.

Emotional cut-off describes a pattern of family interaction that can be observed fairly easily. Generalizations about the social consequences of cut-offs and about the incidence of cut-offs in the wider society may be inferred from accumulated data on families. Data collected in clinical settings suggest some practical applications and implications of the concept of cut-off. The Bowen theory views emotional cut-off as an integral part of emotional process and change within families and in society.

A few meaning elements of the concept of emotional cut-off can be highlighted by referring to Bowen family theory ideas that describe obverse processes. Whereas an effective differentiation of self culminates in changes in basic self, emotional cut-off is an immature and less successful attempt to separate self from fused family relationships. Whereas fusion is intense togetherness, with each participant sacrificing self to the unit twosome, an emotional cut-off is an attempt to deal with the same relationship intensity without sacrificing self. However, in spite of the contrived distance, other characteristics of the rigidly fused relationships remain. Fusion is a significant counterpart of an emotional cut-off.

Emotional cut-offs are generally less apparent within nuclear families than is fusion. Cut-offs are easier to observe between parent and grandparent generations, and this kind of cut-off intensifies the emotions of the nuclear system. If a cut-off between generations is acute and persists for a long period of time, behavior symptoms will surface when the nuclear family is anxious.

Triangles are a substructure of a family that can generate emotional cut-offs. An emotional cut-off may develop when a close togetherness is created by extreme distancing from a third person in a triangle. In contrast to detriangling processes, by which the person in the outside position in a triangle purposely maintains emotional contact with each party in the fused twosome, the distanced third person in an emotional cut-off loses contact with the other two. The members of the togetherness are so caught up in their cocoon of sharing each others' beliefs and perceptions that each loses contact with the third party. In contrast to family projection, by which a third person is trapped in the emotional field between the fused twosome, a cut-off essentially expels the third person from the triangle. Nevertheless, the twosome may maintain strong bonds with that person, and these latent ties may surface in a time of stress or they may be driven further underground through time.

Cut-offs are often repeated between succeeding generations. These repetitions intensity, rather than neutralize, the multigenerational transmission process. When cut-offs persist without being bridged, patterns of related symptomatic behavior may be automatically repeated by members of different generations, and the symptoms may intensify in this process. Making attempts to bridge cut-offs and maintaining emotional contact with members of several generations in the same family are some of the means that can be used to protect self and others from the crystallization of problem behavior in a family.

Research

Formal research is needed to describe and define the characteristics of cut-offs in families. The perceptions of individuals who are emotionally estranged from each other can be used as a basis for selecting indicators to describe emotional cut-offs. An individual who is cut off from a parent is more likely to express either strongly antagonistic or completely indifferent feelings for that parent than someone who has a viable day-to-day relationship with a parent. The estranged person's views can provide a tentative measure of the intensity and quality of emotional cut-offs in the family network. The greatest distortion of objectivity occurs in the midst of the most intense cut-off processes.

A measure of the frequency of cut-offs in a family can indicate the extent to which the distribution of cut-offs influences the behavior of family members. Research in this area could assess the consequences of the intensity and number of emotional cut-offs for a family. The extent of symptomatic behavior in a family appears positively correlated with a high frequency of emotional cut-offs or with fewer more intense emotional cut-offs. This evidence suggests that the existence of emotional cut-offs can be detrimental to the functioning of all family members. Clinical data indicate that cut-offs are generally pervasive and intense in families that have the most difficulty with maintaining viable patterns of behavior.

Emotional cut-offs can be researched to determine their predictability, especially for times of stress. Another aspect of emotional cut-offs that could be documented is the consequences of bridging cut-offs. Exploratory clinical research tends to substantiate the hypothesis than when an individual is able to bridge a cut-off and maintain emotional contact with other family members, this person and eventually other family members function more effectively and become more differentiated than they were prior to the cut-off. A description of the ways that cut-offs can be bridged in a family may provide further indicators of the qualities of emotional cut-offs.

Emotional cut-offs are relationship phenomena. Systematic research efforts are needed to delineate the part all family members play in perpetuating emotional cut-offs in the relationship system and the ways individuals contribute to the processes of separation. An emotional cut-off is not a single person's achievement, even though an estrangement is frequently described by key participants in the cut-off as the result of the behavior of the one who ends up outside the overt togetherness of the other family members.

Therapeutic Considerations
Effective psychotherapy with families frequently includes or results in bridging emotional cut-offs in those families. When a cut-off relationship is meaningfully reestablished, anxiety in the family is visibly reduced and behavior symptoms are, at least, temporarily relieved. The family members most active in bridging the cut-offs and maintaining emotional contact with other family members may eventually become more differentiated in their behavior, thereby improving the functioning of other family members. A fairly accurate indicator of improved family functioning is that children's behavior often becomes symptom-free at the same time that a parent or other key member of the family invests feelings in previously estranged relationships. This kind of change is particularly apparent in families where there have been cut-offs between the parents of symptomatic children and their parents or significant members of their families of origin.

A therapist can encourage the bridging of cut-offs in a family by suggesting to the individuals coached that estranged family members might have interesting perceptions about inner-core family members and nodal events in the family. One can become more objective about one's perceptions of one's family by comparing views with individuals who have withdrawn from the relationship system and who have been pushed out of the active emotional exchanges between family members.

In some families, cut-offs that occurred several generations earlier may affect the functioning level of living family members. If family members can discover information in the past about these cut-offs, some bridging becomes possible, even though the parties concerned may be deceased. An initiation of personal contacts with relatives or close friends of a deceased cut-off family member can improve an individual's functioning and open up the entire family system. For these constructive consequences to occur during a course of therapy, there must first be sufficient symptom relief. Only when some objectivity has been attained, can systematic moves to bridge cut-offs be made.

Emotional cut-offs in a family may develop after the geographical separation of family members. Geographical separation may also follow the development of emotional cut-offs. Moves away from the locale of one's family of origin are generally precipitated more by persisting estrangements between family members than by the conventionally stated reasons, such as a promotion or a more temperate climate.

Families who request therapy are often geographically scattered or splintered. Therapeutic effort may be successful in creating or reestablishing meaningful contact between family members in spite of geographical separations. This kind of bridging activity can be exhausting, but visits and communications with distant relatives can reinvest feelings in isolated parts of the family system, resulting in a variety of beneficial outcomes for the whole family.

Although such extensions of psychotherapy are possible, many families in a clinical setting remain cut off from their families of origin in a variety of ways. Most symptom relief and differentiation appear to occur where the complex effects of emotional cut-offs with parents and grandparents are minimized.

One's Own Family

It is much easier to accept others' perceptions of one's family than to formulate one's own perceptions. For example, most people share their dominant parents' view of other family members. In the early years of life, the depth of this programming is not questioned. One grows to accept certain family members as "in" the family, and others as essentially "out" of the family. The dividing line between being in or being out of a family usually reflects the outreach of the more active and viable part of the family emotional network. Cut-off processes generally exist at points where certain members are defined or viewed as being outside the core family group. One way to identify cut-offs in one's own family is to question others about who makes up the family. The repeated exclusion of particular family members and the degree of negative resistance to such questioning frequently indicate the number and intensity of cut-offs in one's family.

In many situations, there are more dividends for self and for one's family if cut-offs are bridged effectively than if other kinds of differentiating moves are made. Consistent bridging of cut-offs while maintaining meaningful contacts with family members may eventually open up the entire family system. Throughout these processes, an individual becomes more centrally significant in the network of communications and feelings in the family.

After bridging a cut-off in one's family, other family members may follow this example by investing feelings in their own relationships with the "outsider." The person who first bridges the cut-off is gradually respected by other family members, even though there may have been considerable opposition to the bridging moves when they first occurred or if one revealed plans and intentions to other family members before making the bridging moves. It is usually more productive not to discuss plans for approaching a cut-off individual with other family members before making these efforts. The negative reactions of other family members can be discouraging and may make one's actions less effective by introducing unnecessary complications into an already difficult situation.

Frequently, the person who has cut off and who has been cut off from a family knows "inside information" or secrets about the family. This knowledge or assumed knowledge may have initially precipitated cut-off processes. Much significant information may be derived from contact with the estranged individual.

Although travel to visit geographically distant family members is costly, the advantages of personally following through these leads can be rewarding. The material costs involved in reaching distant family members may be more than offset by the "priceless" gains of enriched perspectives, a new view of self, and a more differentiated or effective functioning position in one's family. Moreover, older family members are generally very receptive to a younger person's efforts to establish contact with them. These older family members appear to thrive from the attention and new investment of feelings, and they frequently contribute unique oral histories of family events.

The process of establishing emotional contact with those who are cut off in one's family of origin draws feelings away from a marriage or from a focused child in a nuclear family. A beneficial consequence of these bridging activities is a reduction in the degree of interdependency or overdependency in one's marital and parent-child relationships. The emotional pullout creates conditions whereby marital and parental relationships can become increasingly flexible, viable, meaningful, and enjoyable.

In some respects, there may be no end to the quantity and quality of cut-offs that one can improve in one's family. Efforts to bridge cut-offs, together with an awareness of the pervasiveness of this phenomenon, must be continual if one is to maintain a differentiated position in one's family.

Multigenerational Transmission Process

The concept of multigenerational transmission process describes broad patterns of behavior between members of different generations in the same family. Although the meaning elements of this concept are based on observations of the life-course of the child who is most impaired by emotional projection in a nuclear family, the applications and implication of multigenerational transmission process have more ramifications than do differentiation of self, nuclear family emotional system, or family projection process. Multigenerational transmission process describes and suggests possible outcomes of differentiation of self, dependencies in the nuclear family emotional system, and family projection over several generations.

Multigenerational transmission process is a living context for the description of qualities of change in various generations of the same family. One of the most important modifications a family system can undergo is shifting levels of differentiation of self of key family members through the influence of multigenerational transmission processes. The open-ended comprehensiveness of the concept of multigenerational transmission process suggests that family emotional systems are an integral part of evolutionary processes and adaptation.

The concept of multigenerational transmission process illustrates sequential projections over continuous generations in a family. The multigenerational process describes ways in which nuclear families program particular ranges of differentiation of self from one generation to another. However, whereas family projection culminates in a lowering of the level of differentiation of self between parents and a child in two generations, multigenerational transmission describes more "open" and diverse processes by relating to a wider range of possible levels of differentiation of self.

The concept of multigenerational transmission process does not explain biological inheritance through the generations. Multigenerational transmission process focuses on specific emotional system mechanisms that influence the differentiation of members of succeeding generations. From this broad perspective, the effects of marital conflict or of dysfunction of a spouse may be as significant for the functioning of members of future generations as the effects of family projection.

Multigenerational transmission describes how a series of succeeding generations manifests trends and tendencies in levels of differentiation of self. The trends and tendencies in multiple generations are formed as successions of children emerge from their parental families with slightly higher, equal, or slightly lower levels of differentiation of self than their parents. Patterns in these processes are most visible when behavior in more than three generations of linear descent is examined and recorded or diagramed.

An example of multigenerational transmission that culminates in a lowering of differentiation in succeeding generations illustrates one way in which this process operates. People generally select spouses whose differentiation is basically the same as their own. When a person emerges from the parental family with a lower level of differentiation than the parents have, a spouse selected by this person will have an equal level of differentiation. If this marriage produces a child with a lower level of differentiation, the next marriage will be to a person who has the same lower level of differentiation. When this marriage produces a child with an even lower level of differentiation who marries on that same level, a transmission process can be considered to move from generation to generation toward lower and lower levels of differentiation.

If a family has trends of maintained or increasingly higher levels of differentiation, children from succeeding generations of marriages have levels of differentiation corresponding to those of their parents. There is no clear evidence that a particular evolutionary direction or momentum automatically generates a rise or decline of differentiation in subsequent generations. Rather, parents seem to produce offspring who cannot easily move beyond the same level of differentiation that the parents have. In most circumstances, a family tends to perpetuate its level of differentiation. As only one or two children in a given generation are focused by a family projection, they, and not their siblings, will have a lower level of differentiation than their parents. Siblings who remain outside the family projection will have about the same level of differentiation as their parents, or they will be slightly more differentiated. When differentiation and projection are delineated in several related nuclear families, some segments of the extended system may appear to be becoming more differentiated at the same time that other sections of the system appear to be becoming less differentiated.

The consequences of multigenerational transmission are limited by the range of changes possible in differentiating self. There cannot be substantial leaps or gaps in levels of differentiation between succeeding generations of a family. What may appear to be significant changes in differentiation in a family are often merely shifts in functioning. More marked differences in levels of differentiation of members of the same family may perhaps be observed at the extreme points of a wide range of generations. These changes in levels of differentiation are the product of an exceedingly slow transmission process, which has raised or lowered specific personal levels of differentiation through many generations.

Influences in Marital Conflict

Case history materials have been used to define and document specific family influences on marital conflict and the patterns of behavior generated by marital conflict. Wherever possible, longitudinal studies of family interaction were made over several generations, and genealogical data was used to supplement this information. These exploratory studies indicate the following trends and tendencies in family relationships:

1. The volume and intensity of marital conflict appear to depend more on past family relationships and experiences than on contingencies and characteristics of the present marriage.

2. The level of intensity of the relationship of each spouse in the marital conflict with the parent of the opposite sex is a fairly accurate predictor of the proclivity for conflict that each spouse manifests. For example, when conflict exists between the husband and the husband's mother, the tendency of the husband and wife to have a conflictual relationship is correspondingly high.

3. The sibling positions and sex distributions in the families of each spouse and of each parent of the marriage partners influence the probability of conflict between the spouses.

4. Although habitual conflict between spouses does not resolve the issues disputed, the intensity of the spouses' feelings invested in the marital conflict shields children from projection as a result of parental anxiety in the family.

5. Where conflict between spouses is not overt, husband or wife may become dysfunctional, or the conflict may be projected to a child or grandchild.

Family interaction cannot be described and defined accurately with reference only to the nuclear family setting and to behavior observed at a few points in time (Mishler and Waxler 1968) or to family networks that include many friends as well as relatives (Speck and Attneave 1973). Conflict is a means of dealing with high levels of anxiety in the entire family (Boszormenyi-Nagy and Spark 1973) and is not "contained" by the two parties who appear to be those most actively engaged in it. Triangular interaction in the family emotional system over several generations selects which spouses are combatants and influences the extent to which tension can be dealt with in a constructive way—that is, without impinging on the behavior of others.

Research

Predictions about individual families can be verified by applications of the concept of multigenerational transmission process. Experimental research that includes this kind of verification describes characteristics of the emotional system of several past generations of a family or families with data accumulated from public records and other documentary courses. From the functioning facts of past generations, some predictions are made about how family members might interact in the present generations of the researched families. When these predictions have been made, characteristics of the emotional system of present generations are examined and the data from current behavior patterns are used to substantiate or refute the trends predicted from the data on past generations.

The research procedures described have limited usefulness because the relatively small number of families that can be examined by these in-depth longitudinal methods cannot provide a numerically representative sample of the whole population. Also, operationalization of these research techniques is extremely time-consuming. In spite of these limitations, multigenerational transmission process is a significant concept to use in the formulation of meaningful hypotheses for examining the impact of emotional processes in a family's past generations on present generations. When predictions about patterns of interaction in present generations of individual families are accurate, multigenerational transmission is an effective means of describing change processes in a family. Furthermore, this concept may provide leads for the more accurate description of broad evolutionary processes.

Unless research on families is conducted with a perspective or a frame of reference that accounts for behavior in several past generations, data selected for scientific analyses tends to be incomplete and skewed by a built-in bias that overestimates the importance of interaction. A present-based research focus of this kind distorts empirical reality and does not accurately represent patterns of behavior that occur throughout the more global aspects of the extended relationship network of a family. An awareness of the consequences of this kind of error recommends three generations as a minimum base for meaningful family research and for representative generalizations about emotional processes in families.

Although the concept of multigenerational transmission is not easy to operationalize, it is fairly limited in its scope compared with other social change concepts. In this respect, the concept may have considerably more practical and more versatile applications and implications than concepts such as social class, which relate to broader and more complex aspects of the wider society.

Some of the possible research on multigenerational transmission can fall into two major categories. First, research could begin with an issue or information relating to past generations and work forward to present generations. This research focus and direction could include predictions for present or future family interaction. Second, research could begin with an issue or information relating to present generations and work backward to past generations. The second research focus and direction could include predictions about how past generations might be reconstructed from information gathered from family members in present generations or from genealogical data.

The information a researcher collects in studying the effects of multigenerational transmission optimally could provide new evidence for an assessment of the degree of order in human life. Indicators of a life-course could include occupation, geographical location, marital status, and the number and spacing of children. From a family systems perspective, a major substantive concern is the circumstances of significant deaths in a family. Questions that relate to this issue might include the following: What changes in family processes followed a significant death? What factors appear to have contributed to the timing of a particular death? Another major substantive concern from a family systems perspective is the circumstances of significant geographical moves or migrations in a family. Questions that relate to this issue might include the following: What factors appeared to precipitate a particular geographical move? What changes in a family preceded, occurred simultaneously with, or followed a migration by some of its members? What circumstances might have prevented the geographical migration of other family members?

When these kinds of events are researched through several generations of a family, findings are more likely to be objectively accurate and representative of the whole system than when only a cross section of present facts and events is researched. Research hypotheses on the impact of death and migration through several generations of a family could constitute ways of documenting and measuring changes in differentiation at the times of death and migration. Some indication might also be given of the extent to which death and migration contribute to lowering, raising, or maintaining differentiation levels in a family.

Research on multigenerational transmission could include studies of the range of family structures that result from specific kinds of emotional processes over several generations. To what extent can the concept of multigenerational transmission suggest how a given family comes to produce more men than women? Which transmission patterns contribute to an increase in separation and divorce over several generations?

Although the examples of research already given largely indicate basic research projects, this concept may also be used in applied research. For example, insofar as emotional impairment is viewed as a culmination of a long chain of events that lowers differentiation, the etiology of emotional disorders can be approached by describing characteristics of the multigenerational transmission processes that have contributed to particular symptom manifestations.

Therapeutic Considerations

The concept of multigenerational transmission suggests that emotional impairment is a product of a sequence of intergenerational processes in a family. One way to describe and define some of the factors that have contributed to dysfunctional behavior is to examine characteristics of the broad family network and the different qualities of emotional processes that have occurred through several generations.

The ongoing work involved in accumulating data that describe the nature of emotional processes in prior generations may be an essential integral part of psychotherapy. Information gathering on past generations is a significant activity not only for the therapist or coach, who needs substantive details on several generations in order to be effective, but also for the "identified patient" or the person being coached. The latter benefits from making contacts and building relationships with an increased number of members of the extended family, as well as from getting the information itself. The acts involved in pinpointing facts about one's family may be as "therapeutic" for the person being coached as the clinical sessions themselves.

A person can only begin to discuss events in past generations objectively when that person is not functioning under stress. However, the increased emotional distance from events in past generations may facilitate overall objectivity about one's family. The working relationship between therapist and client may also be improved by a focus on behavior in past generations of a family, especially when dependency issues between the therapist and client have dominated previous sessions.

Psychotherapy is usually most effective when a client is able to increase personal relationships in the extended family system. Clinical sessions are productive to the extent that they contribute to motivating an individual to take stands for self on day-to-day happenings in the family. Multigenerational detriangling is one way to achieve or maintain an effective "I" position in relation to the relentless forces of multigenerational transmission while also relating to members of the extended system.

In most cases, people attend clinical sessions with minimal information about their family structures and processes. Under optimal conditions, a systems psychotherapist "coaches" the other on how to collect information to describe the quality of emotional processes in a few generatios of that person's family. To ensure that therapy is as effective as possible, this information should be gathered for self and not for other family members or for the therapist. Through the therapist's indication of the other's responsibility for self in this task, the client may become more responsible for self in a variety of behavior and contexts.

Some of the dangers inherent for a therapist in examining

processes of interaction in different generations with other relatives include the strong tendency to become overly involved with a client's perceptions of these generations. A therapist may also be influenced by a client's perceptions of multigenerational patterns of behavior. Individuals easily allow themselves to become impeded in their explorations for information by overreacting to the content of past emotional issues without an examination of the quality of intergenerational exchanges around the issues and their impact on the entire family. Making personal contacts with more family members is usually an effective means, for both client and therapist, of safeguarding against difficulties of this kind.

One's Own Family

Some of the most effective kinds of contacts that one can have in one's family of origin are with family "leaders" in the oldest generations. Members of the grandparent generation frequently have more information about the family than do other relatives. Intergenerational contacts also provide the broadest possible range of ages for personal relationships in one's family.

A significant outcome for a person from a young generation who relates to members of older generations is that parents or others in intermediate generations are affected emotionally by the contacts made. Some of the most effective detriangling in one's family may be accomplished on such a multigenerational level.

Documents may have to be ·used to detail research on multigenerational transmission in one's family. For example, genealogical records can complement and check the memories of elders. However, the systematic research of genealogical records is time-consuming and demands personal commitment, and this project may necessitate taking an unpopular "I" position in relation to other family members. In spite of these difficulties, the dividends from one's efforts to research several generations are usually qualitatively superior to research focused solely on living generations.

Differentiation through studying multigenerational transmission in one's family may include making known some of the findings of one's research. An indiscriminate dissemination of information is not as effective or constructive for differentiating self as making careful choices to communicate particular details to specific family members. A tentative guide in this selection process is to give information to family members who will respond emotionally to the disclosures. In this way, the information can precipitate different patterns of interaction and activate a rigid system.

Additional care and thought are necessarily involved when one decides to divulge astonishing or shocking information. This content is emotion-laden, and family members may easily overreact to its communication. Information about events in earlier generations are sometimes more difficult for a family to deal with than are other kinds of information because of the length of time that the facts have been not known. However, differentiation can occur most effectively in one's family when there is some degree of anxiety in the system.

Sibling Position

Bowen has referred to general ideas about sibling position in families throughout most of the period he has been developing his family theory. During the 1960s, he became more familiar with Toman's research on sibling position (Toman 1972), and recognized that Toman's findings were largely consistent with his own. Toman's particularly significant contribution, in light of Bowen's own interests and work, is in his detailed observations and descriptions of behavior considered typical of different sibling positions. Bowen made similar observations and arrived at similar conclusions in a less structured way than Toman did and from a systems perspective as opposed to the psychoanalytic frame of reference Toman used.

As well as describing behavior in particular sibling positions, the Bowen concept of sibling position relates to ways in which levels of functioning and differentiation are influenced by certain sibling positions and distributions. Bowen accounts for how the family emotional system modifies sibling behavior expectations based on chronology or sex. One's functioning sibling position in one's family of origin is considered a major determining influence on one's differentiation of self and on one's vulnerability to family projection and multigenerational transmission. Functioning sibling position strongly influences the probability of becoming emotionally trapped in a family.

One of the most frequent uses made of the concept of sibling position is as a notation category in family histories. Information about sibling positions is collected routinely in family systems clinical work. In this respect, some of the applications of this concept are more visible and are easier to make than are other concepts in the Bowen theory.

The idea that structural sibling position in a family is an important influence on behavior is modified by viewing a person's "functioning" sibling position as a more accurate guide to behavioral expectations and predictions than chronological sibling position. Bowen's conceptualization of sibling position embraces this distinction, whereas Toman did not account for such differences in his work on sibling position. The difference between functioning and chronological position is illustrated by an only sister of brothers who may function as a youngest in her family, even though she is chronologically the middle child of five. Another example is the parental perception and functioning of twins. People are not used to dealing with twins, and parents frequently view one twin as being much older than the other. Although the first born twin is usually treated as the older of the two, the age difference between them tends to be exaggerated.

Family projecton is the strongest influence on the discrepancies that can exist between chronological and functioning sibling positions. Regardless of chronological position, the child who is the "object" of a family projection is frequently treated as a youngest, and that child behaves accordingly. One impairing consequence of being the focus of a family projection is that a child is encouraged to be more dependent on the parents than are the other siblings in the family. Family projection may be viewed as a strong neutralizing influence on the effects of the chronological ordering or sex distribution in a family and this process is an integral part of the family emotional system.

Studies of sibling position behavior add another dimension to predicting family interaction. The collection of data on sibling positions can be an important step in identifying the essential characteristics of a family. Information about sibling positions in earlier generations makes prediction more accurate because the distribution of sibling positions reflects characteristics of the broader emotional network.

The most predictable sibling behavior occurs when there is no oversaturation of emotional intensity in the family system. Lower functioning levels than the predicted profiles are attributable to the intensity of the impact of emotional influences, such as family projection, multigenerational transmission, loss, or cut-off.

Data on the sibling position of parents and an assessment of whether the functioning of each parent is typical of those sibling positions are fairly reliable indicators how a family may adapt itself to life, to emotional forces in the extended family, and to a course of psychotherapy. This information is particularly useful for predicting behavior in families with an only child, where the sibling position of the parent of like sex may strongly influence that child's development and perceptions.

Quality of fusion also depends on sibling position. For example, the intensity of fusion is influenced by the sibling positions of participants in the relationship. Depending on which sibling positions are involved, the twosome behaves distinctively in conflict, in routine exchanges, and under stress.

Research

Chronological sibling position is easy to record accurately and control in an experimental setting. Whether research focuses on families or on behavior in the wider society, sibling position is an objective category of information generally not distorted by the emotional investment of family members.

The major sibling position categories outlined by Toman are the following: the oldest brother of brother(s), the youngest brother of brother(s), the oldest brother of sister(s), the youngest brother of sister(s), the oldest sister of sister(s), the youngest sister of sister(s), the oldest sister of brother(s), and the youngest sister of brother(s). In addition to the eight basic sibling positions are two intermediary positions: the only child and twins. Individual sibling positions can be further classified by noting the sibling position of parents. This more complex categorization suggests that the life-style and differentiation level of two oldest brothers of brothers contrast with each other if the father of one is the oldest brother of brothers and the father of the other is the youngest brother of sisters (Toman 1972).

The sibling position of children and parents can be used as a basis for mapping structural and process characteristics of a family. For example, diagrammatic presentation of several generations of sibling distributions highlights any clustering or thinning out of family members. From a scientific standpoint, this information provides leads for more detailed descriptions of emotional forces in a family. The accuracy of oral reports and the overall objectivity of the study can be checked by referring to written records.

Scientific research on sibling positions optimally includes the study of sibling behavior in a variety of social settings. Performance in groups other than families is influenced by differentiation. Both social performance and family activity can be used to assess variations in behavior in identical sibling positions. For example, one person's behavior may appear more effective in social groups than in that person's family. Although it can be postulated that oldests rather than other sibling positions tend to become leaders in society, only oldests who function effectively in both social groups and the family are well differentiated. An oldest who appears an effective leader in society but simultaneously participates in a significant family cut-off or does not function as an oldest in the family is less differentiated. In this instance, apparent social differentiation is neutralized or negated by low family differentiation. Documentation of this sort may contribute toward the substantiation of the hypothesis that sibling position influences the life-course of less differentiated persons more strongly than that of more differentiated individuals.

Research studies could compare the capacity of individuals in different sibling positions to initiate and accomplish change in self. Another research focus could be descriptions of the tendencies to deviate from the behavioral expectations for particular sibling positions. Sibling behavior that differs from expectations may reflect the impact of emotional forces and processes within a family, including the strivings for differentiation of self.

Another influence on sibling position behavior that could be documented by systematic research is the impact of the loss of a significant family member through death, divorce, or institutionalization. For example, an oldest brother of sisters whose father had died when he was young and whose mother had not remarried would behave differently from an oldest brother of sisters who had not lost his father. The oldest brother who lost his father would probably be pressured and programmed into taking his father's place in the family emotional system.

Research on sibling positions from a family systems perspective could begin to describe and define ranges of behavior characteristic of each major sibling position. For example, expectations for youngests could include behavior of more differentiated youngests as well as of less differentiated youngests. Such comparisons of different levels of differentiation in the same sibling position might indicate some of the most significant properties of becoming trapped in the family's emotional processes.

Therapeutic Considerations

Descriptions of sibling position differences for the purposes of psychotherapy optimally include an assessment of the "emotional vulnerability" of the different positions. The assumption of responsibility is another behavioral characteristic that differs according to sibling position and influences the course of psychotherapy. For example, oldests frequently assume more responsibility than their siblings, and youngests may assume correspondingly less responsibility than their siblings. Felt responsibility for others, or taking responsibility for the whole family, are major influences in a person's day-to-day behavior and long-range planning. However, it is easier to coach an overresponsible person to become responsible for self than it is an underresponsible person.

Another issue related to sibling position and psychotherapy is the kinds of responsibilities expected of an oldest in a family. The specific emotional forces that reinforce a youngest's being viewed as irresponsible are also significant. The togetherness pressures that define the degree of responsibility for sibling positions substantially influence how a family selects a patient or problem.

Although overresponsibility in certain sibling positions may be problematic, the characteristics of underresponsibility are generally considered more severe. Conventional public opinion and more traditional psychotherapy are relatively unconcerned about symptoms or problems of overresponsibility. Overly dependent behavior becomes a focus for family and therapeutic concerns more readily than overly independent behavior.

A child who is the object of a family projection is more likely to become an identified patient than a child who is in a particular chronological position in a family. In a family where the child who is object of a family projection is not the youngest, the youngest in that family will have correspondingly fewer characteristics of a youngest.

One's Own Family

Sibling position characteristics can suggest criteria for evaluating one's own functioning in relation to the expectations for behavior in one's sibling position. A contrast between expected and actual behavior may indicate a particular level of differentiation. For example, better functioning and more effective behavior in a particular sibling position than the expectations for that position suggest a high level of differentiation of self. An oldest who is not overly responsible in conducting daily affairs appears more differentiated than an oldest who acts in overresponsible ways. Also, a youngest who is responsible in conducting daily affairs, especially in relationships with other family members, is perhaps more differentiated than a youngest who is not responsible for self.

A useful starting point for assessing and comparing sibling behavior in one's family is to document characteristics of functioning in the various sibling positions. A disadvantage of defining sibling position in functional rather than chronological terms is that subjective and intuitive perception can displace factual components of the more crude chronological descriptions.

The intervals between births in a family influence sibling behavior. A lengthy spacing of more than five years can have a more significant influence on behavior than a particular rank order of birth or the sex distribution among siblings. Children born a considerable number of years before or after their siblings may resemble an only child in their behavior or they may essentially create another family within the family.

The sibling positions of a multigenerational "line" of same-sex ancestors appears to be a significant influence on behavior in the younger generations of a family. For some women, the sibling position influence of the mother, grandmother, and other maternal ancestors may be more significant than that of the father and paternal ancestors.

Data on the sibling positions of relatives in early generations of a family can add useful dimensions to the limited information of names, birth, marriage, and death dates. The "horizontal" information on sibling positions is essential for making an accurate estimate of the quality of a particular family emotional system. Productive descriptions of emotional forces in past generations largely depend on the extent of information available on sibling distributions in several of those generations.

Emotional Process in Society

Emotional process in society, along with emotional cut-off, is one of Bowen's most recently developed concepts, and it is less refined than other concepts of the Bowen family theory. Emotional process in society represents the broadest possible tensions between individuation and togetherness, tensions that Bowen had already described and conceptualized in the context of individual family units. This concept expands Bowen's theoretical system through its accounting for the impact of social influences on family processes and for the impact of family processes on wider society.

Some of the emotional processes in society move toward societal extinction over long periods of time. Constructive and effective adaptation is another possible outcome of the interdependency and interaction of emotional processes in society. When adaptation is successful, the related emotional processes are more flexible and more conducive to growth. These processes generate constructive social changes in the wider society. Although particular sections of society may manifest different qualities and rates of change at any given point in time, an overall trend toward adaptation or toward extinction is frequently suggested by a variety of evidence.

In families, one of the two strongest overall thrusts of emotional process is toward togetherness. In society also, one of the two major thrusts of emotional process is toward shared togetherness. Insofar as togetherness or fusion forces predominate in society, they impede the differentiation of individuals and groups. Growth and development are stunted in the conditions of fusion, as individuals and groups are unable to function effectively in such an intense and restrictive emotional climate. Differentiation continues to be extremely difficult to accomplish as long as it is counteracted by the strong togetherness forces in society.

Bowen suggests that in certain periods in history, there have been tendencies for society to move in the direction of either differentiation or togetherness, and these tendencies are likely to continue. When differentiation predominates, social improvements and constructive developments follow: When fusion predominates, a society is considered stagnant, manifesting destructive forms of change. In times of high anxiety fusion predominates and people are pressured to make short-term, tension-ridden decisions rather than more deliberate, long-range decisions. Responsible decision making is more apparent in societies where differentiation forces are more prevalent than togetherness forces. High crime rates, violence, arbitrary political leadership, and high rates of divorce can be considered indicators of the potency and dysfunctional consequences of togetherness forces in a societal regression.

The quality or intensity of emotional process in society is an important influence on the level of functioning of individual families. Although family systems are significant emotional units in themselves, they are generally sufficiently open that they can be strongly influenced by broader societal forces. When the emotional process in society is intense, individuals frequently try to avoid responsibility for self both in the context of their own families and in other social groups.

The concept of emotional process in society has broader ramifications than Bowen's other concepts in that it represents a variety of large-scale trends over extended periods of time. The complex network of emotional interaction examined and described is more than an accumulation of isolated family experiences. Emotional process in society is an abstraction that epitomizes how families interact with each other within particular social settings and within particular historical time periods.

Both families and societies manifest differentiation and fusion tensions. The level of anxiety in society largely determines whether the emotional process in society will move toward differentiation or toward togetherness. When anxiety is low, differentiation is more possible. When anxiety is high, togetherness is automatic. These broad emotional forces influence family and individual behavior, just as individual and family behavior influence emotional process in society. Thus, emotional process in society is more than a background for viewing specific patterns of family interaction.

When phenomena such as large numbers of emotional cut-offs and high anxiety levels in families are pervasive in society, they intensify emotional process in society and increase tendencies toward regression and extinction. If sufficient numbers of people are triangled into family emotional processes, conditions that are more conducive to societal regression or extinction will develop.

Research

The global perspective implied by the concept of emotional process in society may improve objectivity in observing family interaction and other patterns of social behavior. An examination of human behavior in this context adds dimensions of reality and accuracy to the more usual short-range observations of family and social behavior. From a conceptual base of emotional process in society, a focus on continuity through time is automatically incorporated with on-the-spot examinations of a variety of behavior. The concept of emotional process in society also provides a basis for comparing and documenting differences of large-scale change in present and past societies.

In addition to their usefulness in the observation of seemingly qualitatively distinct kinds of human behavior, the meaning elements of emotional process in society suggest that specific degrees of predictability and probability exist in complex social and emotional forces. One hypothesis is that where togetherness or fusion prevails as the dominant emotional force in society, patterns of behavior are less productive than if differentiating forces are dominant. A related hypothesis is that the more anxious a society is, the more individual members strive for togetherness. The more a society strives for togetherness, the greater is the probability that problem behavior will be manifested, leading to increased societal regression. A high level of societal anxiety precedes and accompanies problem behavior in a societal regression. If a society follows these tendencies for a long period of time, one outcome may be gradual extinction of that society.

Some tentative predictions can also be made for societal processes of differentiation or effective and constructive adaptation. To the extent that there is a low level of societal anxiety, there are more constructive patterns of behavior, more individual contributions, and more progressive trends of social change. Relationships are freer, and there is less frequent reactivity between individuals and groups. A conceptualization of the diverging tendencies of regression and progression within emotional process in society suggests that a continuum ranging between fusion and differentiation could be used as a tool to order the vast variety of social and individual behavior manifested.

Although the scientific usefulness of the concept of emotional process in society is perhaps more difficult to substantiate than that of other concepts of the Bowen family theory, emotional process in society may provide a more accurate and realistic context for understanding the consequences of differentiation and togetherness forces for families and society than Bowen's other concepts owing to its broader scope of application.

Perhaps it is in the context of emotional process in society that complex patterns of behavior, such as multigenerational transmission, may be defined and observed more accurately.

At present, the concept of societal regression is a working hypothesis that cannot be operationalized in specific research terms. In the present exploratory phase of formulation, it is useful to accumulate a wide range of descriptive data to clarify salient meaning elements of the concept and to design appropriate methodologies for more rigorous research. Data on societal trends in crime, violence, and political activities can be used as indicators of different levels of societal anxiety and different degrees of differentiation or fusion. Although testing for direct or inverse correlations between certain kinds of social behavior and specific patterns of interaction in families is an overly simplistic way of establishing the validity of the concept of emotional process in society, research that describes and defines linkages between social and family behavior may provide constructive leads for understanding some of the complexities in the interplay of these influences.

Comparative research on trends of human behavior in different societies is another means of describing the range of qualities of emotional process in society. Although the Bowen family theory was developed in the modernized society of contemporary United States, each concept suggests directions for research on other kinds of societies and for the study of animal behavior.

To the extent that emotional process in society describes social trends over long periods of time, historical source materials may be used to articulate the substance and interplay of constructive and destructive modes of adaptation. Anthropological data may indicate characteristics of emotional process in society that lead toward extinction. Such data sources would have limited usefulness as a means of substantiating this concept and related hypotheses, however, as the data were not originally collected for this purpose.

The difficulties involved in specifying viable research procedures for confirming the validity of the concept of emotional process in society should not minimize this concept's importance as an innovative context for viewing and understanding family and social interaction. The unique strength of the Bowen family theory largely reflects its focus on a little-researched order of phenomena. It will take a considerable period of time before formal research can begin to definitively substantiate or refute hypotheses generated by the concept of emotional process in society.

Therapeutic Considerations

The concept of emotional process in society suggests a shorthand description of the climate of anxiety in society, one of the most significant influences on family interaction. It also facilitates deeper understanding of human interaction and dependency. The pervasiveness of characteristics such as cut-offs between generations, divorce, influence of peer groups, loneliness, and denial of death appear to have a strong and significant impact on the lives of individuals and families. Well-differentiated and flexible family systems are more durable and more able to withstand these kinds of external impairing influences than are fused family systems. Fused relationship networks are brittle and, because of their rigidity and intensity, may collapse or explode under stress.

An effective course of psychotherapy gradually dilutes an individual's overinvestment in nuclear family relationships or in social groups by increasing that person's emotional investment in the family of origin or extended family. This rechanneling of feelings increases the flexibility of the individual's position in a family, and eventually increases the flexibility of the entire intimate relationship network.

Effective psychotherapy in large numbers of families may reduce anxiety and symptomatic behavior in the wider society, thereby increasing the possibility of more widespread differentiation. Where psychotherapy is not effective or not sufficiently pervasive to have such an impact, the societal level of anxiety may be raised by the perpetuation or increase of anxiety in families. Increased differentiation or continued fusion during a course of psychotherapy indicates whether a particular family contributes toward societal regression or toward effective adaptation.

One's Own Family

Although changing one's position in one's own family does not appear directly related to the concept of emotional process in society, the overall climate of anxiety in the broader social setting has some impact on the facility or effectiveness of one's level of differentiation and on how one's differentiation is viewed by other family members. Where togetherness forces in society are strong, differentiating moves are correspondingly difficult for the individuals making these efforts and for members of their families.

When the emotional process in society is intense, socially accepted goals and standards of behavior tend to be incompatible with responsible individual inner beliefs. When togetherness forces are strong, one tends to sacrifice self for others' needs and to act from pseudo-self. In such an emotional environment, individual thinking is so difficult that action integrated with self and personal convictions is almost impossible; decisions tend to be made in response to anxiety of the moment; and one is less able to formulate an effective plan for differentiating moves in one's family. As geographical moves under conditions of fusion may be followed by continued overinvolvement in substitute feeling systems, spatial distance cannot increase objectivity about one's family. In general, emotional dependency is transferred, rather than dealt with, when societal fusion is strong.

Emotional process in society may be less easy to apply to one's own family than are other Bowen concepts. However, the concept of emotional process in society can be used to some extent, and some implications of this broad influence for individual emotional functioning in one's family, can be explored.

Part II

Applications

Chapter 4

ONE'S OWN FAMILY OF ORIGIN

The efforts described here are selected from six different contacts with my families of origin over a period of eighteen months. During five of these visits, I went to my parental home in England. For one visit, my mother came to the United States. This was her first visit to the United States, even though I had lived in the United States for more than ten years before her visit. I describe my families of origin before my attempts to differentiate self, focusing on the location of significant triangles and multigenerational transmission in my family. A chronology of family contacts made and a review of precipitating events for each family visit from May 1971 to August 1972 precedes a description of the six visits. Changes in self and in my family during the eighteen-month period are assessed, and some tentative conclusions and theoretical proposition are formulated.

I had been exposed to the Bowen family theory for several years before I tried to apply some of the systems concepts to my own position in my family. The research I describe here attempts to replicate some of Bowen's work on differentiating a self in one's own family (1972). I was motivated, for personal reasons, to make organized efforts to free self in my family in this particular time period.

Before the six visits with my family of origin took place, I gave much thought to the particular kinds of family processes I had already observed in my family. Two major ideas from the Bowen theory guided my preparations:

1. An individual can differentiate self in a family more effectively at a time of slight unrest in the system.

2. After differentiating moves in one part of the family, there are automatic related changes in other parts if the person differentiating self simultaneously maintains emotional contact with other family members.

Some of the specific family systems concepts and strategies I used to increase the effectiveness of my efforts to differentiate self included the identification of significant triangles and multigenerational transmission in my family of origin; the construction of fairly specific plans before each visit; and an articulation of detriangling moves, including multigenerational detriangling, and the creative use of reversals. An important assumption made at this time was that the outcome and effectiveness of my efforts to differentiate self in my family of origin would very much depend on the accuracy and comprehensiveness of my plans before and during the visits with my family.

Family of Origin

Location. For several generations, both my father's and my mother's families have lived in the same small industrial town in the north of England. I left England after my marriage in 1959 and have lived in the United States since 1962. The practical considerations and dramatic implications of this geographical separation are significant. Visits to England are necessarily limited, as they involve great financial sacrifice and much investment of effort. On the more positive side, my presence is usually welcomed by my family because of the infrequency of my appearance, and I am also usually given immediate audience when I choose to make contacts.

Significant triangles. I am the only child of a father who was the only son and middle child of three children and of a mother who is the younger sister of a brother. My father ran a family business, which was started by his paternal grandfather and continued by his father. My father became deaf when he was a teenager.

Since the death of my mother's mother in 1963 and the death of my mother's brother in 1968, my maternal grandfather became an increasingly significant person in my family of origin. Although my maternal grandfather did not live with my parents, my mother or my father visited his home daily with food, laundry, and other personal items. My mother idealized her relationship with her father, which she frequently referred to with the names "Romeo" and "Juliet."

Several important triangles can be identified in my family of origin, such as those with the siblings of my parents or with my only cousin. I decided to focus on two triangles in which I am usually the outsider of an intense twosome. These two triangles were with my father and mother and with my mother and grandfather.

Multigenerational transmission. An examination of five generations of my father's and mother's extended families indicates that there is an increasing tendency for both systems to "die out." Both families show less frequent marriage, less reproduction, and more deaths, including accidental deaths and suicides. I have only one cousin, who is in my father's family, and

I was the only grandchild of my maternal grandparents. From 1963 to 1969, there were eight deaths in these extended systems and only three births. In each family, there were at least three cut-offs between "close" relatives. These characteristics of my family of origin suggest rigidity and relative closure in the emotional system.

Events

Visit 1. May–June 1971 (nine days, with all three daughters): "Getting reacquainted."

I had not been to my home in England for almost four years prior to this visit, and my visit in 1967 had also been made after an interval of four years. Although I had been in touch with my family by letter throughout this time, relationships had been considerably strained and distant. This tension was partly the result of anxiety waves following the three deaths of my mother's mother, my father's sister, and my mother's brother and strains in my own nuclear family in the United States. As well as wanting to reestablish general contacts with my family of origin, I planned to follow up a visit my cousin had made to me in the United States in 1970. She had come to my home on her way to a visit with one of her friends after I had initiated contact with her by letter. This was a new exchange in our relationship; my cousin is nine years older and our respective families had played a part in our being separate from each other for most of our lives.

Visit 2. January 1972 (five days, alone): "A breakthrough visit."

I reached what I thought was an impasse in the work I was doing by letter in my family of origin. I also wanted this visit to England to be an introduction to a first visit to my "cut-off" maternal grandfather's brother and his son, who live in Massachusetts. This great uncle left England in 1911, but because of an estrangement between him and my grandfather over the past sixty years, I had only recently learned of his presence in the United States.

Visit 3. April 1972 (five days, with my oldest and youngest daughters): "Maintaining an 'I' position."

After a second visit to my great uncle in Massachusetts, I wanted to consolidate what I thought were differentiating moves of self in my earlier January visit to England. I wanted to put in action my decision not to "two-step" in my family of origin.

Visit 4. July 1972 (two weeks, with all three daughters): "My father's funeral."

My father died suddenly of a first heart attack at the beginning of July at his place of business. My mother opposed my bringing my daughters with me for the funeral.

Visit 5. July 1972 (two weeks, alone): "My grandfather's funeral."

My grandfather fell and had to be hospitalized on the day that my father's ashes were interred. He died from pneumonia sixteen days after my father's death.

Visit 6. August 1972 (four weeks, mother with me, my husband, and my three daughters): "My mother in the United States."

Neither of my parents had visited me in the United States during the ten-and-a-half years I had lived here. I wanted to improve my personal relationship with my mother and to introduce her to her uncle and her cousin in Massachusetts, who she had never met.

Observations

Visits 1, 2, and 3. Visits 1 and 3 were necessary initiating and consolidating stages of my more specific efforts to differentiate a self in visit 2. Much of the uniqueness of these visits was the result

of changes made in my relationship with my only cousin. Before
her trip to the United States in 1970, I had not seen my cousin for
twelve years. In January 1972, I met her two children, aged
twenty-two and twenty years old, for the first time.

I created a "tempest in a teapot" by my letters before visit 2.
Messages included my anxiety about my nuclear family, a report
on the health of different family members with "reversal"
suggestions about how they might be cared for, and my
observations on a "suspiciously" intimate relationship between
the husband of my father's sister and my mother.

A working knowledge of triangles in my family emotional
system gave way to fairly effective detriangling efforts. I made
visit 2 to my parents' home alone. This was my first visit alone
with my parents in fourteen years. For the first two hours of this
visit, my parents voiced their "united" disapproval of my recent
letters and ideas. Neither had wanted me to visit at this particular
time, and so my very presence was a theme for argument. Both
parents emphasized their distress at the "changes" in me. My
mother accused me of taking drugs, and my father told me I was
"crazy" like his younger sister. Some modifications of the
emotional system of the two basic triangles in my family of origin
seemed to follow the conflict that developed. After some efforts
to change my part in the usual patterns of communication in
these two triangles, the system became calmer and more
"respectful" to my changed "I" position. My father and I had
more personal exchanges than we had had in many years,
perhaps in a lifetime, and I went to his parents' grave with him at
the end of this visit.

As well as the differentiating moves described, I made new
contacts in the extended families of my parents during these
visits. Each parent reacted emotionally to any new contact I made
in the extended system, and triangles between myself, mother or
father, and the person contacted were activated. I was able to

detriangle myself from my relationship with the parent involved in each new triangle by diffusing some of the feelings that had previously been invested in me. I freed self, to some extent, by creating a situation where my parent would react to a significant other in the emotional system rather than directly to me.

Visits 4, 5, and 6. Against my mother's wishes, I took all three of my daughters to my father's funeral. Owing to some of my detriangling efforts, I was able to participate in many different activities, often with my children, related to the death of my father without denying the reality of his death or evading this involvement. Although my father's only living sister refused to come to my father's funeral, the increased contacts between family members seemed to open up my father's family system, at least during this period.

Visit 5 occurred when I learned that my grandfather had died while I was leaving England after visit 4. My children and I were the last people to see my grandfather alive, as he died at the same time that our plane left England. There were two days between visits 4 and 5.

My mother's family was also somewhat opened by the death of my grandfather. I met many members of my mother's family whom I had not known prior to my grandfather's death. Within sixteen days, my mother lost both her husband and her father, who had become increasingly significant to her since I left my parental home in 1955. This untimely and unwanted "gap" in her life moved my mother to accompany me to the United States for the first time ever and to my own home for the first time in twelve years.

Not one of visits 4, 5, or 6 was conflict-free, especially not in relation to my mother. Conflictual exchanges and disagreement provided opportunities for me to establish a more solid "I" position with my mother and my family of origin. During visit 6, my mother met her uncle and her cousin in Massachusetts for the first time.

Throughout visit 6, there were many opportunities to communicate with my mother in mature and personal ways, and sometimes I was able to do so. My mother invested much feeling in her three granddaughters, especially in my youngest daughter. For the first time I allowed myself to feel the depth of my emotional attachment to my mother, and for the first time the relationship between my mother and my daughters came alive. Although these changes perhaps indicate some improvement in my functioning position in my family of origin, my greatest awareness was how much more sustained effort is needed to continue differentiating self effectively in my family of origin.

Changes

A precondition of any changes in self was the maintenance of continuous emotional contact with other family members when attempting to differentiate self. Apart from the structural changes in my family of origin as a result of the deaths of my father and grandfather, the quality of emotional relationships in this system appears to have changed considerably. By increasing the number of personal contacts in the system, relationships between myself and other family members became more fluid and diffuse. My anxiety was reduced, and the anxiety in both my family of origin and my nuclear family was also lowered.

Throughout the year prior to my father's death, members of the extended system and community commented to me and to my mother on how much improved my father's health had seemed and on how he had appeared to be less anxious and worried. During the same period of time, there was a marked improvement in the health of some family members. The increased flexibility of relationships in my family of origin is also manifested by the tendency for more humor and less seriousness in the system. During visit 3, my mother commented that she could not remember a time she and my father had enjoyed themselves as much as they had during that visit with myself and two of my daughters.

There were also shifts in more extended parts of the system. For example, my cousin's husband and both her children have been able to make career decisions that had previously proved too difficult for them to make.

Conclusions and Propositions

These six visits provide some data to support the hypothesis that a person can differentiate self more effectively in a time of slight unrest in a family than in a climate of congenial togetherness. Another hypothesis supported by data from these efforts is that after a person makes differentiating moves in one part of the system, there will be automatic and related changes in self and in other parts of the system if the person differentiating self is able to maintain emotional contact with other members of the system.

A series of unrelated propositions include the following:

1. The effectiveness of differentiating moves depends on an adequate working knowledge of family systems concepts and the degree to which moves can be planned and predicted before actual encounters with family members.

2. Detriangling self is the achievement of an "I" position that is relatively outside the automatic emotional system. Detriangling is a means to attain a comparatively calm level of self, to reach a level of relative objectivity, and to become a more responsible "I."

3. Gathering information about extended family creates a personal relationship with the person who gives the information and at the same time checks perceptions about different family

members, thereby increasing the degree of objectivity of these observations.

4. Family members who are cut off from the family frequently supply markedly more and different information from those who are "in" the system.

5. Similarities in the thought and behavior patterns of family members both "in" and "out" of the system suggest that geographical and physical separation from the family does not necessarily imply emotional separation from the system.

6. With repeated efforts to differentiate self, one gains objectivity in viewing self and other family members. Levels of anxiety in the family, especially in response to differentiating moves, become increasingly predictable.

7. After the conflict and tension that necessarily accompany differentiation, the respect and apprecition of other family members for the differentiating efforts become more apparent.

These findings appear to endorse others' findings on factors that contribute toward or that limit the differentiation of self in one's family of origin. Perhaps additional common denominators will be identified among detailed case history data from many more families.

Chapter 5

HEALING PROCESSES

It is difficult to assess when and where healing processes begin and end. The following examination of healing is based on the period that is conventionally known as recuperation, or the time after a physical disability has occurred in someone's life. Specific patterns of family interaction are hypothesized to encourage or inhibit recovery and to delay or prevent disability.

A crisis such as sickness can be a turning point in the emotional processes that produce the crisis. It is more likely that individual behavior can be modified and successfully changed in a crisis than in ordinary circumstances. Some families cannot begin to modify their own impairing behavior patterns unless a sickness occurs.

Healing

The concept of healing has been interpreted on many different levels. Historically, the term included mystical or spiritual elements. An individual is generally not considered healed unless both body and mind are "well." Becoming whole or sound or being cured are other ways of describing healing.

One way to organize traditional and conventional meanings of healing is to compare the extent to which healing is thought to occur within a person with the extent to which healing is assumed to occur between the person who is sick and the expert treating the sickness. The intent of this examination of the part family interaction plays in healing processes is to broaden this range of understanding of conventional concepts of healing.

The observations described focus on a variety of emotionally charged intimate exchanges with and about the symptomatic person. Some generalizations about outcomes of particular patterns of interaction with a symptomatic individual are made, using the family as the unit of investigation. One key assumption is that the family is ultimately the most intimate and most emotionally charged group human beings participate in and respond to, whether or not the individuals concerned recognize this participation and responsiveness and whether or not the participation is visible or invisible (Boszormenyi-Nagy and Spark 1973).

A wide range of patterns of behavior in families accompanies the symptomatic behavior of one family member. Different responses to the symptoms may be represented by points along a continuum that has unsuccessful adaptation or extinction at one end and successful adaptation or survival at the other end. Depending on the extent to which family interaction can be identified as being either relatively constructive or relatively destructive, particular patterns can be documented as precipitating or inhibiting the healing of the incapacitated person and the entire family.

Maladaptive Behavior
Certain conditions inhibit effective healing. Maladaptive

behavior patterns that retard healing emerge from a family emotional system that is tightly bonded and rigidly inter-dependent. In this setting, behavior patterns are continually repeated, and each reactive response in the system has a high level of emotional intensity. Secrets between family members and cut-offs in the relationship system raise the level of anxiety of the incapacitated person and of the other family members. Such families that interact in this way tend to manifest ineffective recoveries or prolonged chronic illness, with the possible impairment of other family members.

Case History 1. Ms. S had not been healthy for two years. She suffered from a wide range of physical ailments. Mr. S was told by Ms. S's doctor that his wife had terminal cancer. Ms. S's life expectancy was estimated at about six months. Mr. S decided to "protect" his wife from this information, as she was elderly and tended to get depressed easily. Mr. S believed that open commu-nication and discussion would cause Ms. S unnecessary harm. Mr. S disclosed the doctor's diagnosis to his two adult daughters, who reacted by intensifying their characteristic activities of care-taking and distancing, respectively. Mr. S and his daughters dis-couraged visits from other family members and informed only a few family members about Ms. S's condition. Ms. S became increasingly depressed and listless and died within four months of the date of her doctor's diagnosis.

Adaptive Behavior

Adaptive behavior enhances effective healing. A family with adaptive behavior patterns is fairly loosely bonded and is flexibly interdependent. Behavior patterns in this kind of family are varied and are not repeated frequently. Interaction is more reflective than "reflexive" and is generally not very emotionally charged. The relationship system is fairly open, and many family members are in touch with each other in meaningful ways. The level of anxiety of a person who becomes sick in this kind of family and of other family members is consistently low. Families with adaptive behavior patterns assume postures that encourage gradual or rapid recovery. There is usually little or no impairment of the health of family members beyond temporary incapacitation.

In adaptive families, there may be some, little, or no awareness of the constructive rehabilitating qualities of these kinds of family interaction. Psychotherapy or coaching may heighten at least one family member's awareness of the impact of particular patterns of interaction on healing. However, a strong motivation to make changes in one's behavior is essential if recovery is to be permanent. A second family crisis, such as the death of a family member, may move anxiety away from the sick person, so that healing can be accelerated.

Case History 2. Mr. G had a first heart attack, and was advised to have bed-rest for eight weeks. Ms. G was anxious about the possibility of losing her husband but was able to control her feelings fairly well. Ms. G was not predictably reactive in her dealings with her husband or with other family members, including her three teenage children. She busied herself with some of the responsibilities for the care of her husband, as well as with her day-to-day activities. She was able to maintain a full-time job and still had frequent contacts with her own elderly parents. Ms. G engaged her children and some members of her husband's family in the daily care of her husband, and she encouraged Mr. G to care for his own needs early in his recovery. As a result of Ms. G's moves, Mr. G was able to return to work shortly after the bed-rest period. He made successful changes in his life-style, and his symptoms did not recur after this first attack.

Family as "Fundamental Health Unit"

These case history materials illustrate different qualities of family response to symptomatic behavior. Although case history data is insufficient to substantiate or refute specific hypotheses about healing, the question of whether the family or the individual is the "fundamental health unit" in society can be explored. If healing processes can meaningfully and accurately be perceived as depending on specific patterns of family interaction, some implications for policy and research can be considered:

1. Intervention measures that facilitate the opening and differentiation of family interaction may be more effective in producing healing or recovery from symptoms than measures based on individual diagnosis, pathology, and institutional care.

2. Health-care costs may be substantially reduced through the creation of home-care services as an alternative to institutionalization. In the United States, the per capita spending over the 1962–1976 period for human services dominated by health programs rose to an estimated $820 from $166, compared with $272–$436 for defense and $13–$46 for natural resources, environment, and energy (Congressional Research Service 1975). The search for alternatives to established health-care systems is indeed pressing (Hall and Sussman 1975).

3. It may be possible to prevent some disability or to delay the onset of its symptoms through educational therapeutic programs that heighten family members' awareness of the outcome of particular patterns of family interaction.

4. The documentation of different kinds of healing processes in families could contribute toward the development of a general theory of human behavior, as well as toward the development of a theory of family interaction. Some behavioral outcomes could be predicted from a knowledge of given relationship conditions and an application of systems thinking, rather than arbitrarily simplistic cause-effect thinking.

Chapter 6

AGING AND INSTITUTIONALIZATION

The increasing proportions of the elderly in our population have heightened professional and personal interest in the topic of aging. Unfortunately, our strong public and private concerns for children and youth have generally been articulated in isolation from concerns for the elderly. Little consistent effort has been made to relate the functioning of younger age-groups to that of older-age groups in society. Young and old are perceived as members of intrinsically different and separate subgroups.

Society cannot meaningfully relate to older people if the elderly are persistently viewed as an isolated group with needs independent of those of young people. Contemporary society may have to deal with many complex relationship problems owing to the widespread refusal or inability to perceive the underlying bonds between all human beings at deep-seated emotional levels. To the extent that public policies precipitate and reinforce cut-offs between generations and cut-offs in the degree of relatedness within each family, current relationship problems are likely to increase.

A family systems approach to aging implies that there is a correlation between a lack of meaningful emotional contact between older and younger family members and the symptomatic behavior of those elderly relatives. An examination of cut-offs in a family, particularly those between members of different generations, can provide a fairly accurate means of predicting the timing and type of symptoms that might appear in the behavior of older family members. An increase in the number and intensity of cut-offs in meaningful emotional relationships in a family tend to precipitate the onset and development of aging processes and problems.

Case history data are used to illustrate the emotional systems phenomena that appear to influence the onset and development of symptomatic behavior in the elderly. The longitudinal methods of gathering and organizing the data are based on concepts and hypotheses generated by the Bowen family theory.

Problems

There are many stereotypical beliefs about aging processes and problems in contemporary society. Four of the most prevalent perceptions about aging processes and problems held in professional and lay circles are discussed here. Although the four areas are interrelated, they are separated arbitrarily to describe some of the specific concerns more clearly.

Physical Debilitation. Aging is frequently believed to be a weakening of bodily capacities. This debilitation is expected to occur more or less at the same time as the onset of "middle age," following a course that is almost as predictable and as inevitable as death itself. The failing physical powers of older individuals are thought to be accompanied by symptoms that precipitate continuing increases in weakness and feebleness.

Senility. The onset and development of physical aging

processes are frequently expected to be accompanied by mental infirmity. In senility, an older person is described as regressing to a childlike state of dependency. When senility occurs, younger family members generally respond with caretaking and helping patterns of behavior.

Loneliness. Loneliness is perceived as being an integral part of aging processes and problems. Retirement from employment, for example, essentially decreases the extent and meaningfulness of social contacts of the elderly at a time when dependency needs usually increase (Rosow 1967).

Poverty. Old age is often characterized by increased economic dependence. Not only are the elderly viewed as incapable of earning their own way in a highly competitive and materialistic society, but they also are considered a financial liability to the community at large. As many elderly persons are not able to pay for the medical care that stereotypical views and beliefs of aging processes and problems have defined as necessary, providing these services becomes a community liability. Families frequently do not assume responsibility for the care of their older members. In some cases institutional care, with its prohibitive costs, may be the only viable option for meeting the needs of the elderly. Society must deal with the widespread poverty of the elderly and the increased financial costs involved in the care of the elderly. The total cost of the services provided for the elderly inevitably places heavy demands on other members of society.

Theoretical Orientation

A focus on aging and family processes from a systems perspective necessitates making several theoretical assumptions. One premise is that there is a direct correlation between the quality of members' participation in the family emotional system and individual behavior patterns. Aging is conceptualized as a product of the older person's position and behavior in the family emotional system. When emotional bonds between an older person and younger family members are tight, rigid, intense, and restrictive—even though these relationships may be manifested as distant—the older person is more likely to become physically debilitated, senile, lonely, or impoverished. When an older person is an active participant in a flexible and open family emotional system, the probability of symptomatic behavior is considerably reduced.

A basic postulate of the Bowen family theory is that symptomatic behavior in older persons and others is a product of the quality of combined emotional relationships in a family. An anxious family with many cut-offs in its relationship system precipitates overdependence, isolation, and senility. When an elderly individual is in a dependent and vulnerable position in a family that is not well differentiated, a projection process focused on the older person is possible.

Patterns of behavior in the multigenerational transmission of a family also influence whether older family members become trapped or triangled in the intensity of the emotional field. In families where older members usually become senile, this behavior may be repeated in subsequent generations. An individual who was very dependent in early life and had symptomatic behavior in times of stress is more likely to repeat these patterns in later years. Intermittent dependency through a life-course can be a frequent pattern of family behavior.

Another basic theoretical assumption is that people are primarily biological beings. Emotional dependence on an intimate group is believed to be a relatively unchanging universal condition that must be dealt with more or less effectively throughout life. Emotional dependency is considered the foundation of all relationship systems. Social norms and mores are conceptualized as specific characterisitics of this emotional field, with the biological, emotional, and social aspects of aging being inextricably interrelated and interdependent.

Hypotheses

Four hypotheses serve as a guide for systematizing observations on aging and family processes:

1. Physical debilitation, symptomatic, and senile behavior of the elderly vary directly with an individual's emotional dependency on the family. Emotional dependency is generally manifested as symbiotic caretaking, helping, or "feeling-sorry-for" behavior patterns.

2. Where symptomatic behavior patterns, including marked economic dependency, occur at an early age, the same or similar patterns are more likely to be repeated at older ages, especially in times of stress.

3. When an individual's parent or grandparent, particularly a parent or grandparent of the same sex, manifests symptoms in old age, that individual is more likely to repeat these behavior patterns in subsequent years.

4. The degree of alienation, isolation, or loneliness of the elderly varies directly with the degree of emotional cut-off with other family members.

Case Histories

Six case histories are used to document these hypotheses. The case histories were selected from several hundred families in clinical and nonclinical settings to illustrate different characteristics of family emotional processes. Three functioning and three dysfunctioning older individuals are presented in the context of their families. The examples are paired; each pair consists of one functioning older person and one dysfunctioning older person. Each pair of examples illustrates functioning and dysfunctioning in different life situations and with different clinical approaches: (1) families where an older person was coached to make changes in functioning in relation to the family; (2) families where a younger person in the family was coached to make changes in functioning, especially in relation to a member of an older generation; and (3) families where there was no clinical intervention. The third pair of families may be viewed as a control group in relation to the other pairs of families.

Families with Older Person Coached

Functioning older person. The older person in this family was a divorced man who was contemplating remarriage. He was the father of two daughters and the grandfather of one grandson. He initiated therapy because he had been concerned that he would be unable to relate meaningfully to the woman who was to be his next spouse. His first wife's divorce action had taken him by surprise, and his present wife-to-be constantly complained about his lack of responsiveness to her needs. The man was a talented musician who worked in the same conservatory as his older daughter. One week before the father began therapy, his older daughter left her husband and child and moved into the home of another man.

After three months of therapy, the father was able to function more effectively in his work. He was also able to act more responsibly in relation to the emotional demands made on him by his daughters and his fiancée than he had been before. Having previously been paralyzed by these relationship concerns, he was now able to formulate plans for himself and put them into action. He had not functioned as effectively since his divorce, which had occurred about ten years before.

Dysfunctioning older person. A grandmother initiated therapy because she had been unable to communicate satisfactorily with the oldest of her three daughters. This oldest daughter had a daughter of her own. The grandmother's wish to see her granddaughter frequently prompted the grandmother to be particularly anxious to resolve the conflict between herself and her daughter. When arguments occurred between mother and daughter, the older woman was not allowed to see her granddaughter.

The grandmother was not able to lower the level of her anxiety in her relationship with her older daughter. The grandmother's father died during the course of therapy, and she became preoccupied with how she could manage to please her mother and cater to her mother's whims in an extended period of mourning. The grandmother's relationship with her oldest daughter continued to be volatile, and eventually the daughter, with her husband and daughter, left town to take up residence in a distant city. In the next few weeks, the grandmother's youngest daughter ran away from home, and the grandmother took increasing numbers of tranquilizers. The grandmother suffered from frequent depressions and a variety of physical ailments. She was unable to focus on self, and she complained about others in her family and blamed them for her difficulties. She terminated therapy at a low point of functioning.

Families with Younger Person Coached

Functioning older person. A woman who had two elderly parents initiated therapy because she had been extremely anxious about the well-being of her incapacitated mother who lived with her and needed round-the-clock physical care. The woman found that the responsibility she had assumed for her mother demanded more tolerance than she was easily able to muster, and she frequently experienced crying spells and depressions.

When the daughter was able to relate to her mother with less of a helping, caretaking posture, the mother began to function more adequately. The mother began to take an active interest in caring for her own needs, and her daughter was able to leave her for longer periods of time than had been possible in the previous few years. Until that point, the daughter had been distancing from her mother through her helping and caretaking activities. When she was able to relate to her mother on a more personal level, her mother was able to function more effectively.

Dysfunctioning older person. A man began therapy when his wife refused to care for his ailing elderly father. Although the father had lived next door to his son for most of his son's marriage, for several years there had been an intense cut-off in the relationship between the son and the father. When clinical sessions began, there had been no meaningful exchanges between the two households for about a year. The son arranged for his niece to live with his father and look after him. As she was divorced and did not have any children, this relationship between the niece and her great uncle worked out fairly well. The son no longer felt trapped by his responsibility to care for his father.

Throughout six months of therapy, the son made no efforts to visit his father or to communicate with him personally. He continued to believe that his father was his wife's responsibility, and he constantly pressured her to look after his father.

The father became increasingly dysfunctional, and eventually his son put him in a nursing home. Although the son, together with other family members, contributed toward his father's expenses, he did not visit his father at the nursing home. He rationalized that his father was senile and would not recognize him even if he did visit him. To alleviate his own anxiety about his estrangement with his father, he also began to encourage other family members to stay away from the nursing home. As the father's isolation from his family became greater, his symptoms of senility increased.

Families Outside the Clinical Setting

Functioning older person. After the death of her husband, an older woman, who was a mother and grandmother, related more openly and more frequently to members of her family. Her relatives responded to the loss of her spouse by increasing their contact with her.

This elderly woman was able to continue making meaningful contacts with her family, including contacts with some members of her family of origin. During the next two-year period, when these relationships were reactivated, she functioned more effectively than she had for many years prior to her husband's death. She was able to make financial decisions independently, and she appeared to decrease some of her direct emotional dependence on her children. She had sufficient economic means of her own to be able to conduct her affairs separately from those of her children.

Dysfunctioning older person. After the unexpected death of his wife, an older man became dysfunctional. For about ten years, he and his wife had become increasingly estranged from their respective families of origin. Their two daughters had moved away and had maintained no more than a superficial level of contact with their parents.

Upon the death of his wife, the man went into a prolonged state of shock. Within four weeks of her death, he had a mild stroke and was hospitalized; and he subsequently returned to his own home. However, as he was unable to care for himself, he sold his home and moved into a nursing home.

Six months after his move to the nursing home, he met a woman who had been a nurse before her retirement and he proposed to her. The two were married and moved into the wife's apartment, where she began to overcare for her husband. An intense, rigid, and emotionally dependent relationship developed between the spouses. The husband became increasingly cut off from his children and from his own family of origin. Neither his children nor his family approved of his remarriage. The husband's symptoms increased, and his financial affairs became too difficult for him to manage. To an increasing extent, his wife supported him both emotionally and financially.

Findings

An older person who was an active participant in a comparatively open emotional system appeared to function more effectively than an older person who was cut off from or trapped into a closed emotional system. When an older person made effective differentiating moves in a family, aging symptoms declined and emotional dependency on the closest family members was reduced. An effectively differentiated older person was generally more adept at coping with life crises, such as death, illness, retirement, or the dysfunction of others.

In families where the elderly were dysfunctional, the number and intensity of emotional cut-offs persisted or increased. The quality of emotional relationships in these families was rigid, superficial, and distant. Crises added stress to an already-tight emotional system, and the symptomatic behavior of the older persons increased.

Conclusion

The onset and development of symptomatic behavior in the elderly, as in the case of other family members, are precipitated and enhanced by crises and stresses in the family, such as the death of a significant family member. Stresses increase the probability that an older person will be triangled into the emotional system of the family, and overadaptiveness after a crisis is a typical dysfunctional response. As symptomatic behavior must be reinforced for it to persist, clinical intervention may reduce the likelihood that an older person will lose self in relation to other family members. The case history data described suggests some tentative generalizations:

1. The degree of closure of a family emotional system precipitates and reinforces physical incapacitation or senile behavior among elderly family members. In some instances, economic dependence of the elderly appears to be a direct consequence of emotional dependence.

2. In times of stress, behavior patterns tend to be repeated automatically. These repetitions may duplicate previously established patterns of symptomatic behavior, or they may repeat symptoms of close family members.

3. Cut-offs are a powerful precipitation of dysfunctional behavior among the elderly. The probability of symptomatic behavior for an older family member increases depending on the degree to which meaningful emotional relationships with other family members are lacking.

4. When intergenerational repetitions of symptomatic behavior occur, the "vertical" relationship of same sex child, parent, and grandparent appears particularly influential. Latent or overt helping and caretaking patterns of behavior between the different generations lead to increased repetitions of symptomatic behavior, particularly in times of stress.

Further Research and Social Policy

Although older people have been referred to as "ex-family members" (Beard 1949), they are equal participants in a family emotional system. Children and neighbors are impervious role-sets, and substitute social activity cannot effectively reduce an older person's family dependence (Rosow 1967). Case history data suggest that aging is more intimately related to family emotional processes than to broader social forces, such as norms or public opinion.

Although the empirical and theoretical validity of the hypotheses discussed cannot be confirmed, policymakers could act from a greater awareness of the extent and degree of interdependence of all members of society than currently exists. Policies and programs for the well-being of children will remain inadequate as long as they do not account for the inextricably linked needs of young and old. In addition to the financial costs involved, institutional care of the elderly tends to intensify the social and relationship problems we have with young and old alike by increasing the number and intensity of emotional cut-offs between young and old.

Enhanced awareness of the extent of emotional relatedness of the elderly to their families may facilitate clearer definitions of the responsibility of each family member and what that responsi-bility means. Questions concerning what aging processes and problems are and how they are related to family and societal emotional processes lead to the critical issue of what it means to die responsibly. How can I conduct my life toward a responsible death? In what ways do I contribute toward the type of death another will experience?

Alternatives to Institutional Care for the Elderly

Care of the elderly is an increasingly problematic topic in a society that must support rising numbers of older people (Rose 1968, Neugarten 1973). In most sociological studies on aging, observations and data about older people are selectively organized, so that the elderly are conceptualized as a distinct subcultural group. The elderly are generally viewed as being in isolation from other individuals and groups in society (Rosenberg 1967, Rosow 1967, Riley 1968) with their own separate needs. However, case history data indicate that the needs of members of all age-groups are inextricably related and that multigenerational family influences may have a significant impact on the functioning of the elderly. Even considering the special care that may be needed for older members of society, family relationships are tentatively conceptualized as a more meaningful and more effective environment than institutionalization. A family with an open and flexible relationship system could delay the incapacitation of older people or even prevent some kinds of physical debilitation.

An older person may be considered primarily a family member rather than a member of a special group in society. A research and theoretical orientation based on that view has not been utilized frequently in the literature (Dinkel 1944, Beard 1949, Bultena 1969). A hypothesis directly related to this view of the elderly and to the public concern for their care is that an older person who is able to maintain meaningful contacts with family members is less likely to need institutionalization than an older person who is emotionally cut off and estranged from other family members (Hall 1976). A related hypothesis is that if economic and service incentives are provided to family members, there will be a reduction in the incidence and need for the institutionalization of the elderly. In this situation, families need not sacrifice their own ambitions or compromise their current efforts to maintain themselves because of the presence of an elderly member in their household (Hall and Sussman 1975).

Research

Many research studies already have dealt with general social or economic aspects of the aged as a distinct social group (Simpson 1966, Solomon 1967). Where research efforts have been directed to observing the elderly within the context of their families (Sussman 1955, Townsend 1957, Streib 1958, Shanas 1961), however, there has been little attempt to link findings to proposals for alternative care systems. Although there have been some descriptive studies of family help systems (Schorr 1960, Streib 1965, Shanas 1961), much of the literature that compares family environments to institutions or to other kinds of actual or proposed health and general care systems is based on unsystematic research or personal and professional opinions (Kaplan 1972, Kistin and Morris 1972, Hochschild 1973, Cohen 1973, Etzioni 1975).

Work on family-bureaucracy linkages, which is a recent international research development, has a bearing on alternative and complementary systems to institutionalization for elderly persons (Litwak, Hollister, and Meyer 1974, Shanas and Sussman 1975). Interaction between families and bureaucracies has been examined within an exchange theory framework. A logical outcome of these studies is to describe the potential of family networks as a living environment for the elderly.

Findings from research on social structural and social participatory aspects of aging (Taietz and Larson 1956, Shanas and Streib 1963, Rose 1968) and on intergenerational, kin-relations aspects of aging (Sussman and Burchinal 1962, Litwak and Szelenyi 1969) indicate that there the degree of social participation of older persons may be related to their physical and mental well-being. A hypothesis generated by this tentative correlation is that when older people interact frequently with others, "high interactors" are more likely to sustain an adequate level of physical and mental health than "low interactors." This factor of "social participation" appears significant within families as well as between older persons and the wider society or members of social groups other than the elderly (Lowenthal 1965, Petroni 1969, Slaker, Sister, Sussman, and Stroud III 1970). These findings and case history data suggest that if older individuals can function well in their own families, they will be grandparents is an important part of the foster grandparent program (HEW 1972). Furthermore, because of the quality of interaction between old and young, there seem to be distinct benefits for the children as well as for the senior citizens participating in the program (Gray and Kasteler 1967, M.A. Hammond 1963). It seems legitimate to raise the question, if increased intergenerational contact is tangibly beneficial to unrelated members of older and younger generations, could there be as many or more dividends for older and younger members of the same family? It will be some time before specific benefits could be empirically substantiated, but data that define the influence of interaction between different generations may be reliable guides for the formulation of effective policy for aging.

Social Policy

Current national practices are frequently geared toward institutional support programs for the elderly. Although no explicit policy has been established, revenue-sharing funds are increasingly being allocated to local communities, some of which support institutional and community-based human services for the elderly. The difficulty of deciding to fund programs for the elderly rather than more attractive and less stigmatized alternatives, such as drug addiction, rape, and alcoholism control, makes the search for institutional alternatives even more imperative.

Even if institutional environments could provide optimal conditions for interpersonal intimacy and gratification of physical and psychological needs for the elderly, which is highly unlikely (Noelker 1975), governments worldwide would find it difficult to increase financing for institution-based programs. Most complex and developing societies have reached their "absorptive capacity" to provide care and services for dependent populations in relation to maintaining a healthy economy and rewarding the producers. Expenses of institutions for the elderly will create burdens that societies cannot bear.

The need for finding alternatives to institutionalization is exacerbated by the imminence of a national health insurance program and the absence of an organized health-care delivery system on the national or local level. The availability of nonstigmatized medical care may encourage people to become "sick." Specialized medical care is generally not needed by most elderly people, and family members are easily able to cope with some of their minor dysfunctions.

Recommendations

There is some evidence of increased national concern and public interest in the topic of aging and its implications for American society (Burger 1969, White House Conference on Aging 1971, United States Senate Committee on Labor and Public Welfare 1975). In my opinion, the following recommendations could be considered:

1. Supported research priorities could be realigned to enable an increase of research on alternatives to institutionalization for the aged (Administration on Aging 1972), as well as on the impact of family interaction on aging and problems conventionally associated with aging.

2. In preparing long-range policy for the elderly (Ellwood 1972), social scientists and policymakers could study quality-of-life issues, such as the dignity and meaningfulness of life for elderly people, in addition to the more routinely addressed issues of economic and physical liabilities.

3. There could be increased support for projects such as the New Jersey negative income tax experiment (Pechman and Timpane 1975), which provides for financial and service incentives to families to establish creative environments for their elderly members.

4. Studies on the positive and negative impacts upon socialization in families of intergenerational living arrangements could be encouraged.

5. Inquiries on the advantages and disadvantages of alternatives to institutional care could be undertaken from the perspective of the older person. The question of who benefits the most and the least from alternatives to institutional care could be explored.

6. Family environments that foster autonomy, intimacy, and intergenerational interaction for the elderly could be designed. The family networks should optimally have access to services for nutrition and health.

7. There could be further research on political and government agency sources of support or opposition to family-oriented and family-controlled alternatives to institutionalization.

8. The linkages of families with nonfamily institutions and bureaucratic organizations could be studied.

Chapter 7

A VOLUNTARISTIC MODEL OF WOMAN

Sociology as an academic discipline has been criticized on many different levels, including its views of women. In spite of a growing awareness of the implications and consequences of the persisting subordinate social position of women in society, sociology's efforts to reach a goal of transcending sex have been ineffective. Biases in substance and methodology have continued to make sociology a science of male society or a male science of society (Bernard 1973).

Owing to its emphasis on the strength of the influence of cultural factors on socialization, particularly on early socialization, sociological research has tended to ignore or even to deny the significance of the personal options available to men and women, minimal though the range of this freedom of choice may be. Many socialization research studies on sexual roles examine cultural influences on females without accounting for the existing diversity in responses to these influences and without indicating how individuals may neutralize the effects of the cultural influences (Weitzman 1972).

The sociological orientations that tend to overemphasize the impact of cultural influences do not tolerate an alternative or ultimate explanation of human behavior in psychological terms (Homans 1964). Perhaps a more accurate appraisal of the present situation in social science research is that we need a "recovery of persons" in sociology, especially in women's studies (Lynd 1939). This refocusing would necessitate a radical shift in theoretical perspectives, so that woman could be found in the center of social studies (Fichter 1972), instead of being an empty statistic.

Unless such a reorientation comes into being, women's studies are likely to continue biased and largely descriptive. In some respects, it is difficult to understand what has influenced the widely held view of woman and man as creatures and products of culture in Western history since World War II and the accompanying lack of interest in thinking of woman and man as creators and producers of culture (Fichter 1972).

Most existing research on women describes patterns of conformity rather than ways in which women deviate from norms (Epstein 1973, Heidensohn 1968). If sociological research is to be action-oriented—that is, participating in social change processes —studies that extend beyond role descriptions and an examination of conformity pressures are essential.

The Bowen family theory can be applied to the position and behavior of women. Some of the concepts of Bowen's family systems theory appear particularly appropriate for an exploration and documentation of sexual role differences in human behavior, including an examination of the wide range of behavior of both sexes. The Bowen theory is used as a middle-range sociological theory to highlight specific interdependency aspects of the reference group and role behavior of women.

Woman as a Self

The Bowen family theory suggests that both women and man are emotionally dependent beings, who are essentially products of the intensity and complex interdependency of emotional field forces in their nuclear and extended families. Unlike many sociologists who suggest that women are intrinsically different from men in their normative behavior (Parsons and Bales 1955), Bowen emphasizes the importance of similarities in the behavior between the sexes. He postulates that both men and women have equal emotional dependency needs; men can be as adaptive to women as women are to men. Only when women or men mature and behave with fewer emotional demands on others, is "liberation," or the achievement of some degree of freedom from family programming and cultural conditioning, likely to occur.

The efforts and processes an individual must initiate to become less emotionally dependent on others are described by Bowen as both challenging and anxiety-provoking. These moves also tend to produce tensions and stresses in the immediate family of the person who is trying to differentiate self. Both men and women experience similar kinds of negative emotional reactivity from close family members after they accomplish some degree of increased autonomy. The slow, tedious, and difficult route toward achieving a modicum of emotional maturity is thought to follow a fairly predictable sequence of events.

Voluntarism

The Bowen family theory suggests that it is prohibitively difficult for an individual to differentiate self if that person has been consistently adaptive to a parent or spouse. Bowen postulates that only a slight degree of change of self is possible in a lifetime. Man or woman can merely become a little less emotionally dependent on each other as a consequence of sustained individual efforts to change self. An important underlying assumption is that although either man or woman may choose to change self, the range of options available to both is narrowly restricted by the emotional programming received in earlier years and by the programming and expectations that have been perpetuated in present relationship systems, especially in one's family of origin.

The restrictions on voluntarism in behavior are largely a product of patterns of behavior that have been repeated through several generations. The family systems perspective endorses the view that the grandmother-mother-daughter reference group has a greater degree of influence on a woman's behavior (Epstein 1973, Toman 1972) than the grandfather-father-daughter influence (DeJong, Brawer and Robin 1971). Also, emotionally intense and closed family systems provide fewer possibilities for voluntarism in behavior than do less emotionally intense and more open family systems.

Voluntarism may be specifically defined as an individual's choice to be an "I," or to be that person's own self. Bowen states that voluntarism is necessarily limited by the push and pull of conformity forces or the togetherness of a group, and most particularly by the intense emotional togetherness of a family. Voluntarism is an integral part of the individuation (differentiation) force in a family—which can be considered a shared drive, or life-force (Bowen 1972). A self, or an "I," is an individual position or a balancing point between the two major forces of differentiation (individuation) and togetherness (fusion) in a family relationship network. The strength of the tension between these two forces makes it particularly difficult for individuals to change their functioning positions in a family and in the wider society.

When a woman attempts to strengthen her position of self in

her family, other family members predictably resist her moves. Those who are emotionally closest to her try to draw her back into the shared togetherness they had at her former functioning level, and they eventually threaten certain consequences for her if she does not revert to former behavior. If the woman maintains her changed position of self in spite of the opposition from other family members and simultaneously stays in meaningful contact with them, she eventually gains their respect and they automatically improve their own levels of functioning.

This fairly predictable sequence of events is illustrated by the case of a husband and wife who have a close togetherness until the wife begins to define herself in ways other than through her relationship with her husband. Her move away from the emotional closeness with her husband predictably provokes at least an initial negative reactiveness from him. The husband may even decide to leave or divorce his wife if she does not conform with his pressures to change back to her former self. If both spouses are able to both withstand the necessary emotional upheaval of the wife's change and sustain meaningful contact with each other throughout this difficult process of differentiation of self, there will be more tolerance and increased respect for each other in their relationship as well as more flexibility and elasticity.

Further Research

The large number of assumptions made and "taken for granted" about the behavior of women should be further questioned in a systematic way. It may be more useful to expand interpersonal or behavioral research on women than to continue the already preponderant culture-focused research (Rubin 1968, Orden and Bradburn 1968, 1969). The Bowen family theory, with its emphasis on the significance of emotional interdependency in human behavior, generates hypotheses regarding influences in the interpersonal behavior of women and ultimately in their participation in events and activities in the wider society.

By conceptualizing woman primarily as a participant in a family emotional system, predictions can be formulated not only about the probability of particular behavior within the family but also about behavior in groups such as friendship and work systems. Moreover, longitudinal studies of patterns of interaction over several generations—for example, between grandmothers, mothers, and daughters in different families— appear to define continuing influences on behavior more clearly and more accurately than do studies that pinpoint only present cultural influences.

Woman is a person and not a robot. She has a choice of responses to cultural conditioning, although this choice may lie within a narrow range of possibilities. Sociological research on women must move beyond the substantiation of theories of social and cultural determinism if research studies are to suggest new options for women and men and new directions for social change.

Chapter 8

FORMAL ORGANIZATIONS

It has long been recognized that emotions have a strong influence on behavior in organizations as well as on family interaction. A wealth of organization theories and management systems have been developed to assist managers in utilizing human emotions in constructive ways. However, these organization theories and management systems have conceptualized emotion as an intrapsychic phenomenon rather than as a systemic response to others and a network phenomenon. Bion (1948) and a few others (Bennis and Shepard 1956, Schutz 1958) have described emotional processes in groups, but their basic emphasis is still on individuals and couples and not on the "systemness" of the group as a whole. According to the individual or couple orientation, a single person under pressure does not respond "normally"; this premise does not imply that the whole system is anxious. Although many authors have noted the impact of stress on groups, these conditions and responses are usually discussed in individual terms.

If groups malfunction, the problem is usually believed to be the result of a specific organizational or social influence rather than the expected response of a group to emotional tension or trauma. Organization theories and strategies based on this segmented view of the system have frequently been unproductive. Managers are often faced with situations where individuals appear stable, where the norms and social structure seem viable, and where the organization and technology are similar to those of successful organizations elsewhere; but at the same time, these situations may manifest high levels of absenteeism, much turnover, alcoholism, conflict, and breakdowns in communications. The Bowen family theory, when applied as a systems theory to formal organizations, pinpoints emotional tendencies and processes in complex organizations and suggests ways to deal with them effectively. The following discussion describes several Bowen family theory propositions in terms of their usefulness for predicting behavior in formal organizations.

Change in Emotional Intensity

Change in the emotional intensity of a group, the most significant component of all modification processes, occurs in a predictable sequence of events. When one member of a given system shifts the functioning position of self in the group, a period of general disruption and reactive responses from other follows. These responses constitute a strong emotional pressure on the person differentiating self to change back to the former functioning level. If the individual trying to change self maintains the new functioning position and simultaneously remains in emotional contact with group members, the others eventually accept the person's new level of functioning and gradually change their way of relating to this person. Owing to the predictability of this sequence of events, a change in the functioning of one group member can modify the functioning level of the whole group.

The same predictable sequence of change can occur when an employee or a manager leaves a work group to undergo human relations training and then returns to the group after training. This person's attempts to relate more openly, more directly, or more independently to associates is likely to meet resistance, even if all members of the group intellectually approve of the employee's or manager's changed behavior. Others' reactions are frequently baffling to the trainee, who cannot understand what is happening when the newly acquired skills fail at producing positive results.

The Bowen family theory as an emotional systems theory suggests that a member of a work group can expect resistance and negative reactivity to a changed posture and that this response may be followed by considerable disruption and dysfunction in the system as a whole. Other members need time to react, readjust, and adapt their own positions and relationships to the trainee and to each other. Maintenance of contact by the trainee is difficult because of the system's automatic tendency to develop cut-offs in relationships during periods of high anxiety.

Managerial skills cannot eliminate this strong emotional process, and they may also be unable to control it. The established patterns of behavior are blocked by the change of one organization member, and it takes time before an effective adaptation by the whole group can be achieved. In the interim period of adjustment, relationship anxiety usually overloads the system and precipitates conflict, dysfunction, or projection to the individuals perceived as "problems" by the more powerful members.

The degree of resistance to change or disruption following change in a work system or formal organization depends on the degree of fusion among group members. An emotionally intense work group, whose members are extremely involved with each other, experiences more disruption than a more loosely related work group. An organization's high level of anxiety and its accompanying characteristics of overly dependent relationships magnify the phenomena of "blocking" or "overload" precipitated by a change in a member's functioning.

Bowen's concept of fusion may be compared with the idea of group cohesiveness originally developed by field theorists (Lewin 1951) and extended by Festinger (1954) in his theory of social comparison processes. Kelman's (1961) idea of the identification process also suggests similar meaning elements. However, these ideas, which generally include a cognitive acceptance and enthusiasm for other members or for the goals of the group, are distinct from the Bowen concept of fusion. Bowen's emotional systems theory suggests that fusion in relationships is not recognized by participants in the togetherness and that fusion inhibits or restricts autonomy.

Loss of a Key Member

When an organization experiences the loss of a significant member, the system frequently responds with unproductive behavior and relationship problems. The severity of these symptoms largely depends on the emotional importance to the whole of the person who has left the organization. Shock wave phenomena or interrelated sequences of disruptive behavior may occur in conditions of temporary as well as permanent loss.

In a formal organization, the loss of a key member through death, dismissal, or voluntary withdrawal frequently results in conflicts, inefficient production, or low morale among the remaining members. Organizational problems following re-assignments of work responsibilities are frequently used as rationalizations for these dislocations in the system. Even if no overt organizational problems follow in the wake of a loss, however, conflict, inefficiency, or low morale tends to appear. These dislocations in the relationship system result whether the person the system loses was positively or negatively significant in the system.

The problem consequences of a loss in a formal organization may be exacerbated by the timing of the loss. When the level of organizational strain is high, additional tension from a loss may easily result in disruption and dysfunction of the system that is markedly out of proportion to the objective reality of the situation.

Advance awareness of the probability of a loss, together with an application of effective managerial strategies, may minimize the impact of a loss. In some instances, it is possible to control the timing of a loss or to provide constructive ways of dissipating emotional tensions resulting from a loss.

Concept of Responsibility

If a significant group member functions responsibly, other members of the group become correspondingly responsible for self in their feelings, thoughts, and actions. In Bowen's family theory, the concept of responsibility refers to behavior consistent with inner beliefs and convictions and motivated by personally selected goals. A responsible person maintains meaningful contact with as many group members as possible. Responsible behavior is characteristic of a differentiated individual, and to some extent this concept of responsibility for self may be compared with Maslow's concept of self actualization (1954) and Riesman's idea of inner directedness (Reisman, Glazer and Denney 1950).

The Bowen definition of responsibility provides an alternative to the concept of responsibility used in most management literature. Traditionally, management at least partly defines responsibility for self in terms of accepting responsibility for the behavior of others. From the viewpoint of emotional systems theory, this kind of behavior is considered overresponsibility and consequently irresponsible. Feeling responsible for others enmeshes them in tight dependency relationships that diminish their opportunities to act autonomously in any given situation.

Emotional systems theory, when applied to organizations, essentially predicts that managers will be more effective if they relinquish their emotional control over others. A manager provides guidance to others through the example of responsible behavior rather than through transmitting emotional pressures to other members of the organization. Under these conditions, subordinates are allowed to be more responsible for self. The automatic spread of responsible action in a group is endemic to an emotional system. The decreased emotional involvement of a manager with subordinates allows all members of the system to mobilize emotional energy previously used to maintain dependent relationships. When emotional demands on others are minimized, overall productivity is increased. The goals of an organization and an individual are not necessarily in conflict (McGregor 1960). In the absence of dependency bonds, the worker's behavior will be more goal-directed and oriented to both organizational and personal objectives. Managers must maintain meaningful emotional contact with subordinates to maximize responsible behavior in an organization.

Triangles

When there is conflict between two members of the same group, a third person is triangled into the twosome to lower the level of anxiety in the relationship. In most triangles, or three-person relationship systems, feelings are invested primarily between two of its members. When there is conflict between the two members of the feeling-invested twosome, the preferred and more comfortable position in the triangle is that of the outsider. When the twosome manifests intense positive feelings, the emotionally preferred position in that triangle is generally that of a participant in the fused twosome. However, the outsider is consistently more autonomous than either of the feeling-invested twosome. An individual is able to function more effectively in the outsider position than in the intense twosome, regardless of whether the feelings in the twosome are positive or negative.

If the inclusion of a third person in the emotional field of a dyadic conflict does not effectively reduce the level of tension in the relationship system, a fourth person is brought into the emotional field. If there continues to be no effective resolution of differences or conflicts between the two key members of the emotional field, the surplus anxiety may be projected to the third person who becomes scapegoated or victimized, or the tension is internalized by one of the original two parties. The person who internalizes the stress tends to become dysfunctional in relation to the group.

This triangling process and the related adjustments to undifferentiation and anxiety frequently surface in an organization. People are unable to keep tension to themselves in families or in other social contexts and automatically involve others in the tension, especially when anxiety is high.

The person in the outsider position of a triangle may or may not see self as more autonomous than members of the twosome. Individuals who become too involved with each other face the serious risk of overloading their relationship, especially when emotional tension in the broader relationship network is high. Undifferentiated individuals are frequently drawn into conflict dyads as they are particularly responsive to emotional tension, and automatically satisfy the emotional demands of others. Young members of a work team, new members, women, or other dependent members in the system are most apt to be caught in the emotional entanglements of others.

Projection occurs when parties to an unresolved conflict "victimize" an individual who is in the lower ranks of the administrative hierarchy. Projection frequently occurs without awareness on the part of the one who is being scapegoated. If two executives are unable or unwilling to work out a conflict, the most uncomfortable one in the twosome directs anxiety and anger to an unsuspecting and less important member of the system. Whenever the conflict between the executives intensifies, feelings are projected to the more vulnerable member of the system, who is low in the hierarchy. As a result, several junior members may mysteriously quit, they may be fired, or they may manifest chronic symptoms of emotional distress. These circumstances evolve in ways disproportionate to the external realities of the jobs of the individuals concerned.

Effective triangling and multitriangling may sufficiently reduce relationship tensions to prevent them from developing into overload, dysfunction, and projection. A supervisor who is aware of a work system's tendency to triangle and to project anxiety to others under stress can deliberately triangle self into a conflictual twosome. If the supervisor refrains from taking sides in the conflict, tensions are lessened and the probability that one of the conflicting members internalizes the anxiety, becomes dysfunctional, or projects tension to a third party is effectively decreased.

Repetition of Behavior Patterns

Past patterns of behavior in an organization, such as the different ways in which the group has dealt with seniority, sex, and race, have a strong impact on present patterns of behavior in the same organization. Individuals can begin to neutralize or even to reverse the strong automatic influence of past patterns of emotional dependency by becoming aware of them and by consciously counteracting them through modified emotional inputs in the system.

Traditional management and human relations theory view stress phenomena as emanating from individuals. However, the Bowen family theory suggests that once behavior patterns become established in an organization, they are automatically perpetuated by the participation of all group members. Even when new people join the organization, they generally respond cooperatively to the strong emotional pressures to conform to the organization's established patterns of interaction.

The perpetual inclination of groups to reinforce past patterns of behavior in the present influences the resistance to change in organizations, such as changes in the position of women or blacks. Strong resistance continues to occur, even when all members of an organization affirm that they are intellectually receptive to change. The organization has an automatic emotional tendency to try to maintain the old system of comfortable established relationships and secure equilibrium.

Managers are more effective if they are aware of the repeated patterns of behavior in their organizations. Emotional dependencies and interactions between young and old, men and women, blacks and whites, and professionals and non-professionals should be observed and diagramed wherever possible. Managers can also profitably realize that changing the structure or policies of the organization does not substantially modify established emotional patterns. The system persists in its efforts to perpetuate the given emotional equilibrium, despite whatever innovations are introduced. People still continue to respond more or less the same way toward each other, whether or not job titles or reporting channels are changed.

Conscious efforts to modify the emotional inputs given to an organization are necessary to facilitate change. The emotional relationships of at least one member of the organization must be effectively changed, or the system will persist in its established relationship patterns for many generations of corporate life.

Changes in the emotional inputs to an organization may have a temporarily disturbing effect upon general productivity and satisfaction. If women, blacks, or young people in an organization initiate changed dependencies and behavior, this shift may disrupt traditional patterns and may precipitate some degree of emotional distress. Instigators of the changes may be pressured to return to their former functioning by the resistance of other members of the system.

Changes in the core groups of an organization, where members are the most emotionally involved with each other, are more instrumental in bringing about changes in the whole group than changes in peripheral groups or in groups that are low in the established hierarchy. A sustained change anywhere in the system eventually affects all members of the organization, as long as emotional contact with the whole is maintained by the changing individual or group.

Conclusion

A conceptualization of formal organizations as emotional systems opens up numerous avenues for investigation. This new frame of reference focuses on the nature and intensity of emotional relationships within an organization, as well as on the dependencies and coalitions that develop in small groups and wider networks. The influence of losses in the organization, the isolation of certain groups through cut-offs in the communication system, and tensions resulting from incompatibilities between the goals of the larger group and individual members' goals are some of the many potential areas of research for family systems theory and applications. The emotional consequences of change in organizations could also be explored.

Emotional systems theory begins to articulate a prediction of the degree of resistance to individual and group change and also suggests a means to minimize resistance. These concepts also further an understanding of those who resist change in a variety of formal organizations and other social settings.

Among the more specific contributions of the Bowen family theory and the emotional systems orientation to formal organizations are conceptualizations of superordinate and subordinate relationships, the influence of seniority in organizations, the difficulties a member encounters in becoming autonomous in relation to the group, and patterns of problem solving, training, evaluation, and informal communication. From a systems perspective many organizational conflicts and tensions are considered particular manifestations of the two major emotional forces of togetherness and individuation.

Emotional systems theory suggests that the frequency of interaction within organizations heightens their emotional intensity. The goals, policies, and structures of an organization are frequently manipulated in response to pressures from the emotional system, even though administrative moves are usually described in terms of furthering the "rational" goals of the organization. Emotional systems theory can be used to delineate some of the rationalizations that disguise the reactiveness of the underlying emotional system of an organization. The Bowen theory can also be used to cope with an organization's resistance to new goals or policies and structural changes. However valid and necessary these modifications are, they pose a threat to the emotional equilibrium of the system.

Emotional systems theory offers a "person-centered" rather than an "object-centered" approach to management. The concepts can enhance administrators' understanding of their organizations.

Problems such as conflict, absenteeism, productivity slowdowns, low morale, and individual inadequacies are viewed as system characteristics rather than as individual behavior. Since any member of an organization can influence changes, emotional systems theory provides managers with a useful new conceptual instrument with which to influence action in their organizations.

Part III

Issues and Implications

Chapter 9

THE BOWEN THEORY AS THEORY

The Bowen family theory abstracts principles of emotional behavior from many kinds of observations of families and society. This process distills and condenses a multitude of unique and specific manifestations of human interaction into a series of more generally applicable core ideas or concepts. The Bowen theory is based on the assumption that there are some natural laws and some degree of order in the universe. Predictions related to these laws are thought to be possible when some qualities of the interrelatedness of emotional phenomena are defined. Any single concept merely suggests the substantive consequences of limited aspects of human behavior. Only by viewing human beings from the perspective of an entire emotional system or from the point of view of the whole network of dependencies can predictions about behavior be made.

The initial conceptualization and subsequent synthesis of concepts of the Bowen theory have been evolving for twenty-five years. During this time, there has been a long and continuing phase of inductive inquiry into the nature of patterns of emotional behavior and dependency. The theory emerged through the formulation and reformulation of hypotheses to correspond with the range of facts observed and recorded.

Unlike many scientific theories or theoretical propositions, the Bowen theory does not offer a causative explanation of emotional interdependencies within families and other social groups. Although prediction is an element of the Bowen theory, the postulation of a simple, dualistic, cause-effect relationship between sequentially related phenomena is contrary to the Bowen systems thinking. Bowen describes and defines the complex patterns of interrelatedness in emotional systems for predictive purposes. No answer to the philosophical question of why phenomena are related is attempted with these goals of inquiry and investigation.

The relative accuracy of a fairly wide range of predictions of behavior at different levels of probability indicates the versatility of the Bowen theory's applications and implications. Hypotheses generated by the Bowen theory can be verified by checking the accuracy of the predictions made. Research applications may be operationalized in experimental settings, in clinical practice, or in one's own family. In clinical practice and in one's own family, changes can be observed more clearly over extended periods of time. When emotional relationships are examined in detail by systematic longitudinal research methods, the Bowen theory's capacity to predict behavior may be verified more rigorously.

The continual formulation and reformulation of hypotheses about emotional behavior in families has disciplined the researchers' ability to make objective observations. Common denominators in the behavior patterns of many families are combined to form the basis of the conceptualization and theoretical refinement of family systems principles and propositions.

Although the Bowen concepts contain many meaning elements

that have already been explored and defined by family researchers, it is the particular "mix" and interrelatedness of Bowen's concepts that make his theory unique. Rather than emphasize the intrapsychic processes of individual family members in isolation from each other, the Bowen theory highlights the many nuances of the emotional dependencies in a family and the degree of responsiveness and reactiveness family members have toward each other. Such a frame of reference is unconventional, and it serves to identify the specific interdependencies that are most critical in creating "problems" and "patients" in a family. The new definition of family problems necessitates a series of innovative research strategies and clinical goals.

The Bowen Theory as a Scientific Theory

Although the Bowen theory claims to be scientific, it departs from the traditions of science in critical ways. The Bowen systems perspective is simultaneously compatible with science and distinctively different from conventional scientific theory.

The development of science has led to an increased consideration of apparently trivial and curious aspects of human interaction as clues and indicators of some of the most basic principles of behavior. In addition to being an achievement of the human mind, science provides a means of testing theories.

Although both science and philosophy aim to understand the world, the approaches of the two disciplines are in many ways diametrically opposed to each other. Whereas science begins with a detailed examination of particulars and moves to more general ideas, philosophy begins with the general and tries to explain the particular. Science is a logical thought system, which may be perceived as a broadly-based "pyramid" resting on a multitude of observed facts.

The validity and reliability of science depends on its component *concepts*. The concepts are more fundamental than the theories that are stated in terms of concepts. Concepts, rather than theories, influence the questions asked by researchers and the answers found. Concepts represent the nature of the universe selectively and do not reflect the totality of minute details. A concept is an approximation of reality, even in cases where definitions appear precise. Each concept of the Bowen theory is subject to these kinds of limitations.

Another property of a concept is that it has a power of growth beyond the original observations or experiments that suggested it. More than twenty years have been needed for the present stage of development of such family systems concepts as differentiation of self, although the rudimentary ideas of the latter had been crudely formulated previously. Articulation of a precise conceptual refinement of differentiation of self will take many more years, as will the substantiation or refutation of its usefulness for understanding the many complexities of family behavior.

A *theory* is a statement of relations between concepts. A theory is more likely to be disproved than proved, as it is not logically possible to test the whole range of experiments or possibilities that a theory could cover. Also, as experiments cannot be replicated exactly, it cannot be maintained that identical experiments give identical results.

In spite of such limitations, a theory can make certain kinds of predictions. Predictions, at different levels of probability, can indicate what will occur under specific conditions. These conditions either may be artificially produced in a laboratory or they may exist in natural environments. If the predicted events are not observed, the theory may eventually be disproved and consequently abandoned or altered. If predictions are fulfilled in repeated instances over a varied range of phenomena, the theory is accepted and ultimately becomes a "law." The law of gravity is an example of this kind of scientific development (Thomson 1961).

Science is invaluable in two principal ways. First, science makes it possible to be forewarned of certain events, enabling the avoidance of more serious and threatening consequences. Second, possession of scientific knowledge about the universe relieves us of a world of fears, rages, and other unpleasant dissipations of energy. However, human relations are not yet generally accepted as proper subjects for serious scientific study (Lundberg 1947). It has taken many centuries for people to begin to apply the scientific systems thinking of astronomy to human phenomena. The Bowen theory is an attempt to make such connections and applications. Through applications of the Bowen systems theory, people may be forewarned and protected from crises in relationship systems and from the more impairing day-to-day patterns of interaction.

The confirmation of a theoretical proposition or hypothesis is a complex and tedious enterprise. Since the process of proof is so long and life is so short, research efforts must be devoted to hypotheses that are strategic. It may be easier to test *systems* of propositions, such as the Bowen family theory, rather than *single* propositions (Zetterberg 1965).

To test the potential or capacity of a scientific theory, a researcher must evaluate whether the theory provides the most concise summary of actual or anticipated research findings. A theory may also be used to coordinate research, so that many separate findings can be consolidated. To be able to use theory and method accurately is to have become a self-conscious thinker who is aware of the assumptions and implications of many kinds of behavior (Mills 1959). The family systems theory evolved from Bowen's attempts to synthesize the evidence of emotional systems. The control of future research efforts on emotional systems can be enhanced by continuing this process of crystallization (Zetterberg 1965).

Delineation of Problems

Only when the interrelationship and interdependency of Bowen's eight working concepts are understood, can the systematic nature of a family and its problems be described accurately. Knowledge of the interlocking nature of these concepts and factual manifestations of the concepts' interdependency generally demand a reidentification of a "presented" family problem in system terms. A systems delineation of a family problem tends to nullify prior definitions made in intrapsychic or other conventional terms. For example, a problem previously thought to be caused by an individual family member's temperament might be reconceptualized as a product of the network of emotional relationships and interdependencies in the entire family.

The Bowen family theory focuses primarily on the quality of emotional relationships and processes in a family. The intensity or rigidity of a family emotional system are viewed as being more problematic for all family members than are particular personality traits of an individual family member. From a systems perspective, behavior symptoms are generally conceptualized as overreactive responses to other family members, or to shifts in the patterns of interdependency in a family. For example, symptoms of individual or relationship dysfunctions may follow the death of a significant family member or may appear as a consequence of cut-offs in meaningful contact between emotionally significant family members.

The description of a family problem as an integral part of an emotional system leads to a reevaluation of what may have been previously defined as "causes" or "effects" by diagnostic procedures. In conventional cause-effect thinking, the sig-

A conceptualization of families as emotional systems necessitates using a multigenerational model for describing nificance of conditions or events immediately prior to and immediately following an observed irregularity or problem in a family is generally overstated by arbitrarily labeling these conditions or events as causes and effects. A central purpose of systems thinking is to delineate a much longer and more comprehensive sequence of events or series of chain reactions that come into play in a consistent manner before and throughout the course of development of a family problem. The process of describing or delineating a family problem in systems terms questions the perceptions of the problem of all family members.

Viewing behavior symptoms as products of a family system is an initial stage in being able to predict interaction in these relationships. Systems thinking necessarily includes conscious attempts to avoid evaluating or diagnosing a family, as these processes tend to perpetuate the symptomatic relationships that already exist in a family. Any identification of members as "patients" reinforces impairing patterns of behavior in a family and endorses the false assumptions and distorted perceptions of those who are most involved in "the problem."

Conceptualization of Problems

Although families are not clinically diagnosed in systems thinking, essential distinguishing characteristics and patterns of behavior are recorded as accurately as possible. Effective working hypotheses in a clinical setting include the immediate goal of alleviation of symptoms, as well as the long-term goal of differentiation of self. To formulate specific hypotheses and clinical applications of the Bowen theory, all eight basic concepts must be utilized. An overemphasis on a single concept or an omission of a concept distorts the data collected and introduces a bias to subsequent predictions of behavior.

structures and processes. When details of extended family characteristics are viewed in relation to a given nuclear family, the nuclear family can be described much more objectively and accurately. An examination of any one part of a family in isolation from the broader relationship system distorts observation of the viable emotional network. For example, family projection in a nuclear unit can be described more accurately when the projection is viewed in relation to the patterns of the multigenerational transmission of which it is a part. Another example that illustrates the necessity of conceptualizing emotional processes in the context of the entire relationship system is the degree of association between differentiation of self and sibling position. Differentiation can be described more accurately if a person is viewed as operating from a specific sibling position that also accounts for the sibling positions of the parents and grandparents of that person.

The global network of the constantly shifting patterns of emotional forces is ultimately the "problem" in any family. To adequately conceptualize this diffuse and defocused problem area, objective observations of many complex and diverse dimensions of a family system must be made. Only after this kind of data has been collected can effective choices of specific research, action strategies, and operational directives be made.

Strategies and Operational Directives

Productive strategies and operational directives for changing an individual position in a family can only be formulated in relation to a consistent and integrated theory. If plans to change one's posture and actions in a family are to surpass a superficial level of assembled techniques, they must be based on interlocking and interrelated concepts.

Some of the difficulties involved in creating an effective plan for changing one's level of participation in a family are precipitated by the side effects and shock wave phenomena that follow unexpected moves or shifts in a family relationship system. The loss of a significant person in a family, such as the death of a mother of young children, would have a strong impact on a family emotional system that shock wave symptoms following the death may be apparent for a considerable period of time. The variety of side effects in this period of adjustment could impede attempts to observe the usual patterns of behavior in the family or one's plans to change position in the family.

In assessing the potential effectiveness of any single strategy or operational directive, there is a temptation to oversimplify an extremely complex process by implying that certain actions precipitate certain consequences. Although family members may react to one person's changes in a fairly predictable emotional way, the particular kinds of emotional responses selected are not as predictable. A detailed examination of intergenerational processes and past behavior patterns may indicate an expected range of possible responses. The Bowen family theory focuses more on general emotional processes than on the particular content or specific modes of manifestation of these processes. A family's initial emotional reaction to a member who attempts functional change can vary greatly in form.

Effective strategies and operational directives should optimally be based on as detailed a knowledge of a family's history as possible. For example, empirical evidence of the degree and extent of family projection in several generations may provide a basis for predicting sibling behavior in present generations. The processes that contribute toward a family's adjustment to a death, rather than the fact of the death itself, may indicate the intensity of anxiety in a family. Consideration of these nuances increases the overall predictive capacity of the Bowen theory and makes the specification of strategies and operational directives more effective.

The most productive blueprints for action in a family are created by the person who will put the plans into action. Plans generally reflect their author's level of theoretical awareness and capacity to deal responsibly with the "fallout," or consequences of changed actions in a family. Acting without sufficient theoretical awareness and putting another person's plan into action can easily boomerang. Thus, irresponsibility can be defined as acting without being aware of or knowing how to handle the consequences of one's actions. An effective plan of action must have a solid theoretical base.

Predictability and Pre-predictability

It appears that the emotional systems influences in human behavior have a higher level of predictability than do other aspects of behavior. This predictability, which is more than an abstract theoretical possibility, is integrally related to the characteristic reactivity and responsiveness of emotional systems themselves. The behavior predicted by emotional systems conceptualizations focuses on what behavior can be rather than on what behavior ought to be.

Pre-predictability describes a phase of exploratory research, which includes compiling sufficient facts of family interaction to make tentative predictions possible. In the pre-predictability phase, a series of objective observations is made, and consistencies are delineated from the data. Ideally, detailed information on emotional processes in all parts of a family system over long periods of time should be gathered. There can be no effective "instant" predictions from a narrow base of facts. Only a full spectrum of nuances can begin to describe the more significant characteristics of family emotional processes. The accuracy of later predictions is contingent upon the effectiveness of these pre-predictive phases of research.

Pre-predictive investigation into the nature of emotional

processes in families is distinct from the "diagnostic thinking" typical of the medical model. In contrast to the relatively static and "fixing" components of diagnostic procedures, a pre-predictive phase of study is essentially open-ended and creative, as it is exploratory and unconfined by an immediate goal of categorization or diagnosis.

Predictions from applications of the Bowen theory can be formulated only at certain levels of probability, with outcomes described in terms of general emotional processes rather than specific manifestations. Whereas the onset of a child's dysfunctioning may be highly predictable within a given period, the specific type of dysfunction or symptom manifestation will not be as predictable. From a detailed history of dysfunctioning of the child and other family members, a series of alternative dysfunctions, in terms of their relative probability and predictability, can be suggested.

Results and Findings

Results and findings from the development and application of the Bowen theory have been accumulating for more than twenty-five years. Some of the preliminary correlations of emotional phenomena have become increasingly predictable in this time, specificity being possible when sufficient details about past and present family circumstances are known.

Clinical or personal applications of the Bowen theory must account for the kinds of changes manifested and the period of time during which applications of the theory were made. The following questions should be raised: To what extent is change solid and relatively permanent or merely a shift in symptoms? To what extent do behavioral changes indicate differentiation of self? What behavior is predictable in a particular period of change after applying the Bowen theory? How can a researcher document change objectively and accurately? How can change in self by distinguished from adaptiveness to others? Although a successful course of therapy cannot be simplistically summarized as an increase in solid self and a decrease in pseudo-self, some degree of inverse correlation between these two parts of self results from increased differentiation.

Results for Self

One of the most important objectives in any attempt to apply the Bowen theory to one's own family is to predict the spectrum of changes that might follow. One of the necessary conditions of real change in self is a modification of the quality of interaction between self and other family members. One cannot grow or change in a vacuum. Differentiation is accompanied by an increased awareness of solid self, without an increase in rigidity. A more differentiated person will not be inflexible in relation to others, except when firm "I" position stands are needed to preserve self. One consequence of differentiation is an increase in one's flexibility toward others. A *no-self* takes rigid and incompatible stands with others, with minimal or no awareness of self.

The person who attempts to differentiate self tends to become the most focal point in the emotional system network. Instead of being a peripheral or cut-off member of one's family, a differentiating person communicates more frequently with a greater number of other family members, who generally begin to communicate more frequently with each other in return. In some respects, this reciprocity reflects emotional rebound or reaction to the contacts initiated in changing one's position in the family. If the newly established lines of communication were mapped on a sociogram, the person trying to differentiate self would appear as a "star," with more lines of contact being traced through, to, and from this person than for other family members.

Although an increase in one's level of functioning is not necessarily correlated with an increase in differentiation of self, increased differentiation is accompanied by improved functioning. The most noticeable characteristic of improved functioning is that a person tends to act from the basis of directed thought rather than automatic, emotionally reactive, and responsive ways.

Functional changes cannot be thought of as dramatic shifts in the level of differentiation. Although one may appear to have made tremendous changes in self-awareness and functioning, only slight changes in one's level of differentiation are possible, even over considerable periods of time. Human limitations make sizable leaps in differentiation impossible. As a result, it is exceedingly difficult to become much more or much less differentiated in a lifetime. Increased differentiation is hard to lose in that one cannot easily slip back to prior levels of differentiation unless a situation is extremely stressful and persistently so. Another result of a successful application of the Bowen theory to self and to one's own family is that differentiation is difficult to reverse owing to the intrinsic tension that exists between the two major emotional forces of togetherness and differentiation.

Clinical Results

In some respects, clinical results are more difficult to document and evaluate than are the more personal results of applying the Bowen theory to one's own family. In cases where contact with a family in a clinical setting is lost or where attendance at clinical sessions is sporadic, evidence and results of the application of the Bowen theory may be obscured. In spite of these inadequacies, some generalizations about the overall results of applying this theory to a spectrum of different kinds of clinical cases for a period of more than twenty years can be suggested.

Changes during a successful course of therapy based on the Bowen theory can be summarized as a relatively predictable sequence of specific emotional events. A phase of effective symptom relief in a family is followed by observable changes in the levels of functioning of significant members in the family. If these changes in levels of functioning and emotional contact with other family members are maintained in face of the others' reactivity, some of the changes made become differentiation of self. If other family members eventually change their functioning positions through contact with the person who already made differentiating moves, the functioning level of the entire family gradually improves and a new level of differentiation of self for the entire family eventually follows.

In a successful course of therapy, this sequence of events occurs over an extended period of time. These changes are accompanied by a gradual opening of the family emotional system. A family with an open emotional system is characterized by meaningful communication between all family members, few or no isolated parts of the family, flexibility in relationships in the family, and few or no symptoms of emotional intensity throughout the family. The improved functioning of family members is accompanied by a reduction in the number and types of dysfunction in a family.

Some predictable characteristics of long-term changes in a successful course of therapy include short-term "seesaw" effects of functional changes in a family, which are precipitated by the intensity of the emotional dependency between family members. Two spouses are generally not able to differentiate self effectively at the same time. A typical pattern of change is that as one spouse improves functioning, the other spouse becomes more adaptive or even dysfunctional. As one spouse strives toward differentiation, the other tends to make reactive moves toward togetherness, responding emotionally and negatively to the other's efforts to differentiate. If the differentiating spouse is able to maintain the position of improved functioning while simultaneously staying in emotional contact with the togetherness spouse, the latter is eventually able to improve functioning and may surpass the differentiating spouse's functioning level. The process of changing one's level of functioning, and of ultimately changing one's level of differentiation, is arduous and time-consuming.

A family that has better differentiated members has increased resilience in times of stress owing to the flexibility of its relationship system. A fairly well-differentiated family is able to deal with the death of a significant member by recognizing feelings of loss and adapting to the loss in a fairly short period of time. A change in the effectiveness of a family's ability to recuperate after a crisis is one indicator of a reduction in the emotional reactiveness and responsiveness of the family emotional system. As a result, there are fewer repetitions of preestablished behavior patterns in the family, especially from a multigenerational perspective.

In addition to overall improvements in a family's capability for dealing with crises after a successful course of therapy, individual family members are able to deal more responsibly with their own reactions and also with the fallout resulting from their changed actions in the family. This increased responsibility for self is evident in all kinds of behavior: the expression of emotion, feelings, thoughts, and actions. Increased responsibility for self also involves a reduction in "overresponsibility" for others.

A successful course of therapy is characterized by reports of what a person does in the family, with a less anxious focus on the original "problem" or relationship concerns. Decreasing dependency on the therapist generates an increased focus on self. Self is considered an active participant in extended families of origin and multigenerational transmission processes as well as a member of a nuclear family. A major concern is how to build person-to-person relationships with members of one's family of origin.

A decrease in the therapist's specific coaching is accompanied by an increase in the client's initiative to work toward personal goals. Personal goals are formulated more clearly, and the capacity to sustain efforts to accomplish moves toward these goals is increasingly evident. There will be increased awareness of "action-level" behavior, and less expenditure of effort and energy on unproductive behavior, such as lengthy discussions about action or debate and argument.

A successful therapy outcome is also reflected in the client's reduced tendency to project undifferentiation to others, especially to children and elderly family members. Levity and humor is an essential part of relationships with others, and personal strengths and limitations are perceived more objectively. One may also be able to act more freely in relation to family members' preestablished expectations for sibling position behavior.

A more profound knowledge of self and an increased capacity to function as a self are predictable consequences deriving from an adequate working knowledge of a particular family emotional system. Someone who has been successfully coached in the Bowen theory is aware of the predictability of triangles in a family and is able to plan effective detriangling moves, including productive multigenerational detriangling.

The Bowen family therapy frequently has a high rate of attrition. Discontinuity in sessions tends to be the result of a client's unwillingness to undertake challenging and difficult projects, such as differentiation of self, and the strength of family members' feelings invested in maintaining the status quo of the emotional system. Where strong motivation and sustained efforts to differentiate self exist, motivation and effort sometimes appear self-generating and self-perpetuating. Although successful moves to differentiate self usually include specific plans, persistent attempts to act for self appear particularly important for increasing effectiveness in differentiating self.

Application of the Bowen Theory as Theory

Throughout the inductive development of the Bowen theory, applications of the concepts have produced increasingly accurate and predictable results. In clinical settings, the more closely this theory is applied, the more predictable the outcome of clinical intervention appears to be. Applications can be made with the same degree of predictability for a wide variety of families.

One of the predictable results of applying the Bowen theory is the resistance or thrust for togetherness that the individual differentiating self meets from other family members. This negative reactivity of closely related others can manifest itself as conflict with the individual differentiating self. The emotional resistance generally follows a fairly predictable pattern. Initially, the opposing response carries the action message that the person changing self should return to the original functioning position. If the differentiating individual refuses to change back to the former operating level, other family members tend to form alliances and threaten joint courses of action that will be taken in the event that this person continues to refuse to return to the former functioning level. If the one who modifies self maintains the changed position and keeps in meaningful emotional contact with other family members, those others eventually are compelled to change their own positions owing to the intensity of their dependency on the person differentiating self. As a result, the level of functioning or differentiation of self of the entire family can gradually be raised.

Throughout these prolonged emotional exchanges, other family members increase their respect for the person who changed position in the group and maintained this change in spite of opposition. In families where a spouse or parent of the person changing self exerted considerable pressure on that person to change back to the original functioning level, the spouse or parent is frequently greatly relieved if the pressures are withstood. The resistance expressed earlier so forcefully begins to show a marked decline, frequently disappearing in times of calm or in periods of extreme anxiety.

Attempts to differentiate self may also result in capitulation to the family togetherness. If the differentiating individual complies with others' demands and wishes and conforms with their expectations, repeating previously established patterns of behavior in the process, any change in functioning is quickly neutralized. As this person's functioning is restored to its original level, the level of differentiation of the entire family remains unchanged.

Application of the Bowen theory heightens awareness among family members of a thrust and propensity to change self. Human beings appear to have a kind of inner life-force that pulls them toward greater differentiation, even during and after differentiating efforts have been met by negative reactivity. Waves or phases of togetherness and differentiation drives may alternate with each other, balancing or stabilizing in a position of tension in relation to each other.

Plans for action can be based on principles that prevent a useless expenditure of energy. The Bowen theory assists in promoting an economy of human effort. The theory is a practical aid to predicting consequences of actions before one acts. When sufficient details of emotional processes in families are known, more specific predictions of outcomes can be made and more energy can be preserved.

Although economy of effort is invaluable in applying this theory to one's own family, the dividends of economy are most evident in clinical settings. When therapeutic strategies have a solid theoretical base, the therapist is more effective with each family coached and is therefore able to work with a large number of families because the energy expended per family is minimized. A therapist's ultimate effectiveness depends on theoretical awareness and functioning position in the therapist's family of origin. Sound clinical results follow effective applications of the Bowen theory to the therapist's own family.

Personal Findings

One of the most significant personal findings for an individual differentiating self is that each move toward differentiation is accompanied by increased responsibility for self at all levels of behavior. By persistently focusing on one's own beliefs, thoughts, and actions, one becomes more responsible for one's emotions and decisions, allowing others to become more responsible. Any slight increase in differentiation is accompanied by increased responsibility for self. Increased responsibility generally implies decreased overresponsibility for others, which is viewed as a form of irresponsibility.

Changes in differentiating self will be more solid if one makes frequent multigenerational contacts, such as multigenerational triangling and multigenerational detriangling. The quality of differentiating efforts is usually improved to the extent that one is able to make effective intergenerational contacts. An action program of this kind can include genealogical research, which is another way to put oneself in meaningful contact with family members in previous generations. Genealogical information about deceased family members can be beneficially disseminated to living relatives. Triangles in the global family system are activated through these kinds of communications, and opportunities to detriangle self from the family are facilitated.

One's capacity to build personal relationships in social settings appears to depend on one's capacity to build personal relationships within one's family. The reciprocal influences of these two capacities can be illustrated only after sustained efforts have been made to build person-to-person relationships in all parts of a family. A person-to-person relationship consists of a series of intimate communications about self made in a one-to-one situation. Such a personal relationship contrasts with depersonalized exchanges, where communications are more anxious and more removed from self. Distancing of this kind frequently results in a third person being pulled into the emotional field of the twosome. The prolonged intimacy of a person-to-person relationship is not possible for an undifferentiated person. Where intimacy and meaningful personal exchanges exist in a person's family relationships, that same individual will function more effectively in all other kinds of social settings.

Another finding related to application of the Bowen theory to one's own family is that a termination of a relationship with a deceased family member can be achieved most effectively through direct participation in that family. The occurrence of a death in one's family provides special opportunities for differentiation of self, both in relation to the person who died and to those who were emotionally close to the deceased family member. Talking about deceased family members with living relatives, visiting grave sites, or tracing ancestors through genealogical research all contribute toward resolving one's emotional attachments to dead family members and to those who were close to the deceased relatives.

Finally, when one is able to effectively bridge a cut-off, this contributes toward changing one's position in the family. Bridging a cut-off can be a means to change the quality of relationships in the entire system. Beneficial outcomes are particularly marked where cut-offs between branches of the same family have persisted through several generations. In some respects, the phenomena of cut-offs and death are similar. Death can be viewed as the ultimate cut-off, and any efforts to discover facts about deceased relatives are an effective way to bridge the cut-offs associated with death.

Research Findings

Research findings from application of the Bowen theory to a large number of families indicate that symptomatic behavior is generally preceded by an emotional cut-off in the system and that the degree or extent of dysfunction tends to be positively correlated with the intensity of the cut-off. The degree of intensity of a cut-off can be gauged by indicators such as duration, frequency in prior generations, or precipitating factors. The timing of the onset of symptomatic behavior can frequently be traced to periods in which a family experiences sufficient anxiety to produce or intensify cut-offs in the emotional system.

Open family systems have freer patterns of communication and more opportunities for individuals to be selfs without the impingement of others' negative responses than closed family systems. Closed family systems manifest a quality of explosiveness resulting from the rigid reactivity of these systems. There is also a distinctive uniformity or similarity of characteristics among members of a closed family system. Research findings indicate that there are more symptoms in closed family systems than in open family systems and that the individual who is able to make successful differentiating moves in a closed system may eventually ease some of the tightness of that network. The probability of reactive behavior is greater in a closed system than in an open system, and it is more difficult to counteract the strong togetherness forces of a closed system than those of an open system.

The most important nodal event in a family is usually a death. In some instances, the occurrence of a death is not as critical as a family's capacity to compensate for the loss precipitated by a death. An unresolved death can generate multiple cut-offs in a family. Shock waves following a death can perpetuate cut-offs or create an emotionally stressful and unstable period of adjustment, when many behavior symptoms will surface.

Relation to Evolution and Science

The degree of predictability of results and findings related to applications of the Bowen theory suggests some linkages with evolution and science. Common denominators in experiences and trends may constitute a beginning foundation for systematic knowledge.

The Bowen theory conceptualizes primitive characteristics of human behavior—that is, those activities closely related to the behavior of other animals. Bowen suggests that primitive interaction can be observed most clearly and most representatively within the context of family emotional systems.

Each concept of the Bowen theory can be applied to social groups and society, as well as to the emotional processes of evolution. No change is a quantum leap in a single generation. Change is considered a product of emotional processes that extend through several generations. Change and interaction are conceptualized as triangular, and emotional projection is viewed as an effective but impairing means of precipitating change in different generations. The basic "units" of interaction in these long-term emotional processes are multigenerational families. Throughout evolution, the increasing differentiation of emotional systems suggests that there has been progress and development. However, the process of differentiation is not automatic, and predisposing factors, such as levels of anxiety and particular nodal events, are necessary before it can occur.

Much of the predictability of the Bowen theory rests on the premise that evolutionary processes can be conceptualized as a product of the balance maintained between the two opposing forces of differentiation, or individuation, and togetherness, or fusion. Although the Bowen theory emphasizes the importance of differentiating decisions and actions, differentiation is only one of two major life-forces in evolution. Togetherness is an equally strong and sometimes stronger force than differentiation. Togetherness binds and bonds individuals in a tightly knit interdependency. As some of the implications of these two concepts remain unclear, more precise research results and findings are needed before Bowen's key ideas can be related more directly to the existing knowledge of evolution and science.

Problems of Ethics

Ethics are a concern in all kinds of research with human subjects. Family life epitomizes a basic human right to many, and sacred values to others. Some attention to the problem of ethics in family research must be given by those working in this field.

Although the specific problems of ethics and family research do not fall into neat, airtight compartments, the complex interplay and interrelatedness of ethics and family research is not considered here. Rather, for discussion purposes, an artificial and somewhat arbitrary distinction is made between ethics and family research.

Definition of Problems

The many diverse problem areas in ethics and family research include the following:

1. The apparent comparatively unquestioning and inflexible allegiance of narrowly trained family researchers to scientific methodology and hypotheses makes them ideologically and operationally insensitive to the intimate personal concerns of subjects and their families. When this professional and

interpersonal rigidity occurs, research methods and findings generally result in an imbalance in the risk-benefit principle for the families involved in the research. In this kind of enterprise, high personal risks are accompanied by abnormally low individual and family benefits.

2. An "overprotection" of rights of subjects easily leads to a sacrifice of the personal and professional integrity of the researcher. Narrow and restrictive limits on research strategies owing to the rules and regulations of the legal system dilute the significance of subsequent research hypotheses and findings.

3. The use of data by third parties, such as funding agencies or government groups, is frequently contrary to the interests of both subjects and researchers. This problem raises the issue of control of research findings and the extent to which the consent of a researcher or a subject may modify a given situation.

4. Many difficulties are involved in reaching a workable consensus on appropriate ethics to observe in family research and in formulating effective guidelines to regulate interaction between researchers, subjects, and third-party groups representing broader interests in society. Ethical problems are particularly salient in family research, as our society views family interaction as intensely private and personal. Family freedom and intimacy are considered intimately related to the democratic principles of our political and social organization. Ethics in family research is consequently a widely shared and deeply emotional concern that precipitates biased input from many different groups in the private and public sectors of society.

Recommendations

In addition to guidelines for professional self-regulation, it seems appropriate to also incorporate the views of other specialists and lay persons in any formulation of ethical policies. Where in-group policing is necessary, blacklisting or professional sanctions may be used to strengthen procedural aspects involved in the application of regulations. On a broader societal basis, existing government agencies and officials may legislate and implement protection procedures or create an independent watchdog agency to take over this task (Szasz 1963).

Such regulation might consider the following points:

1. The voluntariness of the participation of both researcher and subject could be protected through such means as

a. Informed consent, including some descriptive detail about the general direction and goals of research. Such a description should optimally specify major concerns rather than discuss particular hypotheses.

b. Communication about the possible effects of participation in the research project, such as certain consequences for family relationships.

c. Restriction or prohibition of involuntary participation in research projects, perhaps with a stipulation that only adult subjects should participate.

d. Explicit terms for the withdrawal of a subject from participation in a research project and the implementation of formal and informal grievance procedures for both subjects and researchers.

2. Ethical problems in family research could be prevented by improving the quality of research training. Such professional education could include specialized degree programs and on-the-project training. Education in ethical concerns should optimally be furthered through increasing opportunities to pool experiences during the course of research.

3. Personal data collected in the course of research could be protected by counteracting procedures that overly objectify family information. The overall goal of maintaining respect for individual subjects and their families, together with the immediate objective of making direct observations, could include

a. Means to preserve the confidentiality and privacy of subjects, such as maintaining the anonymity of data and findings or purposely not recording names and other "inessential" classifying data during the course of research. These moves preserve confidentiality and privacy and at the same time keep the researcher out of possible legal binds.

b. Formulation of specific measures to control access to and use of data for nonresearch purposes. Trust is an essential ingredient of an effective researcher-subject-citizen system of relationships, and the protection of personal data is necessary for establishing confidence in research procedures.

4. Protection of the personal concerns of subjects beyond the duration of a particular research project. This extension of protection may neutralize hazardous and unintended consequences of the research process and could partly be accomplished by

a. Control of strategies used to collect initial data through the encouragement of procedures in the least violation of informal norms that conventionally regulate the dissemination of personal information. This control of strategies at best culminates in "preventive" methods of research.

b. Responsible follow-up procedures by family researchers in projects where the identity of subjects has been recorded. Later contact might be made to report some of the research findings. Such an exchange would provide an opportunity for both researcher and subject to deal with any unexpected fallout from the earlier research process.

Implications of the Bowen Theory

Principles of the Bowen theory can be applied to many kinds of social groups, identifying microsociological and macrosociological implications at both theoretical and empirical levels.

From a pragmatic standpoint, the Bowen theory can be used to conceptualize some of the contemporary behavioral and social crises.

Bowen hypothesizes that people tend to replicate patterns of family behavior in diverse social settings. Another postulation is that family and social systems function interdependently; each network of emotional forces influences the other. Both societal and environmental crises can be described from Bowen's emotional systems perspective (Bowen 1973). In these respects, the Bowen family theory has implications for social concerns beyond narrow family boundaries and for different social science disciplines.

Societal Problems

There appear to be few areas in which societal behavioral patterns are qualitatively different from family behavior patterns. Hypothetically, it is as possible to estimate societal levels of functioning as it is to estimate differentiation in families. A well-differentiated person can live an orderly life alone or in the midst of social interaction, such as densely populated conditions or a large bureaucracy. A less differentiated person cannot be productive alone, and the powerful togetherness forces draw this person into the discomfort of fusion with others. The impingement of one self on another follows, and the relationship system attempts to deal with the tensions of excess togetherness.

As society develops more urban centers, physical proximity may precipitate alienation and estrangement. The increased density also appears to predispose people to participate in many group activities, with the hope of overcoming this social distance and anxiety. Whereas in the past people used physical separation to relieve tension, effective distance from others is too difficult to accomplish in the present circumstances of a growing population. The population explosion, with its components of togetherness and fusion, is perhaps the base of many current anxieties, and may play a more significant role in human problems than is generally recognized. A point can be reached where the balance of nature is sufficiently disturbed that human life may become extinct. Fear of extinction adds further anxiety to spiraling tension in society.

The disappearance of frontiers and the accompanying sense of the decreasing size of the earth generate anxiety in society. Reactions to feeling trapped on earth are similar to feeling trapped in other situations. One such example is marriage, where spouses may describe themselves as trapped or caught. Similar anxiety produced by overcloseness appears to exist in other social groups, although these cases may not be as easy to identify.

Mobility is one way to deal with population density. In contemporary society, families are frequently required to move as part of work or careers. Also, there has been an increase in the number of occupations that require individuals to travel most of the time. The constant flow of population exchanges "ventilates" some of the overload of societal anxiety.

Projection processes are as prevalent in society as a whole as they are in families. Institutionalized "mental patients" are one of the largest groups to become an object of projection. In the course of this projection, society gains functioning strength from its benevolent posture toward "mental patients."

Other objects of projection processes in society are minority groups. The necessary conditions for such projections are sufficient anxiety and emotionally dependent human beings. The projections have operated for so long that they are extremely difficult to reverse or to change in any way. If a projection is modified successfully, the excess emotional investment is transferred to another minority group. Just as the least functional child in a family becomes more emotionally and physically impaired as the focus of the family's attention and concern, the least functional segment of society becomes more impaired by the measures that are supposed to help it.

Human and Environmental Crises

The Bowen theory is an application of systems thinking to the human universe. There has been much resistance toward this application, as it is difficult for people to question their own behavior and responsibility. When systems thinking is applied to human relationships and emotional functioning, it encourages change in one's functioning, even though any change may at the same time be resisted.

Environmental problems can be viewed as a functional part of other social problems rather than as separate from them. This systems approach suggests that environmental problems have been created by human beings themselves. People have allowed these problems to threaten their very existence.

Constructive solutions to environmental problems must be derived from a holistic viewpoint. At present, society's usual approach to environmental problems is a disjointed series of partial measures applied to narrowly defined problems. These measures are similar to an anxious family's attempts to relieve present symptoms. When corrective efforts are directed solely toward the symptoms of problems, they complicate and fixate the original problems. Giving attention only to symptoms in the environment aggravates the original problems.

Conclusion

Policies to bring about a rise in the societal level of differentiation of self are difficult to design or implement. If the most influential or powerful segment of society—sometimes political leaders—improves differentiation, this change could gradually raise the general functioning level of society.

The poweful togetherness forces in contemporary society

oppose all efforts to differentiate self. However, the improved differentiation of self of a leader in society has a beneficial effect on others. A key person in society can generally modify others' functioning in society, just as a key person in a family influences behavior in the entire emotional network.

Chapter 10

SCIENCE

Throughout the construction of his theory, Bowen made explicit use of conceptual models used in biology, such as symbiosis. Bowen's efforts have consistently striven toward the disciplines and knowledge in natural sciences such as biology, although his resulting theory cannot yet be described as rigorously scientific. Bowen goes beyond recording impressions to observe and accumulate facts. However, in spite of these systematic measures, the Bowen theory is not made up of a series of equations or formulas about highly predictable relationships between clearly defined variables. Many of Bowen's hypotheses remain relatively unsubstantiated and cannot produce the definitively accurate formulas or equations characteristic of more developed sciences.

There are some important similarities between the Bowen theory and science. In general, scientific theory may be described as a shorthand representation of patterns of phenomena that occur repeatedly and are relatively predictable. The Bowen theory consists of concepts that describe repeated and predictable patterns of behavior and that are fairly consistent with each other. Each concept has distinctive qualities but is at the same time fairly congruent with physical and natural sciences, especially with biology. For example, differentiation can be used to describe cellular processes, as well as qualities of human relationships.

An example of a fairly predictable pattern of behavior in a family is that physical symptoms of dysfunction run a more rapid and irreversible course in a tight emotional system than in a loose emotional system. Also, under most circumstances, life expectancy appears longer in a relatively calm emotional system than in an intense emotional system.

Although much of the Bowen theory may be perceived as abstract, the concepts have been developed from family observations. Attempts to concretize these abstractions may "fix" or "freeze" the theory and inhibit its primary function of summarizing empirical reality. Concretizing the abstractions of any theory makes its intrinsic limitations disproportionately narrow and rigid.

Perhaps the most useful characteristic of a theory is its potential for generating questions that can be asked in any given research situation. A scientist cannot observe behavior objectively from a posture of "knowing what is wrong." Under optimal conditions, a researcher works with a hypothesis that can be reformulated in response to observed facts rather than in reaction to opinion. This exchange between thought and observation ensures a focus on working ideas rather than on preformulated answers. A theory generated by observation and experiment becomes part of a thinking system. By contrast, conceptualization that proceeds on an intuitive basis becomes part of a feeling system. The Bowen theory is oriented toward a goal of objectivity in observation, thinking, and research.

Science suggests a frame of reference and a series of principles applicable to the study of family behavior. A scientific perspective may indicate the extent to which family interaction may be viewed as orderly behavior. The Bowen theory delineates facts of functioning in human relationship systems taking into account some of the circumstances of particular events. Bowen's systems thinking is an effort to avoid a preoccupation with why something happens. The Bowen theory focuses on what people do and largely discounts verbal explanation of why they do it. In contrast, cause-effect thinking can be viewed as an emotional response to empirical reality. Cause-effect thinking suggests a much narrower theoretical base than the intrinsic inter-relatedness of systems concepts.

Family Systems

Several theories of human behavior have been based on scientific models in attempts to conceptualize psychic and emotional functioning with some degree of objectivity. Although the medical sciences have tried to apply neurophysiology to the study of emotional functions, a solid bridge between the two fields does not exist. Most theories about emotional illness have been developed in isolation from other sciences. Bowen's use of the family systems concept is an attempt to relate human emotional functioning to the natural and physical sciences. Through the use of this frame of reference, the assumptions of the Bowen theory are generally broader than those of more conventional theories of human behavior.

Some contrasts can be drawn between Bowen's work and that of traditional scientists. For example, the scope of Bowen's perspective is comprehensive rather than selectively analytical. The assumptions underlying Bowen's conceptualizations suggest a more inclusive, long-range relatedness than many specialized scientific inquiries.

A preliminary phase in the formulation of the Bowen theory was the structuring of hard-to-define observations into facts of functioning. This effort was an attempt to find some form and consistency in the shifting, subjective world of human experience. Bowen's focus on facts of functioning eventually provided a formula for the initial stages of the development of his emotional systems theory. An example of a delineation of a functional fact is the following proposition: It is a fact that people dream, think, feel, talk, love, or hate, but what people dream, think, feel, say, love, or hate is not a fact. The content of people's dreams, thoughts, and feelings is largely determined by particular affective states that occur in response to a variety of stimuli. The affective states are manifested in many ways and in varying degrees of intensity. Experiences are behavioral consequences of given emotional systems. Functional definitions of these kinds of feeling states may be viewed as relationship facts. Although it is difficult to give an accurate functional definition of love, it is a fact that statements to another important person about the presence or absence of love in self or in the other predictably result in an emotional reaction in the relationship.

The Bowen theory developed in response to the dilemma created when conventional medical and psychiatric practices excluded family members, other than a patient's parents, from treatment. Conventional theory, which is based on the study of individuals, postulates that illness in a patient developed in relation to the parents or to other close family members. In contrast to this rather narrowly defined frame of reference, the Bowen theory views each person as an occupant of a position in an extended family emotional field or network. This network includes each parent's extended families of origin. Instead of requiring diagnosis and treatment directed only toward patient and parents, the Bowen theory considers a multitude of relationships in several generations of the same family. A person is coached on how to interact more maturely with many family members, with the goal of becoming a more responsible self.

Bowen's systems concepts describe family behavior rather than explain it in terms of cause and effect. Without using a cause-effect model, the Bowen theory defines a chain of events. In characterizing relationships between physical symptoms of dysfunction and a family emotional field, emotional factors are perceived as "having something to do with" the symptoms rather specifically causing them.

People tend to be so deeply entrenched in cause-effect thinking that the use of these concepts becomes fixed. Cause-effect thinking appears particularly rigid where conceptualizations that "explain" social relations are examined. In the fields of medicine and psychiatry, the cause-effect medical model has remained the cornerstone of most practice. The Bowen theory is considered conceptually and therapeutically out of step with medicine and conventional psychiatry in spite of its working effectiveness in treating emotional problems.

The ability to think or theorize in terms of family systems appears inversely correlated with the degree to which one is emotionally involved in one's family. The ability to observe and understand a family system depends on the level of emotional tension a therapist or researcher experiences. A molecular scientist may move beyond cause-effect thinking in his specialty area but will generally lose objectivity and revert to cause-effect thinking when participating in an emotional system. A family therapist who uses an emotional systems perspective may also be able to remain objective and to refrain from blaming others as long as emotional tension in the clinical setting is within comfortable limits. The therapist automatically reverts to cause-effect thinking in conditions of high tension.

In general, people think in terms of cause and effect most of the time in calm periods and all of the time in tense periods. In its assignment of specific causality to human problems, such thinking is frequently inaccurate, unrealistic, irrational, and overly righteous. In this respect, some contemporary scientists may be viewed as imitating their "expert" ancestors, although they may pursue different kinds of evil influences, eliminate different kinds of witches and dragons, and build different kinds of temples to benevolent spirits (Bowen 1973).

Although there are several critical differences and discrepancies between a systems frame of reference and what is generally considered to be the realm of science, there are some important similarities. Systems thinking tends to be a more general and a more comprehensive means of description and conceptualization than is usually found in science. Scientific analysis does not adequately account for the interdependency implicit in systems thinking. However, prediction remains a primary goal for both systems thinking and science, and the thrust of both kinds of inquiry is similar.

When a family is selected as a unit of study in scientific research, boundaries are defined in terms of membership and nonmembership. Although ascribed membership (being born or adopted into a family) is generally a more potent emotional relatedness than achieved membership (being married into a family), both kinds of membership are significant within the complexities of overlapping and interdependent relationships.

A family may be regarded as a large system when viewed from a multigenerational perspective, even though family membership may be more restricted than membership in social or work systems. Examining several generations in the same family increases objectivity, as this focus broadens the basis for comparing different processes and behavior. This broad definition of family is relatively alien to conventional definitions of family, although research based exclusively on nuclear families is necessarily fragmented and unrepresentative of the entire emotional field of a family. Scientific inquiry may be more productive if it is focused on the extended parts of a family system.

Scientific Reality

Science is a way of perceiving and describing phenomena. Science is widely thought of as "superior" knowledge in that it is derived from relatively objective observation and records of changes in phenomena. The ultimate test of a scientific proposition is generally considered the verifiability and accuracy of its predictions (Cotgrove 1967).

Through observations and experiments based on a perceived underlying order of varied physical and chemical phenomena, scientists have articulated discovered regularities as compact scientific laws. Laws that have been combined and related to each other become theories, which are regarded as a reliable basis for further calculation and prediction. A scientific theory is essentially a system of information-laden descriptions of already-known facts and a system of general explanations. In physics, for example, the theory of relativity and the quantum theory are inclusive theories with which most laws of physics can be explained. Since these theories explain many laws, they can also explain a multitude of different phenomena. An important objective of science is the construction of such comprehensive theories (Zetterberg 1965). Science defines the interdependence of phenomena. In families, this focus can be on the complex network of emotional relationships in several generations (Kerlinger 1964).

Scientific knowledge tends to emphasize shared uniformities and regularities in phenomena. The accepted reference point of "natural law" within physical sciences suggests that there are certain relatively fixed or settled aspects of human behavior. In contrast, religion and the humanities focus on unique, unpredictable, and unexpected aspects of human behavior. The supernatural and miraculous are thought to be manifested infrequently rather than continuously or periodically. They are perceived to break through natural laws by interrupting a sequence of predictable events (Darwin 1896). As a result of some of these distinctive differences, science is frequently considered antireligious or irreligious.

Science and evolutionary frames of reference juxtapose human beings and animals with the implication that there are ways to know more about human beings through studying animals. Although this kind of thinking is much criticized, a comparison of human beings and animals implies no more of a lowering of human dignity than does a recognition of the origin of the species. The essence of creative organic evolution may be that it produces completely new and higher characters that are in no way indicated or even implicit in the preceding state of evolution where they originated (Lorenz 1954).

One of the most significant revolutions in the natural sciences during the last thirty years took place in our understanding of animal behavior and human links to the animal world. Primatology and sociobiology are two of the research endeavors that point out the relatedness of human and animal behavior. Until this time, science's unwillingness to reappraise the evolutionary basis of human society appears to have done much to maintain the traditional religious doctrine of human uniqueness, which upholds the concept of human separateness and distinctiveness from other animals.

From an historical perspective, science is a relatively new kind of knowledge. The view that human relations are not yet generally considered proper subjects for serious scientific study could perhaps be substantiated by public opinion measures. Resistance to the application of scientific methods to human behavior is in some respects the result of tradition. Contemporary conventional social theory and social thought tend to regard social problems as essentially legalistic or moralistic. These "literary" perspectives, which are products of literary traditions, are deeply entrenched in the emotional and aesthetic feelings of people and are difficult to change. Although vested interests in society's status quo generally oppose scientific "progress" in these areas, scientific findings appear to carry with them certain compulsions for acceptance. As scientific methods provide increasing numbers of reliable predictions, scientific criteria become increasingly widely accepted as decisive (Lundberg 1947).

Scientific Process

Scientific process is the objective study and prediction of relations among varied phenomena. This enterprise has a unique characteristic of self-correction. Checks are used to control and verify research findings to attain dependable knowledge. The formulation and application of theories are means of attaining increased objectivity (Kerlinger 1964).

Owing to the many difficulties inherent in empirical measurement, a scientist often has to accept an explanation "in principle" (Bertalanffy 1968). Scientific concepts characteristic of organized wholes or systems include interaction, sum, mechanization, centralization, competition, and finality (Bertalanffy 1968). Laboratory control in applying these concepts varies considerably among different scientific disciplines. For example, the solar system has never been brought into the laboratory (Lundberg 1947).

Scientific research moves from a phase of definition, during which terminology is formulated, to a phase of proposition and theory construction (Zetterberg 1965). In both stages of development, facts are accumulated and categorized until laws emerge. A distinction that can be made between findings and laws relates to the different degrees of generality and empirical support that findings and laws have. "Lawlike" propositions may be confirmed into systems or theories depending on the strictness of the selected criteria of verification (Zetterberg 1965).

One paradigm of scientific assertion is frequently expressed as "If so . . . , then so." This model indicates that certain deductions can be drawn from a specific set of circumstances. This criterion of predictability is considered an indispensable component of scientific truth, and it is a cornerstone of the Bowen theory. In more developed sciences, equations are used to represent rich, substantive concepts and highlight relationships between concepts. Where possible, the overly simplistic and commonly accepted language of causality may be replaced by the formulation of relationships that describe systems (Buckley 1968).

Science is frequently an analytical process that includes isolating variables and tracing their relationship with each other. In this way, some systems and subsystems of interrelated elements can be mapped out (Cotgrove 1967). This process involves abstracting certain aspects of complex phenomena. Although some subsystems of natural phenomena may be isolated and examined with respect to their functions for larger systems, families are very complex and difficult to examine in relation to larger social systems. Bowen focuses on a family as a relatively independent emotional unit.

Modern science tends to move in a direction of ever-increasing specialization. This specialization appears necessary because of the vast amounts of available data and the complexity of techniques and theoretical structures used. Such a development has precipitated a breakdown of science as one integrated realm and a move toward the compartmentalization of different sciences (Demerath 1967).

One difference between general systems theory and more traditional sciences is that characteristics of organization such as wholeness, growth, differentiation, hierarchical order, dominance, and control appear in systems theory but are not generally found in sciences such as physics. The many levels of organization constitute a frequently cited unifying principle in a systems perspective (Demerath 1967). The fragmentation of any single science into schools is not uncommon, even in as rigorous a discipline as mathematics. What is striking in behavioral science is how unsympathetic and even hostile to one another such schools tend to be (Kaplan 1964).

Although fact gathering is necessary in all kinds of research, science does not primarily consist of data collection. Without a hypothesis, a researcher cannot determine which facts are important for substantiation or refutation and which facts are less significant. Effective experiments cannot be made without several preconceived ideas, and the adequate statement of research problems is a critical research activity.

A research problem generally involves the definition of a particular relationship between two or more variables. A hypothesis is a conjectural statement or tentative proposition that begins to specify the nature of this relationship. Optimally, hypotheses incorporate theory or part of a theory into testable or near-testable forms. A hypothesis may be viewed as a bridge between theory and empirical inquiry, and it may be one of the most useful tools invented to develop dependable knowledge (Kerlinger 1964).

Human Nature and Scientific Process

Recent developments in the natural sciences suggest that human beings are not unique and that human nature, like a body, may be largely a product of evolution (Ardrey 1966). Although some studies have examined human reflexes or reactive behavior, the observation of spontaneous human behavior was undertaken largely by vitalists or mystics until comparatively recently.

Perception of and participation in scientific activities is limited by inherent personal characteristics. Human perception of relationships between systems in the universe is very much influenced by the system of human nature itself. All living species, particularly human beings, can be viewed as a system. Through striving for some understanding of the inner workings of nature, a scientist is a mechanist or a physicalist in believing that the universe is a unit that can be explained, at least in principle (Lorenz 1971). Most human interests to date have focused on a scientific or systems understanding of the universe outside of self, and not on human relationship systems. Even though a physical technology may be gradually supplanted by a psychological technology, science appears to have relatively conquered the universe while at the same time forgetting or even actively suppressing investigation into the essential characteristics of human nature (Bertalanffy 1967).

One important influence on the reticence shown in this area of study is that human beings are necessarily instruments of observation in the scientific process. A posture of objectivity is perhaps one of the most difficult achievements toward which a human being can work. With view to this difficulty, there can be an inclination to become overly rigid in conceptualizing research on behavior. A danger associated with the necessity of theoretical orientation for a scientific observer, for example, is the possibility of premature closure of ideas. The use of concepts that demand exact definitions of meaning and terms may serve to inhibit an observer who would not normally operate with such controls (Kaplan 1964).

The Bowen theory is based on the observation that similarities exist in all forms of animal behavior. The concepts reflect some awareness of the fact that scientific knowledge has provided a more conscious view of human life. Human beings perceive the universe in entirely different ways than do animals, even though in many respects people's behavior may not be so different. Human beings alone know that their bodies and behavior have evolved and are still evolving and that existence can be placed into a conceptual framework of space and time. Although people have limited options, they possess purpose and exercise choice to a unique degree. Although much human behavior may be perceived as emotionally reactive and responsive, only human beings have a conscious and orderly sense of values.

Accumulated knowledge, though perhaps a relatively ineffective "force" compared to emotional reactivity, may be important in evolution. Through knowledge, especially scientific knowledge, people can exert some control over their lives and a degree of influence in their own evolution. However, this power may frequently be potential rather than actual, and possible choices are inevitably bound by strict limits (Simpson 1949). Belief in the human capacity to increase awareness through knowledge replaces a robotlike concept of human nature with a systems concept. A systems concept includes imminent activity as well as outwardly directed reactivity and has the potential to account for the specificity of human nature and human culture as well as similarities with animal behavior (Bertalanffy 1968).

There are many opposing views within science. These do not appear to reflect irreducible differences between physical and biological laws as much as the complexity of life processes. One way to overcome some of these contradictions and inconsistencies may be to focus on ways in which systems components are organized (Buckley 1968). By a focus on systems' interrelatedness, common denominators between different disciplines may be identified more clearly.

Society and Science

The scientific understanding of inanimate and animate phenomena is part of a broader process of secularization in society. In many respects, modern science has supplanted the view that human beings were specially created and are subject to divine guidance. Purposive vital urges are symbolic descriptions of evolution rather than realistic scientific explanations (Huxley 1942). The development of science has brought about a demystification of society and life processes.

Science has altered the frame of reference used by most people in contemporary industrialized society. Systems theory offers a new and different perspective on society, even though this frame of reference cannot always be clearly articulated. Owing to its recent development, systems thinking is not widely practiced and is used by only a few professionals, academicians, and researchers (Bertalanffy 1968). Although some parallels have been drawn with engineering, systems concepts can represent living phenomena adequately.

Science has revealed that many facts fail to accord with the wishes or logical preconceptions of human beings. Faced with the necessity for some kind of organization, society faces the dilemma of seeking goals that are not in accord with the limits set by nature (Huxley 1942). One adaptation is to focus scientific investigation on examining limits to which social organization must minimally conform if it is to be viable. Human freedom exists when a group is not subject to widespread victimization through ignorance of the relationship between natural laws and human desires and aspirations.

In recent years, scientists have become more naturalistic in their studies of animal behavior. As a consequence, society has begun to acknowledge the possibility that individual and social behavior may be based on a wide range of animallike reactiveness. Whereas past studies of animal behavior were based on observations of animals in captivity, recent studies have examined animal behavior in relatively free environmental conditions. Freud's generation knew comparatively little about these kinds of broad patterns of animal instincts. Society's acceptance of Freud's theories was conditioned before discoveries about animal behavior in natural settings were made (Ardrey 1968). Recent findings from animal studies have provided additional support for the development of the Bowen theory.

Although group behavior is widely acknowledged as more predictable than individual behavior, the application of scientific and systems perspectives to human behavior has been resisted by those who hold traditional beliefs and who view such endeavors as attempts to control relations in society. In society's everyday activities, some degree of predictability is assumed for minimal social organization. If human behavior were unpredictable, people would not be able to have viable relationships with each other (Cotgrove 1967).

When social behavior is a focus for scientific research, relatively predictable characteristics are suggested and described in the hypotheses formulated. "Understanding," a subjective state in which one feels that things make sense, is qualitatively distinct from scientific proof, which depends on the actual demonstration of the interrelatedness of phenomena. As science is ultimately based on verification, one goal is to discover ways of testing "understanding" empirically (Cotgrove 1967). In its applications to social phenomena, science may be described as a search for constancies and invariants in social behavior. Scientific laws are not mere generalizations that are made when facts have been established. The laws themselves play a significant part in determining what the facts are (Kaplan 1964).

Scientific inquiry is frequently specific and limited. Scientists or researchers do not generally study society but focus instead on some restricted portion or aspect of it. Observation also frequently consists of an active search for what is ·not readily apparent or is even hidden. Through exposure or discovery, an intimate, sustained, and productive relationship between scientist and social phenomena may be facilitated (Kaplan 1964).

Science is frequently thought to have added a fatalistic or deterministic dimension to interpretations of social reality. However, if society has been evolving automatically under the influence of irresistible impersonal forces, this assertion is far from suggesting that individuals must submit to these forces. Science has increased social freedom in that one can be said to have a more reliable range of options when one's limits in relation to the universe are defined. Social resistance to such a science of society may itself be described as a product of social education largely derived from deduction, dogma, revelation, and guesswork (Keller 1931).

Conclusion

Bowen's research on interrelationships and behavior within families is distinct from cause-effect studies that generally focus on fewer variables. From the Bowen systems perspective, interaction within the whole family is examined, whereas in cause-effect studies only certain aspects of the whole are analyzed.

Although the prediction of behavior is an important long-range goal for both scientific analysis and systems thinking, the "essence" of the two approaches is different. Scientific analysis generally consists of explanations articulated in terms of "why," whereas systems thinking focuses more on functional descriptions of "how" parts relate to the whole and to each other.

As the most significant family memberships are generally

ascribed, it is frequently easier to isolate variables related to behavior in these groups than in less clearly defined work and social systems. The probability of attaining some degree of precision or reality in the study of families may be markedly greater than in the study of other groups. As family interaction is a primary means of socialization throughout life, a family is a significant emotional system to research in an overall effort to describe some of the principles of the most complex human interaction. By a close examination of family dependencies, concepts for a general theory of human behavior can be developed. It is perhaps only through an adequate knowledge of basic principles of family interaction that behavior in other social settings will be understood.

Chapter 11

EVOLUTION

Bowen (1973) suggests that human beings are intimately related to less evolved forms of animal life and that different levels of behavior are more similar than is generally recognized. A proposition generated by this hypothesized kinship with other animals is that emotional illness can be viewed as a dysfunction of the characteristics human beings share with other animals.

Evolutionary processes provide a comprehensive context in which families may be examined. Evolutionary processes tend to create, maintain, or destroy families. Family interaction is an integral part of broad natural systems that serve primary functions of procreation, socialization, and adaptation. Emotional systems, which are considered present in behavior at all levels of evolution, operate in ways that reflect different stages of phylogenetic history. Although emotional systems have almost constnat influence over human lives, this influence is usually rationalized as self-determined (Kerr 1972). In fact, human perception may be distorted to the extent that behavior is regarded as anything other than a product of emotional systems.

Evolutionary changes can be either regular or irregular, and the types of change may be markedly different from each other. The various products of evolutionary processes are particularly salient: interdependency, togetherness, differentiation, dislocation, and adaptiveness.

Any measure that attempts to represent the time dimensions of evolutionary change is so vast tht figures are usually beyond comprehension. Estimates of the period of time that has elapsed since the earth was formed differ and are constantly being revised. Although it is generally recognized that human evolution is a slow process, from an overall viewpoint it has occurred fairly rapidly. If the earth was formed about four billion years ago and the first life appeared on earth only about five hundred million years ago, seven eighths of the earth's existence did not experience any life. It has been predicted that the earth will last another ten billion to fifteen billion years before it becomes a dead planet. We are faced with additional awesome data if we consider that human beings first walked upright about seven hundred fifty thousand years ago, and first became "civilized" twenty thousand years ago. People began to read and write about ten thousand years ago.

One way to bring these complex developmental processes into sharper relief, so that the relative rapidity of some of the evolutionary changes may be seen, is to convert the earth's four-billion-year time span into a unit of one hundred years. Using this unit as a base, one can say that the earth was formed one hundred years ago, the first primitive human life appeared twelve years ago, and people walked upright about seven days ago. A person became a thinking being about four days ago, and some evidence of civilization appeared at this time. Reading and writing skills were acquired approximately two hours ago, Jesus lived for a fraction of a second only twenty-four minutes ago, and Columbus discovered America six minutes ago. In relation to the timing of these events, the earth would be expected to exist for another three hundred and fifty more years before it would become a dead planet (Bowen 1973).

Human life is one of the most highly developed forms of animal existence. The most rapid form of human evolution has been what may be described as a disproportionate increase in the size of the brain. Since highly developed forms of life usually have a greater probability of becoming extinct, as refinement of function is concomitant with increased dependency, the human brain may be an overspecialization that could ultimately lead to extinction of the human race. This idea contradicts the more widespread opinion that human beings can dominate the environment and can choose between perpetuating themselves and destroying the planet. In relation to these and other broad evolutionary trends and changes, the Bowen theory is an attempt to view human life as an integral part of other kinds of life on earth.

Evolutionary Perspective

After observing a wide variety of behavior in families, Bowen purposely selected an evolutionary-biological model as the most effective way to describe and define multigenerational emotional processes. This theoretical model is sensitive to both segmental and comprehensive multigenerational interdependencies and provides a context for depicting some of the most significant intricacies and complexities in family relationships. An evolutionary perspective suggests that human nature is related to less evolved animal forms. One aspect of this emphasis on the basic animal qualities of human nature is a related deemphasis on the widely held view that human nature is unique and distinct from other kinds of animal life.

An evolutionary-biological frame of reference highlights the

234 The Bowen Family Theory and Its Uses

relative powerlessness and defenselessness of human nature. From this perspective, human freedom to act appears to be bound by strict and narrow limits, and the related ability to change self seems extremely restricted. Faced with complex and powerful external and internal forces, the most effective human efforts to survive as individuals largely consist of ways to avoid or escape the inexorable and merciless laws of evolution. Even though the species may be protected through evolution, individual well-being is not.

Adaptation describes a key process in evolution. Animal and human adaptive mechanisms generally facilitate development of greater elasticity or flexibility in behavior. Darwin suggested that the highest stage of evolution in moral culture would be to recognize that human beings have the capacity to control thoughts (Darwin 1871). Development and retrogression are both adaptations to an environment, however, and the present widespread breakdown of family forms and functions (Cooper 1970) can be viewed as a phase of retrogressive adaptation in evolution.

Evolutionary Processes

Evolution describes life's interrelatedness more clearly than do other theoretical frameworks. Competition, an evolutionary process, may precipitate overspecialization, which frequently becomes a condition of extinction (Simpson 1949). Irregularities, dislocations, or disharmony in evolutionary processes may be products of developments in competition and overspecialization.

Opportunism may also be observed in evolutionary processes, and the course of evolution has been described as typically following the lead of opportunity rather than plan. From this point of view, evolutionary parallelism and convergence may be conceptualized as consequences of the development of the same kinds of opportunities by different groups of organisms (Simpson 1949).

A fairly well substantiated hypothesis about evolutionary processes is the proposition that organisms tend to increase in size (Simpson 1949). However, the number of effective adaptive characteristics of an organism appears more significant for its progressive evolution than an increase in size. A key characteristic of an organism's effective adaptability is its usefulness under the conditions in which it lives (Simpson 1949). Extinction is the ultimate outcome of regressive adaptation, which can be described as changes or paralysis in the organism-environment relationship that inhibit progressive adaptation (Simpson 1949).

Pierre Teilhard de Chardin's concept of atomism, the universal trend toward granulation, is another way of describing evolutionary processes. Atomism takes place in relation not only to the atoms and molecules of inorganic matter but also to plants, animals, and even human consciousness (Teilhard 1970). Teilhard's "law of recurrence" in evolution describes successive temporal phases that develop into a new plurality or atomism, and a higher synthesis. Teilhard's use of the concept of entropy, the dissipation of energy, and his thesis of development toward continuously heightened consciousness and increased spontaneity suggest that human beings evolve as their powers of reflection and thought increase (Teilhard 1970). Evolutionary processes appear to move toward a greater plasticity of behavior, with increased learning and insight (Lorenz 1965).

A serious consideration of the influence of evolutionary processes on human behavior challenges the central assumptions of rational though—for example, that human beings are able to control their lives. An evolutionary perspective suggests that human behavior is not attributed to factors lying solely within the human experience (Ardrey 1968). Furthermore, from an evolutionary perspective, any single stimulus cannot usefully be conceptualized as causing a process in an otherwise inert system. However, a stimulus may modify some of the many complex processes in a comprehensive and already autonomously active system (Bertalanffy 1968).

Evolutionary theory, although considered scientifically weak by many researchers owing to its tendencies to emphasize "single factors" or unilinear direction, is potentially the greatest unifying theory of animal and human behavior. A focus on evolutionary processes can give meaning and some coherence to a wide range of seemingly chaotic facts.

Human Nature

Huxley and other social theorists have suggested that human adaptation to the environment may be achieved by manipulation of the environment to fit human needs and desires (Keller 1931). From this perspective, human beings become rulers of the universe. People cannot oppose the forces that produced them, however, and as human survival and interests are an integral part of the natural schema of the universe, their dependence on natural forces must be acknowledged. Power over nature can only be achieved to the extent that people are able to adapt or conform to natural laws, since people are in large part the helpless playthings of natural forces (Keller 1931). Knowing how natural laws operate affords some degree of control by making obedience to the laws possible.

For the last thirty years, naturalists and zoologists have researched animal behavior in natural conditions rather than in captivity or domestication. Some attention has been paid to patterns of behavior that appear to be shared by both animals and human beings (Ardrey 1968). For example, the expression of aggressive drives may preserve rather than destroy the life of both animals and human beings (Lorenz 1963). Furthermore, many human problems appear to be derived from conditions associated with the loss of the outward expression of instincts, such as domestication (Darwin 1896) or the overcrowding of the population and increased urbanization.

Darwin's description of natural selection from random variations denies the idea of any given "divine" plan in the universe. He suggested that variations favoring survival are preserved by automatic natural selection processes and not by any form of divine intervention. For Darwin, the sum of accidents of life acts upon the sum of accidents of variation and provide a mechanical or materialistic system in which human beings try to account for changes that have appeared and continue to appear in living forms (Barzun 1941).

Although Darwin's model of human nature is undoubtedly limited, he viewed more evolved animals as relatively free, nonspecialized "creatures of curiosity." A human being may be defined as a specialist in nonspecialization, who possesses only a few distinctive motor patterns with a small degree of differentiation. Human behavior is perceived as consisting of a wide range of general rather than highly specialized motor patterns. Furthermore, this characteristic flexibility in human behavior contrasts with the relatively rigid adaptive behavior of less evolved animal forms (Lorenz 1971). The capacity of human beings to utilize a wide range of behavior patterns may depend on their having fewer instinctual drives than other animals. The degree of variability of potential forms and types of action may be one of the most important characteristics of the human condition. Flexibility tends to enhance human adaptiveness and contributes to evolutionary developments (Parsons 1966).

The overall trend in human evolution may be conceptualized as an increase in this generalized adaptive capacity. Overspecialization, with its attendant rigidity and lack of adaptiveness, appears to be one of the greatest threats to extinction. Bowen suggests that the brain tends to blur instinctive awareness of the vital human need to adapt to the environment, as people are too preoccupied with attempts to manipulate the environment.

Means-end capacities, conscious awareness, ideation and even inventive ideation are found, to some degree, throughout the animal kingdom. Although speech and introspection are the sole prerogative of human beings, primitive forms of these processes can be observed in a variety of animal behaviors (Tolman 1932). Complex emotions appear to be experienced primarily by more evolved animals, and human behavior is not as cerebral as is generally believed. Human ideas frequently derive more from emotional imitation than from intellectual reason (Darwin 1871).

Learning and spontaneity may be described as more significant in human life than in most animal life (Darwin 1871). "Instinct" and "drive" do not necessarily denote disorderly, unmanageable tendencies. Procreation and child rearing, for example, are more or less orderly processes. A related idea to consider is that a recognition of order in instinctive behavior may increase freedom or choice in behavior more than a denial of instincts (Keller 1931).

Society

Society is not merely a human product. Cultural values shape patterns of social interaction but do not determine them. Society may be thought of as being more a consequence of an evolutionary past than as a result of a cultural present (Ardrey 1968). It has been suggested that behavior may be as characteristic of human nature as the shape of a human thigh bone or the configuration of nerves in a corner of the human brain (Ardrey 1966).

Insofar as there is a continuous tendency for entropy to increase in human affairs (Buckley 1968), people can aspire to only limited control over their lives. They may, perhaps, choose between alternative postures to the natural forces that move all living beings but not from among the unlimited range of options that they frequently imagine they have.

Human beings appear to be able to check their aggressive drives through social contacts and rituals. These interactions do not weaken or hinder the drives' species-preserving function. One of the greatest dangers of the human aggressive drive has been defined by Freud and some of his followers as its unpredictability. Freud showed that lack and deprivation of social contact and rituals facilitate aggression (Lorenz 1963). People seem to need a variety of contacts with other human beings to preserve themselves as a living species. Without these controls of interdependency, aggression becomes a destructive force in society.

The evolutionary origin of the most complex social organizations has frequently been considered related to kinship groupings (Parsons 1966). Some preliterate societies remain at highly undifferentiated levels of social, cultural, and personality development, whereas more evolved societies appear to be moving toward both progressive individuation and progressive centralization. For one social structure to emerge from another, grouping around certain individuals may be necessary (Bertalanffy 1968).

A society may be most adequately defined as a living, open system that as a whole functions in accordance with the interdependence of its parts (Buckley 1968). In more complex groupings, parts assume certain properties because they are components of the larger whole. Some research findings indicate that differences between inert matter and living material are based not on intrinsic qualitative differences but on the way substances are organized. In applying this concern to social organization, it can be postulated that a rigid differentiation of parts within society poses problems of integration for the whole (Parson 1966), whereas continuity between society and culture generally enhances the quality of life of the whole (Parsons 1971).

There is no single rate of evolution in society. Evolution is by no means an overall cosmic influence that has changed all living things in a regular way throughout the earth's history. Structural change and diversification have been described as two specific kinds of evolutionary processes that have produced some of the most significant developments in societies. However, the rates of these changes are highly variable, and discrepancies and discontinuities are the rule rather than the exception (Simpson 1949).

Bowen Theory as an Evolutionary Theory

In some respects, the Bowen theory can be considered an evolutionary theory. Bowen's concepts describe qualities of emotional interdependencies between members of successive generations. "Vertical" relationships and patterns of emotional dependency manifested in patterns of interaction between members of different generations can be viewed as minuscule prototypes of evolutionary change. Although the overall direction of evolutionary development in a family and in wider society cannot be measured with precision, each system appears to adapt and function in relation to other systems and to the whole.

The Bowen family theory conceptualizes basic patterns of interdependency as principles of process and organization in evolution. The eight basic concepts of the Bowen theory address the most significant facets of the ways in which relationships provide closure or opportunities for individuation. These selective representations of empirical reality describe trends in family interaction and broader social processes.

Differentiation of Self. The emotional process of differentiation in human relationship systems can be viewed as an integral part of evolution. Following Darwin's contributions in the mid-nineteenth century, biologists and zoologists have used the concept of differentiation to describe evolutionary processes of increasing complexity in biological specificity and functioning, and an increasing multiplicity of zoological species. Increasing heterogeneity or differentiation in organic phenomena is frequently specified by concepts such as adaptation, natural selection, and survival of the fittest. Adaptation, maladaptation, natural selection, extinction and survival of the fittest suggest particular aspects of differentiation.

About the time that mid-nineteenth-century biologists and zoologists began to describe evolution, social theorists produced parallel formulations for social processes. For example, before Darwin published *The Origin of Species*, Herbert Spencer, the English social philosopher, published a paper, "Development Hypothesis," that described and defended a theory of organic evolution with applications to biology, psychology, ethics, and sociology (Ruitenbeek 1963). Spencer emphasized the importance of differentiation, or increasing specificity, and heterogeneity within evolution.

Emile Durkheim, a sociologist who wrote at the turn of the century, also viewed evolution as diversification. He emphasized the importance of qualities of social cohesiveness or solidarity in evolutionary processes. Durkheim suggested that social structures and functions in societies become increasingly heterogeneous through time.

Bowen views differentiation as a vital emotional process that influences each individual's behavior. He conceptualizes families as primary units within societies and evolutionary change. However, Bowen does not suggest that differentiation is an "automatic" or irreversible development.

Bowen's key process of differentiation specifies characteristics of goal directedness, increased awareness of self, and more effective functioning in relationship systems. Individuals and families considered less differentiated frequently behave in symptomatic ways and are more emotionally reactive in their responsiveness to others. Lower levels of differentiation represent less advanced stages of evolution, and higher levels of differentiation are conceptualized as optimal or effective adaptations for self and families.

Triangles. Bowen's concept of triangles can be used to describe and define basic microscopic and macroscopic evolutionary changes. If the delineation of triangles in families provides reliable indicators of patterns of intergenerational change, the delineation of triangles in other human and animal groups may provide indicators of broad emotional processes, including evolutionary change.

The concept of differentiation of self implies that human behavior in less evolved states may be conceptualized as emotionally reactive and largely undirected by thought processes. At earlier stages of development, individuals can be considered undifferentiated in their functioning and in their relationships with others. Less evolved human beings are predictably influenced by the primitive or instinctive needs of the groups in which they participate.

The concept of triangles suggests that patterns of emotional forces in less evolved behavior are more intense and more easily identifiable than are patterns of interdependency in more evolved behavior. Reactivity and repeated sequences of interaction are more predictable where triangles are more intense. Triangular patterns of emotional forces in more evolved conditions are less intense and less easily identifiable. Predictability is less accurate and less apparent in more developed stages, and chain reactions are shorter and less easy to identify because the triangles in the later stages are more flexible.

The fact that a person can change self to a certain extent indicates that individuals are able to play some part in broad evolutionary processes. When one is aware of the predictability of emotional processes, one can initiate change in relation to these forces, thereby acting voluntarily. One can, of course, refuse this opportunity to create self and participate in evolution by opting to act automatically and choosing to have little plan or direction throughout life.

Nuclear Family Emotional System. A goal related to viewing self in evolutionary change is increasing self-awareness within the context of the nuclear family emotional system. An individual is able to assume responsibility for the position taken in a nuclear family emotional system and thereby control it to some extent. A more evolved posture in the nuclear family emotional system implies that one can maintain emotional contact with this system and simultaneously think and direct behavior as an autonomous self.

Knowing the most predictable patterns of behavior in one's family is synonymous with being aware of the less evolved forms of behavior in one's family. Observing and at least partially understanding these processes are preconditions of being able to control one's posture in relation to evolutionary forces. Only when human beings recognize some of the influences of evolutionary forces and automatic behavior on their lives will they be able to be more than pawns in the processes of evolutionary change.

Family Projection Process. Family projection describes microscopic evolutionary change insofar as this concept outlines ways in which parents project their undifferentiation and anxiety to one or more offspring. Children who remain outside a projection process in a nuclear family appear to have a level of differentiation higher than that of their parents. When a nuclear family emotional system produces a strong projection process, the differentiation level of a "projected" child is generally lower than that of the parents. A child who becomes the "object" of the family projection develops an "impaired" self. The responses demanded of this child are directly related to the emotional needs of the parents and to the needs of the nuclear and extended families. A child who is object of the parental projection may function in the family or in the wider society as a "savior." or "prima donna," rather than as a patient. In each kind of projection, the relationship between the parents is stabilized by the processes involved, and a minuscule evolutionary adaptation is made.

Emotional Cut-off. Any discussion of the concept of emotional cut-off in relation to evolution is highly tentative and hypothetical. As more data about animal behavior in natural surroundings are accumulated, the identified behavior patterns shared by both animals and human beings may increase.

The emotional forces that influence cut-offs between human beings may be viewed as an integral part of attraction-repulsion activities and drives among all living creatures. The phenomenon documented as repulsion between animals can be considered the moving force in emotional cut-offs between human beings. Insofar as emotional cut-off is a far-reaching activity rather than an intrapsychic defense, the propensity to cut off from intimate others may be a human manifestation of an animal drive. Emotional cut-off can be described as an unlearned developmental response that is deeply rooted in evolutionary processes.

Different phases of evolution and rates of evolutionary change may be characterized by varying distortions of cut-offs in human relationships. When more cut-offs occur, the evolutionary phase may be an anxious period, with differentiation of self being either difficult or impossible. Under these conditions, a society may be assessed as regressive rather than progressive. The existence of fewer cut-offs suggests an evolutionary phase where relationship systems are flexible, with individuals acting for self rather than reacting to anxiety. A decrease in the number of emotional cut-offs may be followed by less loneliness and more effective communication between generations. Societies at this evolutionary stage may be progressive in their qualities of interpersonal behavior and achievements.

Genealogical research into relatively recent generations and the investigation of events in earlier periods of time are ways in which individuals or societies may avoid some of the detrimental aspects of being cut off from the evolutionary past. A natural history perspective on the present may also have a beneficial bridging effect on any estrangement with the evolutionary past.

If emotional cut-offs between animals precipitate aggressive behavior, an examination of cut-offs among human beings may lead to a greater understanding of aggression and other kinds of human behavior. Although the concept of emotional cut-off describes processes opposite to those of fusion, these two relationship phenomena—both products of anxiety—are not qualitatively different from each other. Animal and human aggression may be intimately related to emotional cut-off as well as to fusion and togetherness in evolutionary adaptation.

Even though the concept of emotional cut-off cannot be described with reference to specific linkages with evolution, behavior that cuts off close relationships appears to be basic in most animal forms. Human beings are not so far removed from their evolutionary origins that they can easily circumvent these primitive ways of dealing with anxiety and intimacy. Although bridging a cut-off may be achieved more or less successfully by conscious and sustained efforts, there is evidence that the human tendency to cut off intimate relationships is automatic and difficult to reverse.

Multigenerational Transmission Process. The scope of

multigenerational transmission process is not limited by the range of generations in which emotional forces operate. The concept describes continuing processes that are activated over succeeding generations and that have consequences of fluctuating levels of functioning and differentiation in the related nuclear families. Multigenerational transmission is a versatile concept that can begin to document minuscule evolutionary processes over many generations.

The clarity and usefulness of the concept of multigenerational transmission is restricted by the current lack of available or measurable data for accurately representing the quality of emotional processes in families over many generations. Many years of systematic empirical research are needed to begin to verify some of the hypotheses and propositions suggested by this concept. Although a fairly adequate reconstruction of short-term multigenerational transmission processes can be derived from genealogical data, any projections regarding specific charac- teristics of long-range multigenerational transmission processes may represent little more than "educated guesses."

Sibling Position. Owing to the lack of multigenerational data, only tentative propositions can be used to describe a relationship between sibling position and evolution. Assuming there is a correlation between sibling position and the capacity to differentiate self, some projections about changing levels of differentiation in past generations can be made, especially for more clearly defined sibling positions, such as oldest, youngest and only chid. For example, the sibling position of an oldest could be considered more conducive to increased differentiation than other sibling positions. On a multigenerational level, it could be hypothesized that differentiation in past generations has been more frequent in periods when oldests were significant participants in the extended family system.

It can be postulated that in less evolved phases, behavior is determined more by sibling position or functioning sibling position than by conscious efforts to differentiate self. When a person lives by self-selected beliefs, thoughts, and goals, the programmed effects of a particular sibling position are less influential than when behavior is emotionally responsive and reactive. Although sibling position may be an inhibiting influence for a person who is less differentiated, a more differentiated individual in the same sibling position may be less confined by sibling position programming.

In considering microscopic evolutionary changes between generations, the sibling position of the same sex parent appears to have a more significant influence on a person's emotional programming than the sibling position of the opposite sex parent. For example, an oldest has a more "crystallized" sibling position if that oldest's parents, grandparents, and great-grandparents were also oldests. Toman (1972) has undertaken more detailed studies on the interplay of these influences than has Bowen, and has specified a particular range of characteristic conflicts between members in two different generations. Bowen generalizes that an oldest son tends to pick up a family's expectations for sons, whereas an oldest daughter generally picks up expectations for daughters. Parents may view an only child as an emotional son or daughter, regardless of the child's actual sex. Where these patterns are repeated through several generations, they may be tentatively conceptualized as microevolutionary trends.

Emotional Process in Society. To some extent, the concept of emotional process in society attempts to describe the quality and diversity of broad trends in evolution. One related hypothesis is that when togetherness forces in society are strong, differentiation and individual contributions are neutralized or negated and societal trends are regressive in general. The suppression of individuality impedes constructively adaptive evolutionary growth, leading to less flexibility and actualization of human potential in the societal emotional system.

Propositions of this kind are partly derived from observations of social trends in contemporary and earlier historical periods. For example, one repeated phenomenon is that great leaders or innovators have been "sacrificed" to the wishes of the masses or castigated by majority public opinion. Some of the herding activities observed in the animal kingdom may be so basic in life that parallel thrusts and tendencies surface in human behavior. Although generalizations from observing animal behavior cannot be applied directly to understanding people, there appear to be some common denominators, such as herding and togetherness, in the behavior of animals and human beings.

The concept of emotional process in society describes a range of evolutionary trends, with each trend depending on the level of anxiety in society. Effective adaptation or extinction of a society both may result from the quality of emotional process in society, which is an important component of evolutionary processes. Evolution is a complex combination of change that is incomprehensible to human beings. To simplify this infinite variety of characteristics of evolutionary change, some properties can be considered more conducive to regression or extinction, and others more conducive to progression or constructive adaptation.

In recent decades, members of our society appear to have been so emotionally bound to each other that relationships in general have been overly intense or estranged. As a result, broader social systems have been rigid and dysfunctional. Such evidence suggests a considerable degree of fusion and togetherness, which are more characteristic of societal regression than of effective adaptation.

In a phase of societal regression within evolution, both family symptoms and social-problem behavior increase. There may be more crime and violence in society in a period of marked societal regression owing to the greater probability of emotional cut-offs, repeated patterns of symptomatic behavior in different generations, and impairing projection in families. In a regressive, maladaptive phase of evolution, this social-problem behavior and the related family symptoms may be continually reinforced for long periods of time, and their pervasiveness and severity may correspondingly increase. In an evolutionary phase of societal regression, significantly effective differentiating efforts are needed by many individuals before the regression can begin to be reversed.

Fertility Patterns

Although Bowen used data from individual families to develop his theory, several of his propositions can be applied to broad social trends. One pertinent application is to link fertility behavior and evolutionary adaptation. It can be postulated that our current world population has resulted from fertility behavior precipitated by both micro and macro levels of emotional processes. Certain fertility patterns may have maladaptive consequences for individual families and society. There appear to be more stresses in individual families and broader social systems where the following patterns of timing and spacing of births occur:

1. When the first birth is within the first year of a marriage or equivalent.

2. When the first birth is after ten years of a marriage or equivalent.

3. When subsequent births are spaced less than one year apart.

4. When subsequent births are spaced more than five years apart.

5. When the total childbearing span exceeds twenty years.

As the Bowen theory is not based on linear cause-effect thinking, the timing of the first birth and the spacing of subsequent births are not considered causes of the accompanying stresses and strains. The births frequently precede intense strains, but the strains result from a complex variety of conditions present before the births occurred. Strains and stresses are as likely to produce births as births are to produce strains and stresses. Particular fertility patterns appear to be fairly reliable indicators of tension in families, and these patterns perhaps also point to strain in societies where these patterns are pervasive.

Hypothetically, societal fertility patterns with early or delayed timing and spacing of births are accompanied by a high frequency of social strains and stresses and less effective evolutionary adaptation. When there is a high frequency of early or delayed timing and spacing of births in a society, there are more social problems than when the frequency of these fertility patterns is low.

In some instances, census and survey data from different cultural and social settings may be used to describe and document the existence or nonexistence of these fertility patterns. Where this can be accomplished with sufficient accuracy, the degree and extent of societal tensions and stresses relating to the patterns may be tentatively predicted.

Examples of the kinds of strains that precipitate or accompany early and delayed births in families include divorce, separation, hospitalization, illness, and accidents. Broader societal stresses include poverty, unemployment, crime, rioting, war, and homicide. Although not all of these diverse manifestations accompany particular fertility patterns, some correlations can be identified.

In a world systems perspective, fertility patterns and societal strains and stresses can be conceptualized as evolutionary processes. When research is organized in this way, accumulated observations and data can extend beyond normative description and move toward the formulation of a general theory of human behavior.

Further Research

Macro-level research in family interaction has a need for new concepts to neutralize some of the existing value-laden normative schemas. If family theory is to develop toward scientific explanation and prediction, some means of comparing and identifying shared behavior patterns on a world system level must be found.

Much scientific discovery is a result of finally being able to see phenomena that have been visible all the time. Researchers can be more open to new observations when previous concepts have been replaced in thinking and formulating activities. One advantage of an evolutionary perspective in family research is that it encourages the observation and explanation of variables that have previously been obscured by an overemphasis on cultural or normative descriptions of family interaction. The Bowen family theory is an effective means of bringing into clearer focus the role of emotional processes in micro-levels and macro-levels of human behavior and social science research. When families are thought of as emotional systems in an ecological and world system perspective, they become an integral part of evolutionary change and adaptation.

Chapter 12

PSYCHOTHERAPY AS A SECULAR RELIGION

The recent emergence of family theory and the strong public interest in family psychotherapy can be considered a sectarian movement with many similarities to religion. These comparisons are perhaps most pertinent when clinical applications of family theory are examined as a secular religion.

Although it is not humanly possible to objectively describe recent social trends in the United States, a few generalizations can be made. During the last two or three decades, our technological society appears to have produced fairly widespread isolation and alienation from essential human values. Dealing with problems of warfare, racial conflict, and violence has plunged our post–World War II society into the midst of a critical "human relations problem" (Ackerman 1971). The mushrooming growth of different kinds of psychotherapy in urban settings since the end of World War II can be viewed as a social response to the invasion of personal freedom, distortion of humanistic values, and loss of human connectedness that have been nurtured by "gesellschaft" developments in the United States.

Durkheim's definition of religion as a "sacred community" perhaps has a new significance in light of the depersonalized characteristics of modern society. In some respects, it is religion that preserves essential parts of the value complex of "gemeinschaft" in an industrial society. By promoting cooperation between men and women, religion can deintensify the lethal quality of the pervasive individualistic competition in modern society. Religion can also provide opportunities for individuals to participate in social interaction rather than merely a place on the sidelines from which to watch others (Bobcock 1970).

Traditional religious forms such as church and sect may not be in sufficiently strategic social positions to foster the greatly needed sacred community in the face of rapid modernization. Religious values and world views are frequently perceived as deviant in relation to modern values such as materialism, technological progress, and the urban way of life. Although religions may have much in common with contemporary protest movements such as the revolt of youth against affluence (Bobcock 1970), it may no longer be possible for religious organizations to maintain their particular world views and activities and at the same time "swim in the societal mainstream" (Demerath and Hammond 1969).

The interplay between the sacred and the secular in society is a topic that has occupied much of the attention and energy of researchers in the sociology of religion throughout the field's history. During the last three decades, the distinctiveness of religion and the separateness of the sacred seem to have broken down with the acceleration of modernization. This blurring of sacred-secular differences is a move from polar ends of a sacred-secular continuum to a middle ground. As the institution of religion continues to lose its apartness from other social institutions and religious activity merges with other types of social activity, the separateness between the sacred and the profane is disappearing (Goode 1968).

American religion has been viewed as an integral part of the dominant system of American values (Wilson 1969), as churches in the United States have more secular activities than churches in European countries (Argyle 1958). Throughout the last thirty years, the church has become more involved in secular affairs. The churches' move toward secular concerns has been so abrupt during these years that some observers view the changes as "revolutionary" (Jacobs 1971). Ministerial roles in community problem solving may be considered a kind of social activism (Nelsen, Yokley and Madron 1973).

Some recent research on the relationship between religion and Americanism has been influenced by Herberg's "generation hypothesis" (Herberg 1960). Religion is thought to occupy a central position in American culture because it was instrumental in the process of Americanization (Nelsen and Allen 1974), and this focus is perhaps a result of the tendency of American culture to stress the importance of belonging to some religious tradition (Herberg 1960).

Just as religious phenomena can be described in secular terms, especially during a period of rapid social change, secular phenomena can be described in religious terms. An examination of the recent psychotherapy movement may bring into sharper relief the world views and beliefs considered the sources of the ferment of our times (Parsons 1967). Using Durkheim's terms, a study of the psychotherapy movement may indicate the nature of the "moral contract" between human beings and the "conscience collective" of society in a period of economic and technological prosperity (Mawson 1970), "anomie" being the social state where individuals cease to accept the moral legitimacy of society. The family movement in general and the Bowen family theory in particular can be viewed as products or consequences of the

breakdown of traditional norms in American society in the last
few decades.

Psychotherapy Movement in the United States

Psychotherapy can be defined as the healing of the human soul,
and it can be traced back to Pinel and Mesmer in the eighteenth
century (Harper 1974). Conventional usage has pathological
associations. Psychotherapy generally implies that an individual
has been diagnosed as needing specific treatment for a mental or
emotional illness. Since World War II, there has been a
proliferation of many different kinds of psychotherapy in the
United States. Although many forms of behavior change have
been attempted throughout history, the self-awareness of man
and woman has not attained the same degree of extensity and
intensity as in our contemporary society. Out of this climate of
heightened self-consciousness psychotherpay has emerged as a
significant process (Harper 1974). For the purposes of this
discussion, emphasis will be placed on the particular aspects of
psychotherapy that promote growth at the deepest levels of a
person's being, and the frame of reference will be exclusively on
theories and techniques that depend on verbal communication.

As some of the early Greeks suggested, human beings think
about themselves only when they become aware of personal
difficulties. Problems directly related to self shake one's
confidence and threaten one's security. People postpone the
necessity of facing themselves and their difficulties as long as
possible.

Personal and social crises sharpen concern for individual and
group well-being. These crises may be precipitated by conditions
such as conflicts between old and new values, rapid social
changes, or a breakdown of traditional social forms. When
human beings can no longer avoid the disagreeable process of

examinining their problems as functioning social animals, they begin the long journey toward self-awareness. From a review of literature on self-conception, it appears that contemporary efforts to look at self are longer, deeper, and more systematic than those of any previous period.

The various schools of psychotherapy that came into existence in the 1960s have tended to be organized by charismatic leaders who attract a large body of followers (Gurman 1973a). Specific principles of whatever forms of psychotherapy are used have been described and criticized as "dogmas" (Gurman 1973b). Many theories and techniques of psychotherapy have been treated as having "transcendental" qualities or as being "sacrosanct" (Bry 1972). Most psychotherapy is nonscientific and can be considered a series of doctrines (Bry 1972).

It is difficult to find consensus on a definition of psychotherapy in the professional literature that does not include acceptance of the centrality of the interview situation. Although psychotherapy is becoming more generally recognized in the population at large, the methods and approaches used have been criticized for being almost as numerous as the practitioners engaged in it (Wells 1972). Sociologists generally consider the concept of emotional health as a culturally determined idea that is a product of public opinion. A psychotherapy perspective suggests that each choice a person makes or chooses not to make affects personal development and results in a change or perpetuation of being. In everyday practical terms, these choices are strictly limited, however, but they may be revoked (Zinberg 1970).

In some of the same ways that religion may maintain psychological stability (Lindenthal 1970), psychotherapy can enhance religious awareness. Interpersonal and intrapsychic experiences during a course of psychotherapy can be compared to religious enlightenment. Major turning points in psychotherapy and in religious conversion may indicate the same or similar phenomena.

Psychotherapy and Religious Experience

People generally consult psychotherapists in order to get "better," an important assumption being that up to now they have been "sick." Individuals who identify themselves as "patients" generally want to discover whether they are sick, whether they are bad, whether they can become good, or whether they cannot change themselves. Psychotherapy is inextricably entangled with many physical-mental-emotional concerns and also with many moral preoccupations (Zinberg 1970).

Perhaps more than anything else, psychotherapy is a way to find self. The impact of psychotherapy largely depends on the quality and degree of conviction the therapist displays in action. In some instances, the fervor of a therapist is thought to inspire faith, hope, and trust in the recipient of the psychotherapy, perhaps assisting in the restoration or development of control of self. As so many influences affect a course of psychotherapy, it is difficult to determine how much of an individual's relief from symptoms or change in self can be attributed to the therapy and how much to other agencies (Bry 1972).

The search for self through psychotherapy may have developed at this point in history because our religious institutions have become increasingly impersonal in a depersonalized culture dedicated to materialistic improvement. The search for self may be an attempt to counteract the meaninglessness and vagueness of existing conventions and values. The standard of psychotherapy may be "love thy neighbor," "to thine own self be true," or "work and love." Once this standard become fixed as a concrete goal, it demands uncritical religious belief, although emotional health itself is necessarily a relative, limited, and variable concept. When health becomes an absolute end, it leads to disappointment, rage and the destruction of the very principles of humanity that psychotherapy is attempting to uphold (Zinberg 1970).

Some parallels can be drawn between psychotherapy and religion in terms of beliefs and practices. A common experience in the beliefs of both systems is that of conversion. Although conversion is usually considered a religious experience, it need not be explained as an extranatural or supernatural occurrence. Conversion can also be viewed as a particular kind of "enlightenment experience," as a result of "therapeutic talk," and as a product of "willpower" (Tremmel 1971). Conversion can be a regular, expected, or predictable occurrence in a successful course of psychotherapy.

An individual who has undergone a conversion appears to become a new person, making uncharacteristic choices and being motivated by a different set of beliefs. Those who have had a conversion experience are able to reverse or stifle specific trends that have dominated their lives. A "converted" person stops conducting life business in one way and starts doing it in another.

It is this kind of freedom, the "converting" choice, that gives people a sense of personal worth. The choice to change self is an explicit goal of both religion and psychotherapy. This choice represents a rebellion to the present structure of dispositions, attitudes, thoughts, hang-ups, and energy expenditures in the existing self. The decision to change self is made insurgently and defiantly, but it is made freely (Tremmel 1971).

In moral or theological conversion, as in the change of self in psychotherapy, there is an increase in an individual's awareness of free will. The extended exercise of free will possible through the conversion increases moral responsibility and enhances the quality of individual activity. This sequence of events can be considered the "emergence of a new role, outlook, belief, group identification, character, or personality" (Moberg 1962).

Perhaps both religion and psychotherapy endorse Americanism in similar ways (Eckhardt 1954). Among other shared characteristics of religion and psychotherapy are the dimensions of experience or "feeling," ritual or "cultic" intellect or knowledge, "practice" or "good works," and ideology or doctrine (Glock 1962).

Psychotherapy, Religion, and Social Class

Correlations between religious beliefs and practices are frequently negative (Demerath 1965). Religiosity, or socially enacted religious fervor, has several identifiable characteristics that are given various emphases by different social classes. In medieval times the church discouraged social mobility, since presuming to raise status was considered the same as flying in the face of an omnipotent, omniscient God. Individualism, as expressed by social and spiritual mobility, was traditionally discouraged by the threat of excommunication (Jacobs 1971). In recent times, however, religion has become an accepted vehicle for social mobility (Laumann 1969, Roberts 1968, Winter 1961). In general, the experiential dimension of religion correlates negatively with social class. The lower the class the more involved an individual is, and the higher the class the less involved a person tends to be. In contrast to the experiential dimension, other aspects of religion, such as church attendance, correlate positively with class (Goode 1968).

Psychotherapy can also be correlated with social class. Members of lower social classes, for example, have much less understanding of psychiatric theory and psychiatric treatment (Hollingshead and Redlich 1958, Myers and Bean 1968) and more negative attitudes toward emotional illness and psychiatric treatment (Jaco 1957, Jones and Kahn 1964, Williams 1957). Members of a lower social class are also much more concerned with and more inhibited by the stigma of mental hospitalization than are members of an upper social class (Myers and Bean 1968). The lower classes see only a narrow range of aggressive, antisocial behavior as suggesting a need for psychotherapy, but the middle and upper classes perceive a much wider range of behavior as indicating a need for psychotherapy (Dohrenwend and Chin-Shong 1967). As social and economic resources facilitate an individual's access to psychotherapy, a person and family from a lower class are less likely to seek psychotherapy than those in the middle and upper classes (Gove and Howell 1974).

The younger, urbanized, better educated, and more modernized segments of the middle-class American population, who attend church infrequently (Luckman 1967), are perhaps the most likely members of our society to initiate psychotherapy. Although psychotherapy does not purport to have ultimate answers, as does religion, involvement in psychotherapy appears to have some of the same personal dividends as religious participation. As religious institutions become more secularized and more depersonalized, psychotherapy can suggest ways to retrieve some qualities of religious experience in a secular setting. Although there is no single doctrine of psychotherapy, different clinical approaches, such as the Bowen theory, can be viewed as secular religions in their own right.

Conclusion

As conversion behavior may describe changes in individuals' religious and personal beliefs (Johnson 1971), the popularity of psychotherapy may indicate more widespread changes in social and religious beliefs. Although the question of whether religion "informs" secular society (P.E. Hammond 1963), or whether secular society "informs" religion (Glock 1960) cannot be resolved, comparisons between psychotherapy and religion suggest that it is difficult to separate the sacred and the secular in modern technocratic society. This merger of the sacred and the secular may even be one of our most significant human relations problems since World War II, as ambiguity of values is difficult for human beings to cope with.

The events of every era seem disorderly while they are happening, and it will only be at a later point in time that clearer strands of meaning and pattern will emerge. The objective of psychotherapy—the attainment of human dignity and a sense of personal worth—is a traditional religious theme. Enhancing self is a significant part of contemporary ideologies of protest and liberation, as well as of the Bowen family theory. Perhaps the complex social processes that have produced startling differences in life views, value assignments, and thinking styles between the post-World War II ("electronic") and previous ("preelectronic") generations can be considered a social mutation, analogous to a genetic mutation (Shands 1969). The family movement is a product of this era. Both psychotherapy and religion assist human beings in their necessary adaptation to a rapidly changing environment. In some respects psychotherapy may be more able to meet the specific personal needs of middle-class urban Americans in a technological age than religion. This is one of the thrusts of the Bowen family theory in our society today.

Chapter 13

TOWARD A GENERAL THEORY OF HUMAN BEHAVIOR

The Bowen theory describes emotional phenomena in families. Although the theory has been used primarily for family therapy and for research on behavior in families, diverse applications are possible. A comprehensive theory of emotional behavior can relate to many circumstances. Emotional pressures and tensions are a powerful influence in any group context.

The relationship between emotional systems theory and other theories in organizational behavior and the social sciences is extremely complex. A review of existing literature suggests that organization theory does not adequately conceptualize emotional pressures and interdependencies in organizations. Emotions tend to be dealt with in fragmented and incomplete ways. Most discussions of emotions in organizations (Roethlisberger 1953, Rogers 1961, Bion 1948) do not extend beyond an individual psychology of emotions and the relevance of this to individual emotional health and interpersonal communications. Some scholars (Lewin 1947, Bales 1950, Homans 1950) incorporate emotionality as part of a broader theory of small group behavior or treat it as a residual element of group processes (Shepherd 1964).

Bion and others of the Tavistock School have described the nonrational, or emotional, behavior of groups. However, they have not dealt with issues such as the quality of emotional interdependencies within groups or the impact of emotional tensions resulting from the past history of the group and the individuals in it. Some theories focus on intimacy and control (Bennis and Shepard 1956, Schutz 1958).

Social systems theory describes a variety of social pressures and outlines the structure of informal groups. However, it does not provide many meaningful leads on the nature of the emotional interdependencies and processes that bind a system together.

Emotional Systems Theory

An Organic Model. Organization theory has already conceptualized human groups as systems (Henderson 1935, Boulding 1956, Wolf 1959) and human relationships within them as being intrinsically organic, flexible, fluid, and evolving (Scott and Mitchell 1972, Burns and Stalker 1961). The Bowen concept of emotional systems may be viewed as a refinement and elaboration of this basic model. Unlike the closed, rigid, and insensitive interrelationships of a machine, an emotional system is living and changing. Like other organic systems emotional systems manifest simultaneous tendencies toward equilibrium, growth, adaptation, interdependency, and increasing differentiation. These processes are considered primarily in terms of reflexive and reactive patterns of emotional interaction and response.

Equilibrium. From the perspective of emotional systems theory, equilibrium is most accurately conceptualized as a steady emotional state that expresses a balance between the two major

countervailing emotional tendencies: a drive toward differentiation of self and an opposing force toward togetherness (fusion).
The opposition of these drives or forces is perhaps most visible in
the nuclear family, where the continuous struggle of children
toward autonomy is balanced by their equally strong yearning for
dependency. Emotional systems theory postulates that these
tendencies exist in all human groups and that the two major
forces influence all individual and social behavior.

Interdependency. One of the principles of general systems
theory is the concept of interdependency. A change in one part of
the system is thought to be followed by changes in other parts of
the system and eventually in the system as a whole. Emotional
systems theory suggests that change in the emotional level or
behavior of a particular member or in the emotional inputs into
the system produces predictable responses and reactions among
system members.

Differentiation. A primary characteristic of an emotional
system is an overall tendency toward differentiation. Bowen's
concept of differentiation is similar to the biological process of
specialization among and within species in nature. Emile
Durkheim documented preliterate groups as more "like-minded"
and more functionally unspecialized than civilized peoples
(Durkheim 1947). He postulated that more evolved groups were
specialized and pluralistically integrated.

Bowen suggests that differentiation occurs largely at deep-
seated emotional levels of behavior. Organizations that
superficially appear alike frequently manifest a wide range of
emotional responses to similar crises. Each organization's
characteristic latent patterns of reactivity persist, regardless of
whether or not the organization is a particular size or structure.

Differentiation is also an individual process. Emotional
systems theory postulates that there is an evolutionary tendency
for individuals to seek greater emotional independence and

autonomy as well as to share togetherness with others. An important part of changing a position in an emotional system is to relinquish reflexive postures and behavior and to substitute thoughtful, reflective, and goal-oriented postures and behavior.

In the context of organizational behavior, career changes can result from the effective differentiation of self. Power and authority displacements, which may temporarily imperil production efforts, can be system responses to changes in the emotional dependence of one or more of its significant members.

Adaptation. Like other organic systems, emotional systems manifest many modes of adaptation. Evolutionary adaptation can be constructive or destructive. Emotional systems theory postulates that constructive adaptation is characterized by increased flexibility in behavior, decreased intensity in dependence, and increased emotional autonomy of individual members. In a better functioning family, for example, a wide range of behavior is "accepted" by both parents and children, and there is a fairly marked degree of independence of each member.

Formal organizations also manifest constructive or destructive adaptations. Although young companies may thrive on high levels of emotional interdependency between their members, in the long run an organization must show a flexible tolerance for individual differences in order to be viable.

Energy. An emotional system is essentially a biological phenomenon characterized by fundamental energy forces. Emotions are more deep-seated than feelings and are more influential in human behavior. Anxiety is a manifestation of basic emotional energy.

An individual who experiences a given level of emotional pressure or strain may express "uptightness" or "stress" in a number of ways. A significant property of an emotional system is that it translates basic emotional energy into a set of clearly identifiable, predictable, and interrelated behavior patterns and feeling responses. An emotional system is sufficiently powerful to be able to effectively "program" its members to respond in certain prescribed ways (Broom and Selznick 1963).

Organizations program their members to respond to frustration or emotional stress in a variety of prescribed ways. However, the effectiveness of an organization appears limited by its members' previous programming experiences, especially in the family, and by individual emotional styles (Athos and Coffey 1968).

Emotional Overload. An emotional system is a network of relationships bonded together and enmeshed by flows of energy. As one member of the system expresses emotion, another may absorb it. The complexities of interdependencies in a given situation precipitate stresses that are reacted to or absorbed by one or more members of the system. The level of absorbed emotional energy, tension, or pressure eventually reaches a saturation point, and individual members of the system are prompted to behave in ways that reduce the overload of stress and tension. Anxiety is relieved most effectively by certain patterns of interaction. When it is not possible to reduce the emotional overload, individuals or the organization become dysfunctional. The potential for emotional overload in organizations is great. The dissatisfaction, tension and productivity problems widely reported in American business (Tarnowiesky 1973, Work in America 1972) may be destructively expressed emotional phenomena.

Loss. A loss has a significant impact on an emotional system. A family and a work system, automatically seek to replace an individual lost through death, dismissal, or voluntary with-drawal. This reactive response is characteristic of an emotional system. The aftermath of a loss is a difficult phase of readjustment. For the system to recuperate from the loss, emotions invested in the lost person must ideally be redirected to a replacement.

The process of striving to replace a loss has not received much attention in management literature. It is recognized that an organization that loses a chief executive faces a difficult transition period, but not that the same process operates to some extent when any member is lost. Even when an individual who has been perceived as destructive to an organization is removed, the displacement of emotional dependencies necessarily precipitates a somewhat disruptive period of readjustment.

A group is also strongly influenced by the intensity and number of its cut-offs, which can produce reactions similar to those generated by a loss. If a member is physically present but does not communicate with the group, there are maladaptive consequences for the group as a whole. The severity of the resulting dysfunctions depends on the intensity of the cut-off.

If an organization has a high level of anxiety, the potential for overload and dysfunction is high. One manifestation or consequence of overload is increased withdrawals or cut-offs in the organization. A loss or closure in an emotionally charged system may result in a chain reaction of other losses and closures, accompanied by disruption and dysfunction.

Concepts

An essential characteristic of emotional systems concepts is that they are interlocking and overlapping. No single concept can be described adequately without considering it alongside the others. The emotional systems orientation identifies dependencies between variables and is not based on cause-effect thinking, which arbitrarily selects particular variables as "cause" and "effect." For purposes of clarity, each concept is described in comparative isolation from the other concepts.

Differentiation of Self. Several writers have observed the powerful emotional processes of differentiation and togetherness in small groups (Bennis and Shepard 1956, Schutz 1958, Bion 1948, Lawrence and Lorsch 1967). Emotional systems theory suggests that there are two major life-forces that operate in all groups. One of these drives moves toward individuation, whereas the other moves toward togetherness (fusion). A member of an emotional system functions from a position of tension resulting from the opposition of these two forces.

When balance or equilibrium between these two drives is characterized by less individuation and more togetherness, behavior manifests emotional dependence, reactivity, and automatic reflexes. A person at this level of functioning may be described as constantly identifying with others—doing what they do and feeling what they feel. This individual tries to merge identity with another or others in the system. This behavior is similar to Kelman's identification process (1961), although Bowen specifies emotional rather than cognitive influences.

When an individual's balance between these two drives consists of strong individuation or differentiation and less striving for togetherness, behavior is directed toward individual goals and is influenced by the approval of others. Differentiated individuals are aware of and comfortable with the distinctions between their thoughts and feelings and those of the group. Differentiated behavior is more reflective and thought directed than automatic and responsive.

Triangles. A triangle, which consists of three participants, describes the smallest relationship unit of an emotional system, as a couple or twosome are not considered stable. Under stress, dyads break down or become emotionally overloaded, predictably drawing a third party into the twosome to relieve the tension.

An organization is a series of interrelated and interlocking triangles. Coalitions within triangles have been conceptualized in detail (Mills 1954, Stryker and Psathas 1960). Hare (1962) notes that coalitions of two against one in three-person groups are so potent and enticing that other characteristics of the group may not be developed.

All kinds of interpersonal relationships can be conceptualized as active or dormant triangles. Overlapping and interrelated triangles are usually more visible in families than in formal organizations. Although each group member has potential relationships with the others, triangles frequently only become activated and externalized around stress-producing or emotionally charged issues.

The concept of triangles is essential for an understanding of emotional systems. Most management and behavioral science literature deals primarily with dyads or group networks, although some discussion on triangles exists (Caplow 1968).

Core Group Emotional System. The concept of core group emotional system describes and defines emotional field forces between "inner group" members in a broad relationship network. An individual perceives members of a core group to be those who are emotionally closest, having interacted with them most persistently and most frequently over a long period of time.

In a work setting, the core group is the informal social group with which an individual identifies most strongly. The core group does not necessarily correspond to an "in" social group, to a leadership group, or to a task group within the organization. Although core groups may follow social or organizational groupings, they frequently cut across them. The determining factor in a core group is the degree of emotional investment of the participants. An organization can be described as a complex of interdependent core groups.

Each core group is characterized by a small number of members and unique patterns of behavior. To a certain extent core groups reflect or respond to dependencies and anxiety in the larger system. Core groups also manifest a higher level of emotional intensity and more frequent interaction than the wider system. A result of the increased activity and intensity in core groups is that emotional overload is common and frequently unavoidable.

Emotional overload in core groups can be handled in several ways. The most usual responses are emotionally reactive: conflict between major participants in the core group, dysfunction of one or more members of the core group, or projection of tensions to another individual or group. Projection or scapegoating is frequently the most ineffective way to handle overload in an emotional system.

Projection Process. Emotional projection is likely to occur when differentiation in a relationship system is low and anxiety is high. When tensions are high between two key members who are unable to differentiate self or function separately from each other, a third person is triangled into the twosome. The third person is trapped in the emotional field between these two members, and eventually symptoms appear in the behavior of the third person. The third person absorbs much of the emotional tension generated by the twosome, the degree of dysfunctioning of the third party resulting from the degree of unresolved tensions between the original two members. This process is often conventionally referred to as scapegoating.

Projection frequently occurs in organizations or between groups in organizations. Projection is most easily observed in cohesive departments of divisions that increase their unity by blaming an outside group for their own internal problems or by viewing an outside group negatively. Projection may occur when there is an increase in the emotional intensity or tensions within and between departments.

Emotional Cut-Off. Emotional cut-offs are breaches and blockages in the relationship network of a group. Bowen points out that the frequency of cut-offs or emotional divorces in families perpetuates relationship difficulties or precipitates symptomatic behavior. Whenever cut-offs are effectively bridged, anxiety is lowered and relationships within the family become more flexible and more viable.

Formal organizations and other social groups frequently manifest emotional cut-offs. Co-workers who find it difficult to get along with each other are inclined to distance themselves to deal with the high level of tension between them. Members of the same organization may be emotionally distant from each other but may work physically close to each other. Proximity is not a sufficient condition for enabling meaningful interaction.

In a large organization, a small group within the whole may be cut off from the rest of the network. This group will predictably function ineffectively unless concerted efforts are made to bridge the gap with meaningful emotional contacts.

The concept of emotional cut-off suggests that the most effective behavior of an individual or a group includes maintaining contacts with a wide range of others or other groups. For example, effective management cannot be focused too intensely on a single work unit if the unit is to function effectively in the long run. All kinds of contacts at each level of the organizational hierarchy, must be activated to ensure that a particular work unit remains or becomes a viable part of the whole.

Emotional cut-offs frequently· develop without conscious effort. They are largely automatic responses to tension, and much effort may be needed to bridge a cut-off successfully. The individual or the group attaining this objective achieves a raised level of functioning.

Multilevel Vertical Transmission Process. This concept describes processes that are activated in a chain-reaction sequence of events at different hierarchical levels of an emotional system. Patterns of behavior are visible and predictable at different levels in an organization. They are integral parts of "up-and-down" processes in the system.

One typical sequence of events in a multilevel vertical transmission process is the increasing intensification and repetition of patterns of reactive behavior. Trends and tendencies at the top or center of an organization become more distinct and more predictable at each lower level of the emotional system. Emotional systems theory suggests that members of an organization who are lower in the hierarchy or newer to the system are more vulnerable to pressures and more responsive to others' emotional dictates. The behavior of these individuals is less independent and less effective. They are more likely to absorb intensity and anxiety from other parts of the organization.

Multilevel repetitions of behavior become increasingly automatic through time. They show a strong inclination to be perpetuated unless individuals or subgroups make conscious efforts to reverse or change them. Patterns of conflict, dysfunction, projection, and other emotional processes—including the isolation of different segments of the system—are frequently manifested across a range of generations or hierarchical levels in an organization.

Personnel changes and logical discussion have little impact on the tenacity of the repeated patterns of behavior. Individual members of a particular group feel an overwhelming pressure to respond in the same ways with which the group has responded over time. The communication of a pattern of behavior may or may not be verbalized, but the selected response is clear, even to an outsider. This emotional reactivity may contradict the external appearances of the situation, norms in the group, rules and policies of the organization, or the verbalized "rational" directives of the group's leader. Changes in behavior patterns are possible only if changes are made in the emotional participation within and between groups.

The automatic tendency to repeat established patterns of behavior can be described as an organizational climate. This concept, which encompasses the total effect of any given situation, was originated by Lewin (1951) and discussed more recently by Litwin and Stringer (1968) among others. These authors do not focus on emotional reactivity, but they suggest that the emotional environment· of an organization has an important relationship to the behavior within it. Emotional systems theory conceptualizes feelings, repeated patterns of behavior, and reactivity as major components of organizational interaction. These responses are considered programmed into the system by multilevel vertical transmission processes that exert a powerful influence on individual and organizational effectiveness.

Sex and Seniority Positions. American cultural mythology has long suggested that the intensity and form of emotional responses in organizations partly depend on sex and seniority. Emotional systems theory hypothesizes that although sex and seniority may have considerable influence in an organization, emotional behavior results from programming within the system rather than from the particular sex, tenure, or age of an individual.

As emotional energy circulates within an organization, it may be transformed into a wide range of emotional responses. To a certain extent the variation in responses depends on the sex and seniority of the individuals involved. Communication may be grossly distorted in this process, and identical messages may elicit contrasting responses from different members. Incentive programs based on power or prestige will also elicit a wide range of responses, depending on the level of anxiety in the system and the level of anxiety of the individual concerned.

Emotional Process in Society. To the extent that the strongest currents of emotional process in society move more toward either differentiation or togetherness, all kinds of activity in that society will be influenced in that direction. If a society is in a crisis of intense togetherness, behavior in organizations and in other groups tends to be more limited and more repetitive than in a society that has a lower level of anxiety. When the overall emotional process in a society is directed more toward differentiation than toward togetherness, behavior in organizations and in other groups tends to be more flexible and less automatic than in a society that has a higher level of anxiety.

Although the emotional climate of any organization largely derives from the intensity of its own relationship network, the boundaries between an organization and society are not impermeable. In the same way that broad organizational drives toward individuation or togetherness affect behavior within any part of an organization, societal processes of individuation or togetherness influence drives and patterns of behavior in an organization.

The Bowen family theory describes a microcosm of emotional processes. Emotional process in society and in organizations is generally less visible and less predictable than emotional process in families, but many of the same principles of reactive dependency operate in all these contexts.

Conclusion

The Bowen family theory can serve as a general theory of emotional systems in human behavior, and its many applications and implications make it extremely versatile. Although the Bowen family concepts have an important set of consequences for family research, new associations become possible when the Bowen family theory is used as a means of understanding interaction in other settings.

The applications and implications of the Bowen family

theory are perhaps more clearly defined in relation to formal organizations than in relation to other social settings. A work system is similar to a family, especially in terms of continuing membership, frequency of interaction, and multi-level organization.

The Bowen family theory suggests a new view of society and human nature. A focus on emotional dependency in personal relationships highlights some generally underemphasized characteristics of interaction. Some of the implications of this innovative perspective on social reality have been described here, but many remain unacknowledged and are subjects for further research.

REFERENCES

Ackerman, N. W. (1971). The growing edge of family therapy. *Family Process* 10:143–156.

Adams, B. N. (1968). *Kinship in an Urban Setting.* New York: Markham.

———(1970). Isolation, function, and beyond: American kinship in the 1960s. *Journal of Marriage and the Family* 32:575–591.

Aldous, J. (1970). Strategies for developing family theory. *Journal of Marriage and the Family* 32:250–257.

Aldous, J., and Hill, R. (1967). *International Bibliography of Research. Marriage and the Family, 1960–1964.* Minneapolis: University of Minnesota Press.

Alexander, J. F. (1973). Defensive and supportive communications in family systems. *Journal of Marriage and the Family* 35:613–617.

Anderson, M. (1971). Family structure in nineteenth century Lancashire. Cambridge Studies in Sociology, no. 5. Cambridge: Cambridge University Press.

Andres, F.D., and Lorio, J.P., ed. (1974). *Georgetown Family Symposia,* Vol. 1 (1971–1972). Washington, D.C.: Georgetown University Medical Center.

Ardrey, R. (1966). *The Territorial Imperative: A Personal Inquiry into the Animal Origins of Property and Nations.* New York: Atheneum.

——— (1968). *African Genesis.* New York: Atheneum.

Argyle, M. (1958). *Religious Behavior.* London: Routledge and Kegan Paul.

Athos, A., and Coffey, R. (1968). *Behavior in Organizations, A Multidimensional View.* New York: Prentice-Hall.

Bales, R. F. (1950). *Interaction Process Analysis.* Cambridge: Addison-Wesley.

Barakat, H. (1969). Alienation: a process of encounter between utopia and reality. *British Journal of Sociology* 20:1-10.

Bartell, G. D. (1971). *Group Sex.* New York: Peter H. Wyden.

Barzun, J. (1941). *Darwin, Marx, Wagner—Critique of a Heritage.* Boston: Little, Brown.

Beard, B. B. (1949). Are the aged ex-family? *Social Forces* 27:274-279.

Bell, C. R. (1968). *Middle Class Families.* London: Routledge and Kegan Paul.

Bennis, W. G., and Shepard, H. A. (1956). A theory of group development. *Human Relations* 9:415-437.

Bernard, J. (1971). *Women and the Public Interest.* Chicago: Aldine-Atherton.

——— (1973). My four revolutions: an autobiographical history of the ASA. *American Journal of Sociology* 78:773-791.

Berne, E. (1967). *Games People Play.* New York: Random House.

Bertalanffy, L. von (1967). *Robots, Men, and Minds.* New York: George Braziller.

——— (1968). *General Systems Theory.* New York: George Braziller.

Bezdek, W., and Strodtbeck, F. L. (1970). Sex-role identity and pragmatic action. *American Sociological Review* 36:491-502.

Bion, W. R (1948). Experience in groups. *Human Relations* 1:314-320.

Bittner, E. (1963). Radicalism and the organization of radical movements. *American Sociological Review* 28:928-940.

Blood, R. O., and Wolfe, D. M. (1960). *Husbands and Wives.* New York: Free Press.

Bobcock, R.J. (1970). Ritual: civic and religious. *British Journal of Sociology* 21:285–297.

Boszormenyi-Nagy, I., and Spark, G.M. (1973). *Invisible Loyalties.* New York: Harper.

Bott, E. (1957). *Family and Social Network.* London: Tavistock.

Boulding, K.E. (1956). General systems theory—the skeleton of a science. *Management Science* 2:197–208.

Bowen, M. (1959). Family relationships in schizophrenia. In *Schizophrenia—An Integrated Approach,* ed. A. Auerback, pp. 147–178. New York: Ronald Press.

——— (1960). A family concept of schizophrenia. In *The Etiology of Schizophrenia,* ed. D. Jackson, pp. 346–372. New York: Basic Books.

——— (1961). Family psychotherapy. *American Journal of Orthopsychiatry* 31:40–60.

——— (1965a). Intrafamily dynamics in emotional illness. In *Family, Church, and Community,* ed. A. D'Agostino, pp. 81–97. New York: P.J. Kennedy and Sons.

——— (1965b). Family psychotherapy with schizophrenia in the hospital and in private practice. In *Intensive Family Therapy,* ed. I. Boszormenyi-Nagy and J.L. Framo, pp. 213–243. New York: Harper.

——— (1966). The use of family theory in clinical practice. *Comprehensive Psychiatry* 7:345–374.

——— (1971a). Family and family group therapy. In *Comprehensive Group Psychotherapy,* ed. H.T. Kaplan and B.J. Sadock, pp. 384–421. Baltimore: Williams and Wilkins.

——— (1971b). Principles and techniques of multiple family therapy. In *Systems Therapy,* ed. J.D. Bradt and C.J. Moynihan, pp. 388–404. Washington, D.C.: Groome Child Guidance Center.

——— (1972). On the differentiation of self. In M. Bowen, *Family Therapy in Clinical Practice,* pp. 467–528. New York: Jason Aronson, 1978.

——— (1973). Cultural myths and realities of problem solving. Paper presented at Environmental Protection Research Symposium on Alternative Futures and Environmental Quality, March.

———(1974). Societal regression: viewed through family systems theory. In *Energy: Today's Choices, Tomorrow's Opportunities,* ed. A.B. Schmalz. Washington, D.C.: World Future Society.

Bowen, M., Dysinger, R.H., and Basamania, B. (1959). The role of the father in families with a schizophrenic patient. *American Journal of Psychiatry* 115:117–120.

Bradt, J.O., and Moynihan, C.J., ed. (1971). *Systems Therapy.* Washington, D.C.: Groome Child Guidance Center.

Britton, J.H., and Britton, J.O. (1971). Children's perceptions of their parents: a comparison of Finnish and American children. *Journal of Marriage and the Family* 33:214–218.

Broderick, C.B. (1971). Beyond the five conceptual frameworks: a decade of development in family theory. *Journal of Marriage and the Family* 33:139–159.

Broom, L., and Selznick, P. (1963). *Sociology.* 3rd ed. New York: Harper.

Bry, A. (1972). *Inside Psychotherapy.* New York: Basic Books.

Buckley, W. (1967). *Sociology and Modern Systems Theory.* Englewood Cliffs, New Jersey: Prentice-Hall.

———(1968). *Modern Systems Research for the Behavioral Scientist—A Sourcebook.* Chicago: Aldine Publishing Company.

Bultena, G.L. (1969). Rural-urban differences in the familial interaction of the aged. *Rural Sociology* 34:5–15.

Burger, R.E. (1969). Who cares for the aged? *Saturday Review* 52:14–17.

Burgess, E.W., Locke, H.J., and Thomes, M.M. (1971). *The Family: From Traditional to Companionship.* New York: Van Nostrand Reinhold.

Burns, T., and Stalker, G. (1961). *The Management of Innovation.* London: Tavistock.

Caplow, T. (1968). *Two Against One: Conditions in Triads.* Englewood Cliffs, New Jersey: Prentice-Hall.

Christensen, H.T. (1964). Development of the family field of study. In *Handbook of Marriage and the Family,* ed. H.T. Christensen. Chicago: Rand McNally.

Cohen, M.G. (1973). *Proceedings and debates of the Ninety-third Congress,* first session, 119 (174). Washington, D.C.

Congressional Research Service (1975). Publication HJ2005 U.S., 75-60E, February 24.

Cooper, D. (1970). *The Death of the Family.* New York: Pantheon.

Cotgrove, S. (1967). *The Science of Society.* New York: Barnes and Noble.

Croog, S., Lipson, A., and Levine, S. (1972). Help patterns in severe illness. *Journal of Marriage and the Family* 34:32–41.

Darwin, C. (1871). *The Descent of Man and on Selection in Relation to Sex.* London: John Murray.

———(1896). *The Origin of the Species by Means of Natural Selection or the Preservation of Favored Races in the Struggle for Life.* New York: Appleton.

DeJong, P.Y., Brawer, M.J., and Robin, S.S. (1971). Patterns of female intergenerational occupational mobility: a comparison with male patterns of intergenerational occupational mobility. *American Sociological Review* 36:1033–1042.

Demerath, N.J., III (1965). *Social Class in American Protestantism.* Chicago: Rand McNally.

Demerath, N.J., III, and Hammond, P.E. (1969). *Religion in Social Context.* New York: Random House.

Demerath, N.J., III, and Peterson, R.A., ed. (1967). *System, Change, and Conflict—A Reader on Contemporary Sociological Theory and the Debate over Functionalism.* New York: Free Press.

Dennis, N. (1962). Secondary group relationships and the preeminence of the family. *International Journal of Comparative Sociology* 3:80–90.

Dinkel, R. (1944). Attitudes of children toward supporting aged parents. *American Sociological Review* 9:370–379.

Dohrenwend, B., and Chin-Shong, E. (1967). Social status and attitudes toward psychological disorder: the problem of tolerance of deviance. *American Sociological Review* 32:417–433.

Durkheim, E. (1947). *The Division of Labor in Society.* Glencoe, Illinois: Free Press.

Dysinger, R. H., and Bowen, M. (1959). Problems for medical practice presented by families with a schizophrenic member. *American Journal of Psychiatry* 116:514–517.

Eckhardt, A. R. (1954). The new look at American piety. In *Religion, Society, and the Individual,* ed. J. M. Yingar. New York: Macmillan.

Edgell, S. (1972). Marriage and the concept of companionship. *British Journal of Sociology* 23:432–461.

Elliott, K., ed. (1970). *The Family and Its Future.* London: J. and A. Churchill.

Ellwood, C. (1972). Preparation for the year 2000. *Adult Education* 45:27–31.

Epstein, C. F. (1973). Positive effects of the multiple negative: explaining the success of Black professional women. *American Journal of Sociology* 78:912–935.

Etzioni, A. (1975). Alternatives to nursing homes. *Human Behavior* 4:10–11.

Farber, B. (1964). *Family: Organization and Interaction.* San Francisco: Chandler Publishing Company.

Ferm, D. W. (1971). *Responsible Sexuality—Now.* New York: Seaburg Press.

Festinger, L. (1954). A theory of social comparison processes. *Human Relations* 7:117–140.

Fichter, J. H. (1972). The concept of man in social science: freedom, values, and second nature. *Journal for the Scientific Study of Religion* 11:109–121.

Finnegan, R. (1970). The kinship of ascription of primitive societies: actuality or myth? *International Journal of Comparative Sociology* 11:171–194.

Fletcher, R. (1962). *The Family and Marriage.* Harmondsworth, Middlesex: Penguin.

Freilich, M. (1964). The natural triad in kinship and complex systems. *American Sociological Review* 29:529–540.

Gibson, G. (1972). Kin family network: overheralded structure in past conceptualizations of family. *Journal of Marriage and the Family* 34:13–23.

Glock, C. Y. (1960). Religion and the integration of society. *Review of Religious Research* 2:49–61.

——— (1962). On the study of religious commitment. *Review of Recent Research Bearing on Religious and Character Formation*, research supplement to *Religious Education*, S98–S110.

Goode, E. (1968). Class styles of religious sociation. *British Journal of Sociology* 19:1–16.

Goode, W.J. (1963a). The process of role bargaining in the impact of urbanization and industrialization on family systems. *Current Sociology* 12:1–13.

——— (1963b). *World Revolution and Family Patterns*. New York: Macmillan.

——— (1971). Force and violence in the family. *Journal of Marriage and the Family* 33:624–636.

Goody, J. (1973). Evolution and communication: the domestication of the savage mind. *British Journal of Sociology* 24:1–12.

Gouldner, A.W. (1970). *The Coming Crisis in Western Sociology*. New York: Basic Books.

Gove: W.R., and Howell, P. (1974). Individual resources and mental hospitalization: a comparison and evaluation of the societal reaction and psychiatric perspectives. *American Sociological Review* 39:86–100.

Gray, R.M., and Kasteler, J.M. (1967). Foster grandparents and retarded children. Research Report, Utah Foster Grandparent Project, Salt Lake City.

Gurman, A.S. (1973a). The effects and effectiveness of marital therapy: a review of outcome research. *Family Process* 12:145–170.

——— (1973b). Marital therapy: emerging trends in research and practice. *Family Process* 12:45–54.

Gursch, W.E. (1967). Quarterly Narrative Report: Foster Grandparent Project. Denton State School.

Hall, C.M. (1971). *The Sociology of Pierre Joseph Proudhon (1809–65)*. New York: Philosophical Library.

——— (1972). The aged and the multigenerational cut-off phenomenon. Paper presented at Georgetown University Pre-

Symposium on Family Psychiatry, Washington, D.C., November.

———(1973). *Vital Life: Questions in Social Thought*. North Quincy, Massachusetts: The Christopher Publishing House.

———(1974). Efforts to differentiate a self in my family of origin. In *Georgetown Family Symposia*, vol. 1 (1971–1972), ed. F. D. Andres and J. P. Lorio. Washington, D.C.: Georgetown University Medical Center.

———(1976). Aging and family processes. *Journal of Family Counseling* 4:28–42.

Hall, C. M., and Sussman, M. B. (1975). Aging and the family: alternatives to institutional care. American Sociological Association Annual Meeting, report and recommendations of Committee on Public Issues and the Family.

Hammond, M. A. (1963). Effects of the foster grandparent project upon the Oral Language Development of Institutionalized Mental Retardates. Ph.D. Dissertation, North Texas State University.

Hammond, P. E. (1963). Religion and the "informing of culture." *Journal for the Scientific Study of Religion* 3:97–106.

Hare, P. (1962). *Handbook of Small Group Research*. New York: The Free Press of Glencoe.

Harper, R. A. (1974). *Psychoanalysis and Psychotherapy—36 Systems*. New York: Jason Aronson.

Harris, C.C. (1969). *The Family*. London: Allen and Unwin.

HEW (U.S. Department of Health, Education, and Welfare) (1972). AOA projects to test alternatives to institutionalization of aged. *Aging*, No. 215–216. Administration on Aging.

———(1972b). *Cost Benefit Profile of the Foster Grandparent Program*. Booz, Allen Public Administration Service.

Heidensohn, F. (1968). The deviance of women: a critique and an enquiry. *British Journal of Sociology* 19:160–175.

Henderson, L. J. (1935). *Pareto's General Sociology*. Cambridge: Harvard University Press.

Herberg, W. (1960). *Protestant-Catholic-Jew*. Garden City, New York: Doubleday.

Hochschild, A. R. (1973). Communal life-styles for the old. *Society* 10:50–57.

Hollingshead, A., and Redlich, F. (1958). *Social Class and Mental Illness.* New York: Wiley.

Homans, G. (1950). *The Human Group.* New York: Harcourt Brace.

——— (1964). Bringing men back in. *American Sociological Review* 29:809–818.

Humphreys, L. (1970). *Tearoom Trade: Impersonal Sex in Public Places.* Chicago: Aldine Publishing Company.

Huxley, J. S. (1942). *Evolution: The Modern Synthesis.* London: Allen and Unwin.

Ibsen, C. A., and Klobus, P. (1972). Fictive kin term use and social relationships: alternative interpretations. *Journal of Marriage and the Family* 34:615–620.

Jaco, E. G. (1957). Attitudes toward an incidence of mental disorder: a research note. *Southwestern Social Science Quarterly* 38:27–38.

Jacobs, J. (1971). From sacred to secular: the rationalization of Christian theology. *Journal for the Scientific Study of Religion* 10:1–9.

Johnson, W. T. (1971). The religious crusade: revival or ritual? *American Journal of Sociology* 76:873–890.

Jones, N. F., and Kahn, M. W. (1964). Patient attitudes as related to social class and other variables concerned with hospitalization. *Journal of Consulting Psychology* 18:403–408.

Kanter, R. M. (1968). Commitment and social organization: a study of commitment mechanisms in utopian communities. *American Sociological Review* 33:499–517.

Kanter, R. M., ed. (1973). *Communes: Creating and Managing the Collective Life.* New York: Harper.

Kaplan, A. (1964). *The Conduct of Inquiry.* San Francisco: Chandler Publishing Company.

Kaplan, H. I., and Sadock, B. J., ed. (1971). *Comprehensive Group Psychotherapy.* Baltimore: Williams and Wilkins.

Kaplan, J. (1972). An editorial: alternatives to nursing home care, fact or fiction? *The Gerontologist* 12:114.

Keller, A. G. (1931). *Societal Evolution—A Study of the Evolutionary Basis of the Science of Society*. New York: Macmillan.

Kelman, H. (1961). Process of opinion change. *Public Opinion Quarterly* 25:57–78.

Kenkel, W. F. (1966). *The Family in Perspective*. New York: Appleton-Century-Crofts.

Kent, D. P., and Matson, M. B. (1972). The impact of health on the aged family. *The Family Coordinator* 21:29–36.

Kerlinger, F. N. (1964). *Foundations of Behavioral Research*. New York: Holt, Rinehart and Winston.

Ketcham, W., Sack, A., and Shore, H. (1974). Annotated bibliography on alternatives to institutional care. *The Gerontologist* 14:34–36.

Kirkendall, L. A., and Whitehurst, R. N. (1971). *The New Sexual Revolution*. New York: Donald W. Brown.

Kistin, H., and Morris, R. (1972). Alternatives to institutional care for the elderly and disabled. *The Gerontologist* 12:139–142.

Lacey, W. K. (1968). *The Family in Classical Greece*. Ithaca, New York: Cornell University Press.

Laumann, E. O. (1969). The social structure of religious and ethno-religious groups in a metropolitan community. *American Sociological Review* 34:182–197.

Lawrence, P. R., and Seiler, J. A. (1965). *Organizational Behavior and Administration*. Homewood, Illinois: Richard D. Irwin, Inc. and The Dorsey Press.

Lawrence, P. R., and Lorsch, J. W. (1967). Organization and environment: managing differentiation and integration. Cambridge: Division of Research, Harvard Business School.

Lee, G. R. (1974). Marriage and anomie: a causal argument. *Journal of Marriage and the Family* 36:523–532.

Lewin, K. (1947). Frontiers in group dynamics. *Human Relations* 1:5–41.

———(1951). *Field Theory in Social Sciences*. New York: Harper.

Lindenthal, J. J. et al. (1970). Mental states and religious behavior. *Journal for the Scientific Study of Religion* 9:143–149.

Litwak, E. (1960a). Geographical mobility and extended family cohesion. *American Sociological Review* 25:385–394.

———(1960b). Occupational mobility and extended family cohesion. *American Sociological Review* 25:9–21.

Litwak, E., and Szelenyi, I. (1969). Primary group structures and their functions: kin, neighbors, and friends. *American Sociological Review* 34:465–481.

Litwak, E., Hollister, D., and Meyer, H.J. (1974). Linkage theory between bureaucracies and community primary groups—education, health, political action as empirical cases in point. Paper presented at the Annual Meeting of the American Sociological Association, Montreal.

Litwin, G., and Stringer, R.A. (1968). *Motivation and organizational climate.* Cambridge: Division of Research, Harvard Business School.

Lorenz, K. (1954). *Man Meets Dog.* London: Methuen.

———(1963). *On Aggression.* Trans. M.K. Wilson. New York: Harcourt Brace.

———(1965). *Evolution and Modification of Behavior.* Chicago: University of Chicago Press.

———(1971). *Studies in Animal and Human Behavior*, vol. 3, Trans. Robert Martin. Cambridge: Harvard University Press.

Loudon, J.B. (1961). Kinship and crisis in South Wales. *British Journal of Sociology* 12:333–350.

Lowenthal, M.F., and Boler, D. (1965). Voluntary versus involuntary social withdrawal. *Journal of Gerontology* 20:363–371.

Luckman, T. (1967). *The Invisible Religion.* New York: Macmillan.

Lundberg, G.A. (1947). *Can Science Save Us?* New York: David McKay.

Lynd, R.S. (1939). *Knowledge for What?* Princeton: Princeton University Press.

Lyness, J.L., and Lipetz, M.E. (1972). Living together: an alternative to marriage. *Journal of Marriage and the Family* 34:305–311.

Marciano, T.D. (1975). Variant family forms in a world perspective. *The Family Coordinator* 24:407–420.

Martin, R. J. (1974). Cultic aspects of sociology: a speculative essay. *British Journal of Sociology* 25:15–31.

Maslow, A. H. (1954). *Motivation and Personality*. New York: Harper.

Mawson, A. R. (1970). Durkheim and contemporary social pathology. *British Journal of Sociology* 21:298–313.

McGregor, D. (1960). *The Human Side of Enterprise*. New York: McGraw-Hill.

Mills, C. W. (1959). *The Sociological Imagination*. London: Oxford University Press.

Mills, T. M. (1954). Coalition pattern in three-person groups. *American Sociological Review* 19:657–667.

Mishler, E. G., and Wazler, N. E. (1968). *Interaction in Families*. New York: Wiley.

Moberg, D. (1962). *The Church as a Social Institution*. Englewood Cliffs, New Jersey: Prentice-Hall.

Muncy, R. L. (1973). *Sex and Marriage in Utopian Communities— 19th Century America*. Bloomington, Indiana: Indiana University Press.

Musil, J. (1971). Some aspects of social organization of the contemporary Czechoslovak family. *Journal of Marriage and the Family* 33:196–206.

Myers, J., and Bean, L. (1968). *A Decade Later: A Follow-up of Social Class and Mental Illness*. New York: Wiley.

Nelson, H. M., and Allen, H. D. (1974). Ethnicity, Americanization, and religious attendance. *American Journal of Sociology* 79:906–922.

Nelson, H. M., Yokley, R. L., and Madron, T. W. (1973). Ministerial roles and societal actionist stance: Protestant clergy and protest in the sixties. *American Sociological Review* 38:375–386.

Neugarten, B. L. (1973). Patterns of aging: past, present, and future. *Social Service Review* 47:571–572.

Nimkoff, M. F., ed. (1965). *Comparative Family Systems*. New York: Houghton Mifflin.

Noble, T. (1970). Family breakdown and social networks. *British Journal of Sociology* 21:135–150.

Noelker, L. (1975). Intimate relationships in a residential home for the elderly. Ph.D. dissertation, Case Western Reserve University.

Olson, D. H. (1972). Marriage of the future: revolutionary or evolutionary change? *The Family Coordinator* 21:383–393.

O'Neill, N., and O'Neill, G. (1972). Open marriage: a synergic model. *The Family Coordinator* 21:403–409.

Orden, S. R., and Bradburn, N. M. (1968). Dimensions of marriage happiness. *American Journal of Sociology* 73:715–731.

———(1969). Working wives and marriage happiness. *American Journal of Sociology* 74:392–407.

Osofsky, J. D., and Osofsky, H. J. (1972). Androgyny as a life style. *The Family Coordinator* 21:411–418.

Paden-Eisenstark, D. (1973). Are Israeli women really equal? Trends and patterns of Israeli women's labor force participation: a comparative analysis. *Journal of Marriage and the Family* 35:538–545.

Parsons, T. (1943). The kinship system of the contemporary U.S. *American Anthropologist* 45:22–38.

———(1966). *Societies—Evolutionary and Comparative Perspectives.* Englewood Cliffs, New Jersey: Prentice-Hall.

———(1967). Christianity and modern industrial society. In *Sociological Theory, Values, and Sociocultural Change,* ed. E. Tiryakian. New York: Harper.

———(1971). *The System of Modern Societies.* Englewood Cliffs, New Jersey: Prentice-Hall.

Parsons, T., and Bales, R. F., eds. (1955). *Family, Socialization, and Interaction Process.* New York: Free Press of Glencoe.

Payne, G. (1973). Comparative sociology: some programs of theory and method. *British Journal of Sociology* 24:13–29.

Pechman, J. A., and Timpane, P. M., ed. (1975). *Work Incentives and Income Guarantees.* Washington, D.C.: The Brookings Institution.

Petroni, F. (1969). Significant others and illness behavior: a much neglected sick role contingency. *Sociological Quarterly* 10:32–41.

Queen, S., and Habenstein, R. (1967). *The Family in Various Cultures.* New York: Lippincott.

Ramey, J. W. (1972). Communes, group marriage, and the upper middle class. *Journal of Marriage and the Family* 34:647–655.

Riesman, D., Glazer, N., and Denney, R. (1950). *Lonely Crowd: A Study of the Changing American Character.* New Haven: Yale Univerity Press.

Riley, M. W. (1968). *Aging and Society, Vol. One: An Inventory of Research Findings.* New York: Russell Sage Foundation.

Roberts, B. S. (1968). Protestant groups and coping with urban life in Guatemala City. *American Journal of Sociology* 73:753–767.

Roethlisberger, F. J. (1953). Administrators skill: communication. *Harvard Business Review* 31:55–62.

Rogers, C. R. (1961). *On Becoming a Person.* Boston: Houghton Mifflin.

Rose, A. M. (1968). The subculture of aging: a topic for sociological research. In *Middle Age and Aging*, ed. B. L. Neugarten. Chicago: University of Chicago Press.

Rose, A. M., and Peterson, W. A., ed. (1965). *Older People and Their Social World.* Philadephia: F. A. Davis Co.

Rosenberg, G. S. (1967). *Poverty, Aging, and Social Isolation.* Washington, D.C.: Bureau of Social Research.

Rosow, I. (1967). *Social Integration of the Aged.* New York: The Free Press.

Rosser, C., and Harris, C. C. (1965). *The Family and Social Change.* London: Routledge and Kegan Paul.

Rubin, Z. (1968). Do American women marry up? *American Sociological Review* 33:750–760.

Ruitenbeek, H. M., ed. (1963). *Varieties of Classic Social Theory.* New York: Dutton.

Schlesinger, B. (1970). Family life in the kibbutz of Israel: utopia gained or paradise lost? *International Journal of Comparative Sociology* 11:251–271.

Schneider, D. M., and Smith, R. T. (1973). *Class Differences and Sex Roles in American Kinship and Family Structure.* Englewood Cliffs, New Jersey: Prentice-Hall.

Schorr, A. (1960). *Filial Responsibility in the Modern American Family.* Washington, D.C.: Social Security Administration Report.

Schutz, W.C. (1958). *FIRO: A Three-Dimensional Theory of Interpersonal Behavior.* New York: Rinehart.

Scott, W.G., and Mitchell, T.R. (1972). *Organization Theory: A Structural and Behavioral Analysis.* Homewood, Illinois: Richard D. Irwin, Inc. and The Dorsey Press.

Shanas, E. (1961). *Family Relationships of Older People: Living Arrangements, Health Status, and Family Ties.* New York: Health Information Foundation.

Shanas, E., and Streib, G.F., ed. (1963). *Social Structure and the Family: Generational Relations.* Englewood Cliffs, New Jersey: Prentice-Hall.

Shanas, E., and Sussman, M.B. (1975). *Older People, Family and Bureaucracy.* Durham, North Carolina: Duke University Press.

Shands, H.C. (1969). Integration, discipline and the concept of shape. *Annals of the New York Academy of Sciences* 174:578–589.

Sheper, J. (1969). Familism and social structure: the case of the kibbutz. *Journal of Marriage and the Family* 31:567–573.

Shepherd, C.R. (1964). *Small Groups: Some Sociological Perspectives.* San Francisco: Chandler Publishing Company.

Sherif, M., and Sherif, C. (1953). *Groups in Harmony and Tension.* New York: Harper.

Shore, H. (1974). What's new about alternatives? *The Gerontologist* 14:6–11.

Simpson, G.G. (1949). *The Meaning of Evolution.* New Haven: Yale University Press.

Simpson, I.H., and McKinney, J.C., ed. (1966). *Social Aspects of Aging.* Durham: Duke University Press.

Slater, P.E. (1963). On societal regression. *American Sociological Review* 28:339–364.

Solomon, B. (1967). Social functioning of economically dependent aged. *The Gerontologist* 7:213–217.

Speck, R., and Attneave, C. (1973). *Family Networks.* New York: Pantheon.

Sprey, J. (1969). The family as a system in conflict. *Journal of Marriage and the Family* 31:699–706.

Streib, G. (1958). Family patterns in retirement. *Journal of Social Issues* 14:46–60.

———(1965). Intergenerational relations: perspectives of the two generations of the older parent. *Journal of Marriage and the Family* 27:469–476.

Stryker, S., and Psathas, G. (1960). Research on coalitions in the triad: findings, problems, and strategy. *Sociometry* 23:217–230.

Sussman, M. B. (1953). The help pattern in the middle class family. *American Sociological Review* 18:22–28.

———(1955). Activity patterns of post-parental couples and their relationship to family continuity. *Marriage and Family Living* 17:338–341.

Sussman, M. B., and Burchinal, L. (1962). Kin family network: unheralded structure in current conceptualizations of family functioning. *Marriage and Family Living* 24:320–332. Also in *Kinship and Family Organization*, ed. B. Farber. New York: Wiley, 1966.

Sussman, M. B., and Cogswell, B. E. (1972). The meaning of variant and experimental marriage styles and family forms in the 1970s. *Family Coordinator* 21:375–381.

Szasz, T. S. (1963). *Law, Liberty, and Psychiatry.* New York: Macmillan.

Taietz, P., and Larson, O. F. (1956). Social participation and old age. *Rural Sociology* 21:229–238.

Talmon, Y. (1959). The case of Israel. *Human Relations* 12:121–146.

———(1972). *Family and Community in the Kibbutz.* Cambridge: Harvard University Press.

Tarnowiesky, D. (1973). The changing success ethic. *American Management Association Survey Report.*

Taylor, I., and Walton, P. (1970). Values in deviancy theory and society. *British Journal of Sociology* 21:362–374.

Teilhard de Chardin, P. (1970). *Let Me Explain.* Trans. R. Hague et al. London: Collins.

Thompson, G. (1961). *The Inspiration of Science.* London: Oxford University Press.

Tolman, E.C. (1932). *Purposive Behavior in Animals and Men.* New York: Appleton-Century.

Toman, W. (1972). *Family Constellation.* New York: Springer.

Townsend, P. (1957). *The Family Life of Old People.* Glencoe, Illinois: Free Press.

Tremmel, W.C. (1971). The converting choice. *Journal for the Scientific Study of Religion* 10:17–25.

Troll, L.E. (1971). The family of later life: a decade review. *Journal of Marriage and the Family* 33:263–290.

Turner, R.H. (1969). The theme of contemporary social movements. *British Journal of Sociology* 20:390–405.

——— (1970). *Family Interaction.* New York: Wiley.

United States Senate Committee on Labor and Public Welfare (1975). Nurse Training and Health Revenue Sharing and Health Services Act. Calendar no. 29, report no. 94-29. Washington, D.C.

Weintraumb, D., and Shapiro, M. (1968). The traditional family in Israel in the process of change—crisis and continuity. *British Journal of Sociology* 19:284–299.

Weitzman, L.J. (1972). Sex-role socialization in picture books for pre-school children. *American Journal of Sociology* 77:1125–1150.

Wells, R.A. et al. (1972). The results of family therapy: a critical review of the literature. *Family Process* 11:189–207.

White House Conference on Aging (1971). *Toward a National Policy on Aging.* Final Report, vol. 2, Washington, D.C.

Whitehurst, R.N. (1972). Some comparisons of conventional and counter-culture families. *The Family Coordinator* 21:395–401.

Williams, W. (1957). Class differences in the attitudes of psychiatric patients. *Social Problems* 4:240–244.

Wilson, B. (1969). *Religion in Secular Society: A Sociological Commentary.* Baltimore: Penguin.

Winer, L.R. (1971). The qualified pronoun count as a measure of change in family psychotherapy. *Family Process* 10:243–247.

Winter, G. (1961). *The Suburban Captivity of the Churches.* Garden City, New York: Doubleday.

Woof, W.B. (1959). Organizational constructs: an approach to understanding organization. *Journal of the Academy of Management,* April.

Wolff, K.H., ed. and trans. (1950). *The Sociology of Georg Simmel.* New York: The Free Press.

Work in America (1972). A report of a special task force to the Secretary of Health, Education, and Welfare. Cambridge: MIT Press.

Young, M., and Willmott, P. (1962). *Family and Kinship in East London.* Harmondsworth, Middlesex: Pelican.

Zelditch, M., Jr. (1955). Role differentiation in the nuclear family: a comparative study. In *Family, Socialization, and Interaction Process,* ed. T. Parsons and R. F. Bales. New York: Free Press of Glencoe.

Zetterberg, H.L. (1965). *On Theory and Verification in Sociology.* Totowa, New Jersey: The Bedminster Press.

Zimmerman, C.C. (1972). The future of the family in America, *Journal of Marriage and the Family* 34:323–333.

Zinberg, N. (1970). The mirage of mental health. *British Journal of Sociology* 21:262–272.

INDEX